Dancing round raindrops

Steph Mason

Copyright © 2011 Steph Mason

Steph Mason has asserted her right under the Copyright, Design and Patents Act 1988 to be identified as the author of this work.

All rights reserved.

ISBN: 1466238070

ISBN-13: 978-1466238077

For Nicola, Catherine, Charlotte, Christopher, Huw, Alice, Nicholas, Amelie, Ella and Henry

"Twenty years from now you will be more disappointed by the things you didn't do than by the ones you did do. So throw off the bowlines. Sail away from the safe harbour. Catch the trade winds in your sails. Explore. Dream. Discover."

Mark Twain

Steph Mason

PROLOGUE

February 1922, Kelvedon, Essex.
The black capitals on the station sign spelt safety for Dorothy as they emerged one by one from the shroud of steam and dusky murk to cross the window, each letter heralding a tiny bubble of relief which escaped up her throat from the Turk's head her stomach had knotted itself into. Pushing down the glass she turned the handle and had one slim ankle hovering above the step before she realised there was no-one there.

A spherical porter was, for some inconceivable reason, looking directly at her as he hurried down the platform, left, right, left, right, the tight blue trousers rising up his stout legs making a fat 'V' of creases at his groin. She shrank back, letting the train's dark interior cocoon her from the waddling grin that seemed intent upon stalking her.

Bracing herself against the yellowing box of walls, her abdomen squirmed then locked tight, her knees no longer seemed able to keep steady and she knew that in a moment her high heels and tailored silk outfit would be incapable of disguising her complete disintegration. She imagined her hips sinking down to her ankles, her arms enfolding her knees, her head hanging almost to the floor while she gave in to the animal moans that were building at her core. With sluggish horror she realised how triumphantly thorough she had been in ensuring she could never go back. Yet what was forward? Where was the end of the line now? She had travelled with nothing but her confidence in him, and a couple of ridiculously dainty suitcases.

A flicker at the corner of her eye forced her to turn slightly as a man in a rumpled beige suit vaulted over the spikes of the green wooden gate and sprinted down the platform, past the wallowing porter, to arrive in front of her, an un-nailed Catherine wheel flailing his arms as he grabbed at her neat leather bags. He was shouting at her above the noise of the engine, still effervescing with the speed of his arrival as she cowered back further into the carriage, unbothered if he should remove her cases so long as she could remain hidden within the shadows.

He stopped abruptly, looking at her for the first time, a frown replacing the frenzied concentration that had marked his efforts so far. She felt herself stiffen as he observed her, she needed to run, she was in a trap, it had all been a trick, the whistle must shrill out and let her escape from all of them, she must keep moving on and on, further and further away until she knew she could not be found and her mind could settle.

"Whatever's wrong Dorothy? I've said I'm sorry!"

He had sprung inside the doorway, clamping her upper arms beneath his firm hands and whirling her out of the narrow passageway to be dumped on the platform, her pointed shoes skittering on the damp stone.

"Where's Harold?" she croaked, long legs sliding from beneath her as the train began to creak, preparing to leave, her haven moving on, abandoning her as she picked herself up, crumpled and exposed.

PART ONE

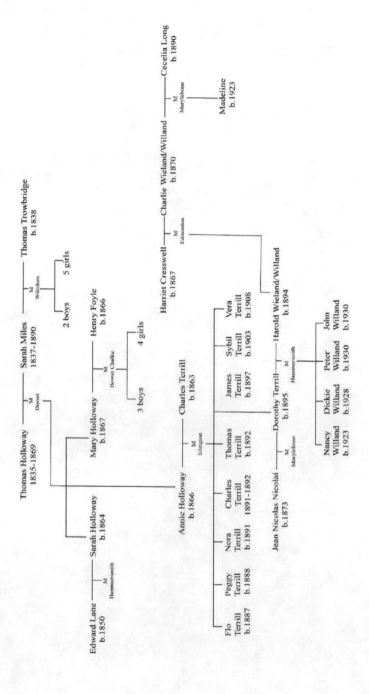

CHAPTER ONE

1900, Wilton, Wiltshire.
(Annie: 34, Peggy: 12, Nora: 9, Dorothy: 5)
There was mud, endless mud, on the year the new century began it seemed as if the rivers surrounding Wilton were continually overflowing and the clouds remained menacing for months at a time. Annie Terrill peered out at the leaking sky from beneath the peeling paint of the cottage door frame, the farmyard was a quagmire that only the most desperate would venture across. In one respect the wretched sogginess was a comfort to her as at least there would be no visit from the Attendance Officer today and she would not have to put up with another ear bashing for failing to ensure Nora and Thomas pursued their meagre education. If it would just keep raining until Friday she could save the tuppence from the week's school fees. She reckoned she worried as much about the Attendance Officer as her husband Charles did over the number of sheep he was losing to hoof infections as rain caused the animals to remain inside week after week. The family had changed from wheat to livestock farming five years before when falling grain prices left the spectre of Wilton Workhouse haunting every struggling moment of their lives. Now it was looming once again and Charles maintained that only the most drastic life changes could prevent the entire family from sliding further into a swamp of hunger and debt that, he claimed, was certain to culminate in residency behind the three rows of cold rectangular windows. Although Annie wasn't sure her husband's proposal to uproot the family was sensible, the prospect of being separated from him and her children within the massive austere red-brick block chilled her so deeply that she was prepared to follow any rainbow in an attempt to avoid it.

The sole occurrence that appeared genuinely hopeful on the family's horizon was that Annie's eldest daughter, Flo, had landed the position of below stairs maid in a large house in Wembley. When Flo had visited the previous autumn she had mentioned there was talk of the position of cowman becoming vacant as the current incumbent was both over sixty and too fond of his powerful homemade cider to waken on time to drive the beasts indoors for their morning relief. Charles had asked his daughter to ensure the farm manager knew he would be interested in the post should it materialise and in February, not a moment too soon for the Terrills, word had arrived that the job was his should he want it. Selling their remaining scrawny stock would pay off the back rent they owed on the farm and just cover their train fares to Middlesex, but even with the burden of trying to scratch a living from thirty tired acres removed, the joint earnings of Flo and Charles would not amount to more than twenty shillings a week, and Annie worried that they would be swapping their current debts for another set, but this time she would have lost her vegetable patch and the eggs from her chickens plus the rabbits Charles regularly snared. This time they might be hungry as well as poor. Twelve-year-old Peggy would need to find a situation as soon as possible, yet even if Peggy were to gain employment it would be two years before Nora could join her and far longer for Thomas, Dorothy and four year old James. Although Annie accepted it was probably impossible for the family to remain at the farm, she was unsure whether Charles's solution moved them further away from the threat of starvation and the workhouse, or closer towards it.

Flo had found some rooms for them to rent in a tenement which she said were clean and only shared a tap with three other families, but Annie was tormented by the idea that their troubles were dragging her children further and further down the social ladder to a level so low they could never hope to claw their way up again. The choices they had made had not been fortuitous, even her younger sister, Mary, seemed to have coped better than she had. Although Mary also produced children at an oppressive rate, she was married to a carpenter whose trade was not subject to the whims of the weather as her own family's was. Sarah, eldest of the three sisters, had avoided the poverty trap completely by managing to align herself to a wealthy stockbroker, fifteen years her senior, who kept her in a style Annie could hardly begin to visualise. It was curious what the fates had handed them, all three girls had entered domestic service when they were twelve but from then on their life paths had diverged so greatly a stranger would never place the trio together as siblings if asked to pick them out of a crowd.

Annie closed the door on her watery world, moving to put a few more sticks on the fire to reheat the stew for tea, there had been an uncomfortable amount of bean and potato stew so far this year but she had promised herself she would give the family a treat this Sunday by killing the oldest hen. She was fairly sure it had stopped laying and it shouldn't be too stringy if it was boiled slowly.

Thomas wandered into the room, a serious lad of seven whose features seemed to register great responsibility at being the family's eldest son. His dark shirt was tucked into a pair of shabby breaches which were hung from his shoulders by leather braces. There was a finger-width gap all round his waist which led Annie to be thankful that he would not be growing out of his trousers any time soon. Gently removing his cap, she dipped a rag into the water bucket and rubbed at his face and hands in an ineffectual effort at cleanliness before their meal.

The smell radiating from the pot above the fire was strong with double cooked kale and pulses, however the speed with which James entered the main room told Annie that her youngest son's stomach was sufficiently empty it could even be enticed by the waft of stewed old vegetables. Dorothy came trailing behind him, a waif of bony arms and knobbly knees topped by a mop of red curls. Within minutes Nora had raced through the front door, removed her brown shawl from over her head and shoulders, leaving it to drip from a nail on the wall. She announced that her father and Peggy were just behind her, dropped a kiss onto her mother's cheek and began slamming bowls and mugs on to the table. Annie moved the cooking pot to the side of the fireplace and took down the kettle, setting it to boil.

When Charles entered his coat streamed water like a dozen milk jugs emptying onto the brown stone flagged floor. Annie fussed around her husband removing his outer clothing and the waistcoat beneath, which was similarly sodden, she mock scolded him that they'd all be done for if he caught his death of cold, while hanging the items carefully on the back of a chair and placing it as close to the fire as she dared without scorching them. The fabric was so thin they were unlikely to be still damp in the morning.

"'ow ever did you get so wet?" Annie asked as she ladled out the stew, making sure there was more potato on Charles' plate than the others.

"Got told there was a message for me in town so I 'ad to walk to Dawlies to pick it up. It was Flo saying I should start in a fortnight."

"That doesn't leave long to get rid of the animals," she said feeling her lips becoming pinched. "People'll be paying less now they know we've gotta go, I bet the 'ole neighbourhood knows by now the way that Olive Dawlie gossips. We'll be lucky to get enough for our train fares let alone pay the first month's rent, I don't know 'ow we'll all be able to manage."

"Stop frettin' Annie," Charles said slowly spooning beans into his mouth while he spoke, his raggedy beard and moustache moving as he chewed methodically. "I've been thinkin', and it's only a thought mind, so don't go yellin' at me if you don't like the idea, but I got to thinkin' that maybe we should write to your elder sister and see if there was a chance she and 'er 'usband might like to 'elp us out a bit by adopting one or two of the little 'uns."

There was a tense silence as a succession of thoughts paraded through Annie's head. First, outrage burned up her neck and cheeks, how could he even consider giving away their children as if they were easily dispensable like rotten cabbages. The anger cooled into sadness as she realised he was only voicing the very thing she already feared, that even with the move they would be unable to support all of them. She saw five pairs of young eyes observing her as Charles kept his gaze fixed on his plate. There was certainly nobody she would trust more than Sarah to care for her precious babes, and the move to Wembley would at least take them closer to her sister's Mayfair home. If they had to sacrifice some of the mouths they were struggling to feed, leaving some of them with Sarah was the sole option Annie would ever consider. Charles risked looking up at his wife and seemed to recognise an expression of resignation.

"If Mr. Lane took in Thomas, or even both the boys, and gave them a bit of learnin' maybe he could use them as apprentices, that would be a heck of a start for the lads ..." he said encouragingly.

"Aunt Sarah told me that Mr. Lane used to be a doctor before he took up stock broking," Nora gabbled, "maybe he'll make Thomas a stockbroker and teach James medicine," she said grabbing her smallest brother and slapping a straw hat on his head before standing him on her chair.

"Imagine James with one of them black bags going round the countryside feeding all the sick people with foul smelling medicines and getting paid a fortune. 'e'd live in a fancy 'ouse with a fancy wife who didn't know nothin' about bringin' up kids, so mother would 'ave to move in and 'elp."

The slight smile that tugged at the corners of Annie's mouth was sufficient to encourage James to visibly enjoy the idea of being the source of the family's largess as he piped up "... and I'd give mother a beautiful shawl with red beads on cos I 'ad so much money, and we'd eat cake every week ..."

"Ahhh, but you've forgotten the rich stockbroker, Thomas Terrill, 'oose living in an 'ouse almost as grand as the Queen's," said Peggy jumping to her feet and hauling Thomas onto another chair where he looked thoroughly bewildered leaving Annie aching to get up and hug her solemn boy.

"Look," Peggy proclaimed, circling her brother theatrically, "at the cut of 'is coat, 'is silken cravat and polished soft leather boots." Thomas wriggled his toes and in an earnest attempt to make his bare feet look more like polished leather carefully rubbed the top of each one up and down the back of his trouser leg.

"Mr Thomas will have spent pounds and pounds on sendin' father the best tobacco for his pipe and will take mother to see the shows at the music 'alls and she'll get to meet all the singers and actors because 'er son's such a classy gent!"

Thomas drew himself up to his full four foot, plumping up the moth-eaten muffler around his neck, becoming entranced by his role as a city toff so that Annie was relieved she hadn't stifled the moment with her urge to enfold him in her arms.

"And I'll buy mother roses and pretty things that make 'er smile," Thomas announced solemnly, "and ribbons for Dorothy's 'air and jewels for Peggy," he concluded.

"I want jewels too," Nora said with a pout, "and I don't think we should forget Flo."

"I'll buy jewels for everyone," said James with ponderous finality, "'cos I'm goin' to give medicine to the Queen and make her young again and then everyone will be so happy they'll give me all their money."

"Yes," said Nora forcing a laugh as she looked pleadingly into her mother's eyes, "and as she gets younger we can have another Diamond Jubilee celebration with a street party like the last time."

"Sit down!" Annie ordered, smiling gently in spite of the turmoil she felt, "we 'aven't even written to your Aunt Sarah yet and you're puttin' it about we've made the family fortune! Tomorrow morning I'll give you a penny," she said turning to Peggy, "and you can go and buy paper and a pencil from Dawlies so we can send a letter. Your father's got a good 'and so he can put down the words, it's far too long since I did my letters and I'm not sure I can remember 'ow," she said feeling as if events were sweeping her along too fast, making her dizzy and confused about the consequences of taking the road they were heading towards, "at least Wembley's close to London so we can all visit regular," she added by way of comforting herself.

The following evening Annie, Charles and the two eldest girls spent over an hour discussing how the letter should be worded to make it most polite, and it was not until the light was already dim in the room that Charles began to write.

Dearest Sister and Mr. Lane,
We hope you are well. There is no sickness in our house but we have been sorely tried by the weather and the deaths of many animals. We are obliged to give up the farm and move to Wembley on Thursday next. We are worried that our monies in Wembley will be greatly stretched and that it will be even harder to support our younger children who are not allowed to work for such a long time. We are writing to see if you could find it in your hearts to adopt one or two of them until our fortunes recover. They are good children and won't give any trouble.
Your loving sister,
Annie

Posted the next day, Annie found herself oscillating between praying the letter never arrived and planning glorious futures for her well educated boys. It was a relief for her tortured mind that most of her waking hours had to be spent packing and preparing for their move. On Tuesday a note came announcing that the Lanes would be arriving on the noon train the following day. Annie would have liked Charles to be present, "to have a man around to talk man-like to Mr. Lane" as she put it, but Charles had to take the last of the animals to market to get what he could for them before they left, and she suspected he was relieved for an unshakeable excuse to avoid spending time with a man with whom he believed he would share absolutely no common experience whatsoever. Annie reckoned men would always bond together, she had watched farmers, travelling salesmen and stall keepers enjoying a jug of beer at the end of a busy market day and did not imagine her sister's husband would be much different from all the other men she had mixed with.

* * *

(Edward Lane: 50, Sarah: 36)
Edward Lane prided himself on hailing from one of the country's most celebrated reformist families, whose refined social conscience had robustly backed everything from Irish Home Rule to contraception for London's prostitutes. Unfortunately these sound ethics had not adequately prepared him for the very real gulf between professional city gentleman and tenant farmer existing below the poverty line.

Addressing the conundrums of social deprivation and lack of education for the masses had provided many afternoons of enjoyable philosophical sparing for Edward as he sat deep within the comfort of the buttoned leather armchairs situated in the lounge of the Constitutional Club on Northumberland Avenue, but actually having to grapple with the same questions in the flesh was already proving to be considerably less pleasant and far more taxing for his polished senses. The stench of the farmyard was truly alarming and the sight of Sarah's sister in her faded blouse with a cleanish apron attempting to hide the patches which made up much of the skirt fabric beneath, was frankly shocking. He could see the resemblance between the sisters in their high cheekbones and the line of their jaw, but their outer trappings were at opposite ends of the fashion scale, it was as if someone were making a crude point that any first impression could be radically altered by a few bits of cloth, jewellery and a shining pair of shoes.

As Edward turned his attention towards the philanthropic reason for his visit, five bland pasty faces stared back at him. He attempted a smile, but the expressions before him remained the same and Edward's stomach began to sink lower in his abdomen as he realised that the family who had requested his assistance did not even possess the grace to welcome him as a selfless saviour when he took the trouble to respond to their plea.

* * *

When Annie heard the station cart rumble up the track she had felt confident of the good impression her scoured house and children would make on her sister's partner. The gallons of glacial water she had drawn from the well the previous day had been used to expunge the worst of the grease stains from clothes, floors, walls and skin. Her kids all looked cleaner and neater than she had ever seen them, although the redness behind Thomas's ears where she had scrubbed to remove encrusted grime was perhaps more noticeable than if she had left the dirt where it was, yet as the couple waited for the driver to fold out the steps so they could climb down, Annie's confidence began to waver. She stared at her sister decked-out in a double-breasted travelling gown, its polka dot collar matching the spotted feather which jauntily adorned the left side of her hat. Wiping her hands nervously down the front of her apron she digested the evidence that on previous visits Sarah had clearly dressed down. The man beside her sported a gleaming top hat, elegantly tailored coat and silver-topped cane. Now that Annie saw her sister with Edward Lane she was at a complete loss to know how their union had ever been accomplished. She remembered the neat starched uniform Sarah had worn when she was in service, looking slim and pretty, but the gulf between that and the, grand, almost haughty, woman she saw in front of her was staggering.

A delicate sun-shaped broach had been used to fasten the scarf around Sarah's slender neck and from every part of its orb and wavy rays transparent stones glistened. Pawning such an item would keep a family for months, Annie thought, and for the first time ever she was unable to meet her sister's eyes as the weight of differences in their circumstances erased the pride she had earlier felt. Before this moment Annie had believed she knew her sister; they had grown up and played together, they would laugh and cry together, they looked out for one another, the three of them forever united by their bond of sisterhood; yet in this outfit, with this man, she couldn't recognise her sister at all.

* * *

Sarah felt grateful that most of Edward's features were covered by well groomed whiskers, however to a practiced observer, such as herself, his eyes gave him away. He was horrified. It was as she had feared. When her sister's letter arrived Sarah had cautioned against the two of them travelling to Wilton, suggesting instead that they send the family a little extra money every month to help with boots and schooling, but Edward had become animated by the idea of transforming one of the country's most disadvantaged youngsters by submerging it in the priviledged lifestyle of Mayfair, his conversation had taken on the air of Mr. Brownlow as he painted himself as a man poised to make a real difference to part of the social life of Britain. In spite of her most earnest efforts Sarah had been unable to draw him away from his fantasy world by gently placing pictures of rural reality before him, now she could see he was being brutally initiated into true country life and every part of his immaculately groomed exterior was recoiling from what he saw. Sarah wished she had a moment to speak to her sister alone, to hatch some kind of plan to guide the children and Edward through the next hour, but such a luxury was impossible and she felt horribly torn between maintaining her habitual London look and a deep wish to embrace her careworn sister and the clutch of ragged offspring. Another glance at Edward's rigid face and the stiffness of his bearing made her capitulate into remaining uncharacteristically aloof in the belief it would somehow support him through an experience which was so far removed from his comfort zone as to be almost physically painful to watch.

    The warmest gesture Sarah managed was a quick squeeze of Annie's hand as her sister ushered Edward Lane to stoop beneath the lintel of the cottage where a bare whitewashed room greeted him. The couple had brought a two-tiered iced cake with them in a large box and Sarah hoped that the sight of it would enliven the children out of their grave silence. The cake, however, seemed to further unnerve Annie who had placed three matching teacups and a screw of tea on the table in preparation for the visit but suddenly claimed all the plates had been packed and sent to Wembley ahead of them. Sarah suspected the cups were borrowed as all the family's china she had ever seen was a mishmash of designs and invariably chipped. Both the sisters had been in service long enough to know what a gentleman expected, and she believed Annie had calculated that Edward would find the experience of eating without porcelain quaint if he believed it was due to the constrains of packing and moving, but would be appalled to see them using her usual tableware which by its very nature underscored the family's level of destitution.

As Sarah handed each of the children their portions she was repaid with mumbled thanks and although she attempted to smile the reticence out of her nieces and nephews their fearful round eyes remained while the silence lengthened as each of them adopted the pretence of taking inordinate care over eating, never lifting their line of sight from cake or floor.

It was clear to Sarah that Edward was slightly rattled by the elongating awkwardness but, not one to be beaten by situations, he began to ask each of Annie's brood what their future ambitions were. Peggy managed to respond to her mother's begging looks, stating politely that she hoped to go into service as soon as they arrived in Wembley. Nora lightened the mood by announcing her aspiration was to work in a cigarette factory as she had heard that quick rollers could earn up to seven shillings a week and everyone knew girls' hands were more nimble than boys' because of the needlework they did.

Then came Thomas, he shifted his weight from one foot to the other, eyes still firmly fixed on his boots, unable to say a word. As Sarah watched him her corseted form wished to crumble as she recognised how hard he was struggling to say the right thing to the man everyone in the tiny room expected to become his mentor. Although Thomas had never seemed to her to be an emotional child, Sarah was almost certain she saw the glint of a sheen beneath his lowered eye lashes and his nose seemed just a little too pink to be solely from the cold clamminess of the day.

"So Thomas," Mr. Lane prompted once again, "Peggy wants to go into service and Nora wants to roll cigarettes in a factory, can't you think of something you would like to do?"

"I'll do whatever I'm told, sir," he finally blurted out before falling mute once again.

"I want to be a dancer and work in the music halls," exclaimed Dorothy, "and I think your spotted waistcoat is very pretty, I've never seen one like that before."

"Dorothy! Mind your manners," Annie interjected sharply. But Dorothy's liveliness acted like a small sigh of normality to Sarah and she smiled as Edward replied he thought Dorothy's hair was very pretty. He really was coping with this experience extraordinarily well she felt, Dorothy's red-blonde curls were the single beautiful thing in the room and he had picked it out and flattered the five-year-old without missing a beat.

The compliment elicited a bobbed curtsey and a "Thank you, Sir" which led to Edward's hairy cheeks lifting into a full smile for the first time since they had arrived. Sarah could see young James become eager to add to his sister's triumph as he leant forward, all shyness gone, preparing to answer the question he knew would be his, but Edward abruptly rose from his seat, thanked Annie for the tea and announced he was going to seek out the cart driver and instruct him to reharness his horses ready for the journey back to the station, as he reached the door he gestured for Sarah to follow him outside.

They walked towards the field in which the horses were grazing, Sarah keeping a step behind him, too concerned at Edward's probable reaction to her family to brave breaking the silence. She had sensed James had been about to announce an exotic career goal and was disappointed the tea party had been truncated just when she felt the atmosphere was thawing and it might be possible for both boys to display their true characters.

"If you've no objection, we'll take Dorothy," he called back to her. "She seems personable and could be quite pretty with a good wash and the right clothes."

"Dorothy!" Sarah stammered, the realisation that he had no idea what would help her family slapped her firmly in the face.

"Yes, best to leave the boys to follow in their father's footsteps and the other girls are both almost of working age."

The retort rose in her throat that their father's footsteps had been so inadequate the family was penniless. She swallowed it down hard, conscious that however ignorant he appeared by his current action, he would be deeply hurt by any comment that might reveal him to be less in touch with reality than those who lived in such abasement on the farm. As she watched him raise his walking cane to hail the driver she knew that whatever she said would bring him no closer to comprehending the realities of Annie's life and that, without doubt, Dorothy probably would fit in with their lifestyle better than any of the others; she was young enough to be moulded and taught, bright enough to remember where she had come from and so be suitably grateful for where she'd ended up. Edward's vision of pious altruism it certainly was not, but a pleasant addition to their already pleasant lives it might become.

Sarah walked slowly back towards the cottage, meandering around the farmyard inspecting stones and the well with its precariously worn rope, taking in the stack of baskets used for apple picking and the old horse-mounting block, now wobbly where part of the soil had sunk beneath it; head down, she was trying to decide what attitude to employ when telling her sister of Edward's decision. There was no doubt that Annie would be shocked, maybe even angry, to educate and aggrandise a girl was a shameless waste when the only outcome it could be expected to generate was a better marriage rather than the improved future prospects for the entire clan that could be gained by educating a boy. Undoubtedly Thomas had not presented himself as a winsome child, but she had expected Edward to take James instead.

Her rational mind knew all the reasons why this decision was insensitive and reprehensible and she bit her lip in an attempt to keep the rigid seriousness on her face that the situation demanded, yet despite her efforts she was engulfed by a heady wave of delight. It had not been her choice so she could not be held accountable for its frivolity, her own deep sense of responsibility would never have permitted her to do anything so utterly delicious, but Edward's ruling handed her the one thing her privileged life was missing, a child. Not just any child, but a charming little girl, her very own walking, talking doll upon whom she could lavish love and attention making rays of sunlight slice their way through the arid adult existence she and Edward had cultivated over the past five years. Looking down she realised that she was still carrying the empty cake box which had been perched on her lap in the cottage. A flock of starlings were aggressively poking the ground beside the muck pile. They rose into the sky at her approach, then dived for the crumbs as she opened the box and tossed them into the air. Watching their concentrated ferocity in the pursuit of the best and biggest morsels, Sarah attempted to edge away from the possibility that this would be how Annie would view her in a few minutes time; like a greedy eagle swooping in upon the nest in her dark travelling cloak, and seizing the choicest chick, before soaring back to her eyrie high above, indifferent to the devastation she had caused below. Guilt was tweaking the edges of her pleasure but it was insufficient to erase the excitement she was only just managing to push down, stopping it from recklessly surging through her and stamping its mark across her usually impassive features. The difficulty of keeping the happiness off her face made Sarah realise she would be unable to deliver the news of Edward's choice with any empathy for the disappointment and anguish it would cause Annie; the predator would have to retain the arrogance her fine plumage permitted. All she could do was make a silent vow to rectify the damage later, when the move had been made and emotions had been soothed by time.

Within twenty minutes Dorothy had been bundled into the cart. Promises of visits had been made and Thomas had lost his boots as well as his fortune to his younger sister who had possessed no footwear of her own, being too young to have to walk to school yet. The Terrills' arms stopped waving even before the travellers had rounded the bend, dropping to their sides openly weary with the incomprehension at what had just occurred.

* * *

Peggy was not usually frightened by her father but the colour of his face darkened and the contempt in his voice dripped ever heavier as he questioned each one of his children individually. One by one Charles instructed them to recount the day's events and Peggy watched her mother attempt to shield Thomas and James as every successive mention of Dorothy's "pretty hair" seemed to add to her father's building fury until disappointment and anger overflowed into derision.

"Pretty 'air!" Charles yelled banging his fist against the flaking cottage wall, "who chooses 'ow to 'elp their kith and kin from pretty 'air? She don't eat nothin', she don't need a penny a week for school and she won't do nothin' 'cept get married to some fancy bloke like 'imself who 'as no more idea of 'ow to 'elp 'is own family than a sheep knows 'ow to plough a field. Pretty 'air! 'e sounds like some daft rich old spinster choosin' a lap dog."

Later, propping herself up on one elbow as she leant to blow out the stub of candle beside the bed, Nora voiced what Peggy was already thinking, it was unsettling to be lying there without Dorothy's little body between them, her red curls mixing on the bolster with their mousy ones.

"We'll end up goodness knows where tomorrow," Peggy replied a little shakily. "And Dorothy'll end up as grand as Aunt Sarah," she said licking her fingers to pinch the wick and stop it smoking.

"Yes, but it'll be a while before she's big enough to ask 'er for 'and-me-downs," Nora grunted sleepily, as Peggy pulled the blanket up high and attempted to ignore the chilly gap at her back.

CHAPTER TWO

When Dorothy awoke her first thought was that she had died. Although this was worrying, she felt glad she had managed to avoid the painful bit. Above her was a high white ceiling with curly plasterwork around the edges and extra swirls, which looked like fluffy stone feathers, at the corners. She was a little confused by her need to pee and wondered if the urge was not real if you were in heaven and whether that meant it would be fine to stay in the warm bed and let go. On the off chance that the afterlife didn't operate quite as efficiently as she imagined, she wriggled over the side of the thick mattress, dropping to the floor where she found a china chamber pot with blue flowers on it and a matching lid. A few pinches and a glance at her toenails, which were thoroughly grubby from the insides of Thomas's boots, convinced her that her initial supposition had been wrong. Everyone knew that when dead people became angels they got white and clean, which her feet were definitely not.

    The events of the previous day reappeared in a jumbled haze; climbing onto the station cart and her mother kissing her in a way that was not quite cross but also not quite cuddly had made her wonder if she had done something wrong; she remembered the train, which had tried to hiss at her, and had gone so fast that when she squashed her nose against the window and stared forward it had made her dizzy, so she had stopped, scared that she might be sick which would make Aunt Sarah angry and waste the wonderful cake whose sugary icing she could still taste around her lips. Then, when they had left the train she recalled getting into a black carriage with dark red cushions and hearing Mr Lane tell the driver to go to Maddox Street, but after that she must have fallen asleep as she had no recollection of how she came to be wearing a white lady's shirt with puffed shoulders, which almost touched her ears. The sleeves had been rolled up four times and were very bunchy, yet Dorothy's fingers only just peeped from the ends when she stretched her arms out in front of her. The bottom of the shirt ended half an inch above her ankles and the high collar was sufficiently wide for her to be able to pop a shoulder out of one side when the other was tight against her neck.

She padded over to the window, it was in two halves with six small panes top and bottom, but as she drew closer her steps became smaller and more nervous as she realised she was higher than she had ever been before. Edging towards the sill in case her negligible weight might be sufficient to over balance the building, she looked down into the street and across at the massive stone columns supporting the front of a church. She was a little disappointed she could not tell Thomas that she was now far higher than he had been in the big tree of the south field and so although he may have climbed further up than she had dared and called her chicken, she had finally out done him by at least half a tree's height.

* * *

Katherine Jones occupied the smallest bedroom of the third floor apartment at Hanover Mansions. She had worked for the Lanes for the past five years and had intended to make Maddox Street her final placement before retiring. The Lanes had proved to be quiet and considerate employers, perfectly suited to Miss Jones' temperament which disliked noise, disruption and, in particular, children. Up until the previous evening Miss Jones had been content to amble towards her twilight years, secure and unruffled by her surroundings, but last night the master and mistress she believed she had got so well trained, had rebelled horribly, returning late at night carrying a child whom they announced they had adopted.

To say Miss Jones was vexed was a vast understatement. After mutely helping Mrs Lane to install the shabby creature in the spare bedroom, Miss Jones had spent the entire night in a state of highly uncomfortable agitation. She wished she could discuss the situation with her cousin whom she met every Sunday for tea but there were more than three days until their ritualistic weekly appointment and in the meantime Miss Jones had no option but to stew.

How, after years of complete predictability, her employers had suddenly hit upon such a hare-brained idea as adopting a child, she had no idea. What possible reason could have driven them to shatter the peace and harmony of their well ordered lives with this red-headed girl? Red heads were known to be the worst, completely wild, she had heard, jumped up little misses who would antagonise staff and cause trouble with normally reasonable employers. She had seen it happen time and again when loyal servants had lost their positions following a little miss or master deciding to have some sport. Furthermore, children always entailed nurses, especially in Mayfair, but there was only one servant's bedroom in the Lane apartment. This was a particular worry, nobody had mentioned a nurse last night so either she would be expected to take on extra child care duties, which she dreaded, or, heaven forbid, she would be asked to make way for a younger more energetic maid who could combine the two rolls. Either option caused Miss Jones to see the new addition to the household as a foul fiend rather than an innocent little nipper.

It was not yet ten in the morning but Miss Jones had already expended considerable energy beating the rugs and had moved on to dusting the contents of the living room with unusual briskness. Turning from the mantelpiece she locked eyes with the miniature intruder who was standing in the doorway. Miss Jones had hoped the child would remain in her room until Mrs Lane returned allowing her the dignity of a formal introduction to the girl at which her employers might impress upon their ward the need for courtesy towards those who served them, but the child stared insolently from the hallway, steadfastly refusing to vanish back to her bedroom.

"'Scuse me, Miss," the trembly voice was sufficiently loud in the empty apartment to command her attention, "do you know where my Aunt Sarah is?"

Ahh, so she was a niece, perhaps there was a chance she would be dispatched back to her family within a few weeks and the household would settle down again.

"Your aunt took a bit of material down to Miss Tremlett to have a dress made up for you. You're to stay as you are until she gets back, although by the look of your feet you should take a bath."

"Oh no," the child stammered, "I can't need one of those, I had one the other day before Aunt Sarah came, although Mother did say the water didn't make much difference to James and I because all the others had been so filthy before us."

Determined not to be foiled in what she had abruptly decided to do, Miss Jones continued, "Cleanliness is next to Godliness; your aunt will be expecting to put a new dress onto a clean body."

"Will you be getting in before me?" the child enquired.

"Indeed I will not! The very thought! Get through that door and I will come and run it in a minute."

* * *

Dorothy scampered down the hallway and in through the door that had been indicated before revolving slowly in a full circle, mouth and eyes wide open as she took in the furnishings and then had to restrain herself from the impulse to twiddle and pull and splash – what a playground!

There was an enormous white bath set along one wall on legs with huge black paws at each corner. Dorothy knelt down running her fingers between the iron claws before turning her attention to the first flushing lavatory she had seen in her life. She reckoned the smooth wooden seat would be fine enough for a princess, even a small child who had to wiggle off the seat rather than just stand up like adults did, would be in no danger of catching splinters off this piece of wood. High above her there was a tank with an arm coming off it to which a chain and porcelain toggle was attached, Dorothy was fairly sure it was for pulling on but she would need to stand on the seat to reach. She was just considering climbing up when the fearsome maid entered carrying two thick folded towels and a bottle of pale purple liquid. Dorothy hoped it wasn't some nasty medicine she was going to be forced to drink.

Although she was longing for an opportunity to pull hard on the toggle, Dorothy stood still with her hands behind her back watching the water spill out from the great metal taps as the black and white clad ogress bent over the bath tub. She tried to look unquestionably obedient hoping that her clearly biddable nature would soften a smile out of the terrifying domestic, but it didn't appear to be working and the housemaid roughly removed Dorothy's shirt, plonking the skinny child into the water and beginning to scrub without taking any more notice of her than if she had been part of a pile of washing on Monday morning. Working upwards from her feet, Dorothy was relieved when her oppressor changed from a brush to a cloth upon reaching her face. Using the same bar of soap that had been employed on the rest of her, two thick freckled arms lathered up the rich red curls before sloshing out the residue with jugs of water deposited on her head before Dorothy realised what was happening and had the foresight to close her eyes. Out of the bath and smarting all over she cringed at the sight of the stopper being loosened from the bottle of lilac liquid, anticipating that a large spoon was about to be extracted from the deep apron pocket and rammed into her throat forcing her to choke down some vile potion. Instead Dorothy was treated to some of the contents being rubbed into her hair whilst she breathed in the dense scent of lavender. Surprise at such a gorgeous indulgence triumphed over muteness, and Dorothy thanked the maid for making her smell like a flower. This small politeness appeared to jolt the ageing spinster into focusing on her charge and she began to comb out the red curls quite gently laying each knot-free section carefully over the child's shoulder.

An hour later Aunt Sarah smiled down at her freshly laundered niece and complimented Miss Jones on the transformation before giving Dorothy a package to unwrap; sliding off the string and slowly bending out the stiff brown paper she extracted a simple frock made of emerald green material which Dorothy believed to be the most beautiful dress ever created. Aunt Sarah had even pressed the dressmaker to use the cut-off from the hem to make a matching hair ribbon and by the time Mr Lane returned from his office, apart from a continued lack of footwear, as Aunt Sarah had posted Thomas's boots back to the family that morning, Dorothy had been remodelled into something not out of place in a genteel living room. Feeling like the prettiest fairy imaginable, Dorothy twirled in front of her uncle, the rich material billowing out as her shining hair spun behind her.

"Quite the Mayfair Miss in a few short hours!" Edward exclaimed, clearly delighted at the metamorphosis, "We need to have the ribbon trimmed in white though," he commented as he circled the now still model with the look of a professional design critic, "then we can buy white shoes and gloves to go with it. The colour's perfect for her hair but accessories must always match, young lady," he said with a twinkle "yet if we buy them in green it will be difficult to use them with any other outfit."

"I won't need anything else for years," Dorothy replied horrified at the notion that her uncle might believe her to be so extravagant, "this one's got lots of room in it and I've got the dress I came in which I should really wear on weekdays and keep this one for best," she said seriously before noticing her Aunt's smile which seemed to be urging her to stop. Sarah carefully explained Edward's generosity and the enjoyment it gave him to see everyone elegantly attired, telling Dorothy that she herself often changed her outfit two or three times a day. Nevertheless, her aunt cautioned, in the case of a growing child, enjoyment at seeing smart clothes must be tempered by the fact that Dorothy would soon outgrow all the items of her wardrobe.

"So you see Uncle Edward is correct that white accessories make the best sense when you're young," she concluded. "We'll draw around your feet and hands so that I can use the outlines to buy shoes and gloves tomorrow and then I can take you for your first walk through Hyde Park." But Dorothy had already ceased listening properly, her mind whirling with the idea of having anything more than one dress in the world, it suddenly seemed a very long time since she had left the farm.

* * *

Wandering along the Serpentine and watching the young boys being taught to swim suspended from ropes and poles like gargantuan baited fishing rods, became one of Dorothy's favourite pastimes. As Aunt Sarah had hinted, her wardrobe grew as she was taken to see ever more amazing things. Almost daily she was presented with a new wonder so that the peacocks in Kensington Gardens were quickly surpassed by the weird beasts Dorothy gawped at in Regent's Park zoo, and the Crystal Palace and

Victoria and Albert museum left her with so many questions that she was pressing her aunt and uncle for answers from sun up until she dropped into bed, exhausted by another day of discovery. Her aunt spent several hours a day teaching her to read and when the fair lashes began to droop with the effort, Aunt Sarah would tell her fables or folk tales, or, best of all, they would play a game where Dorothy would choose four of the most bizarre characters she could conjure up and her aunt would have to weave them into a story.

Even in the evenings Dorothy's appetite for her new life style didn't wane and she would coax her uncle away from his armchair and on to the piano stool where she would balance precariously beside him watching his fingers and attempting to copy them until she was finally chased beneath the feather eiderdown to recharge for the following day.

The Lane's piano was a simple black Chappell upright but its casing had been carved all over; tall cornflowers grew up the sides whilst the lid and front panels were emblazoned with musical adages produced in perfect copperplate script, even the narrow strips of the music stand itself were bedecked with leaves. The carvings had transformed a bog standard instrument into a work of art and Dorothy would cajole her uncle into recounting the story of his mother being asked by a travelling carpenter if he might beautify her piano, and her agreement born out of pity at his frayed appearance. The carpenter had worked swiftly and by the end of the day the piano had been fully adorned and Mrs Lane senior willingly paid the four shillings that had been agreed upon. Visitors to the Lane house frequently admired the carvings and were eager to arrange for the young man to work on personalising their own furniture but the only clue to his name were the initials H.W. carved next to the date of 1890. Nobody had ever seen him in the area again and so the Lane piano remained unique, a fact that made Dorothy even more eager to learn to play it.

For Dorothy, the daily lessons and outings with her aunt and uncle took over almost seamlessly from the routines of searching for eggs around the farmyard and helping her mother in the vegetable garden. The months passed in busy contentment and at the start of the New Year, just after Queen Victoria had finally expired, Dorothy started school at the local convent attached to St. George's church, an impressive building which faced her bedroom window and whose bells called the family of three to do penance every Sunday.

It was more than a year later, in the early autumn of 1902, when Dorothy finally went to visit her parents and siblings in Wembley for the first time.

* * *

1902, Wembley.
(Dorothy: 7, Nora: 11, Peggy: 14)
James was playing in the road with most of the other lads from Gladstone V tenement, it was Sunday morning, a time when children were 'shushed' and even a normal amount of noise was likely to be punished by a clip round the ear. James always felt such chastisement to be unjust given the amount of singing and shouting the grown-ups indulged in on a Friday and Saturday night, but to say so would have earned him the strap. Dorothy's younger brother had lost his infant chubbiness and stretched out into a streetwise six-year-old dappled with the normal grazes, cuts and smuts and topped with an untidy mop of brown hair which covered his ears, and often his eyes, except for when violent head flicking kept it back. He often soaked his head under the tap so that the unruly mass would clump together allowing him to see. It was the closest thing to washing that he regularly managed. James's best friends were the two Henrys. Henry Rickman lived on the ground floor and so was considered to be the poshest of the trio by virtue of living closest to the tap and the privy, while Henry Reed was lowest in the pecking order because his parents lived on the top floor. James was in the middle of the two and could see no way of bettering his social status because Henry Rickman was also half a head taller than him, owned a jacket with pockets, and had an ugly looking scar across his left cheek where his Dad's belt had caught him, all of which were badges of honour James could not mimic, but when a finely dressed lady and pristine child turned into the street and he recognised his Aunt, James saw the fleeting possibility of a leg up.

"That's my sister," he announced to the Henrys who were gawping at the strangers in a particularly slack-mouthed manner.

"Don't be daft," said the jacket-clad Henry, "you don't know no one what looks like 'er."

"Na," the other Henry agreed whilst perfecting the art of picking up pebbles and throwing them with his toes, "but I dare you a farthin' to go up and talk to 'er."

"You don't 'ave a farthin'," James pointed out.

"But I do," Henry One chimed in, "and it says you don't know that young miss."

"Done," said James marching off up the street in the direction of the visitors. He was determined not to look back at his friends, knowing that with every unhesitant step worry would be creeping further up their faces as they realised the farthing was being neatly transported into his pocket.

James half dragged his giggling sister back to the Henrys whilst Aunt Sarah progressed at a more sedate pace. The two lads appeared far less perturbed at their financial loss than they were engrossed by their efforts to compete with each other through tales of their individual valour as they regaled Dorothy with stories of foiling local robbers and scaling impossibly high walls, and with each courageous invention James knew his standing in Gladstone V had gone up another notch and wondered how regularly he could arrange for his sister to visit.

Proudly leading the way up the stairs to the four rooms occupied by the seven Terrills, James thought back to Wilton and how it had been fun to have Dorothy around. With a twinge of surprise he recognised that he had missed her, especially now that Thomas seemed to spend most of his time with their father leaving James marooned in the midst of his many older sisters.

Opening the door to the living room was like unstopping a bottle of shaken beer, Annie, Flo, Peggy and Nora enveloped Sarah and Dorothy in a shower of hugs, kisses and questions. The preliminaries accomplished, Dorothy was soon the centre of a circle of siblings as she told stories of the giraffe's blue tongue and the terrifying occupants of the Reptile House at the zoo. James honoured Dorothy with his full attention and carefully asked every pertinent question to ensure he was supremely knowledgeable in front of the Henrys, so cementing his superiority even after Dorothy had been evacuated back to Mayfair.

* * *

Directly Dorothy had gained the attention of her sisters and James, Sarah touched Annie's arm and softly jerked her head in the direction of the next door room. She had spent many hours perfecting her apology to her sister for hijacking the wrong child, but as she embarked upon her speech Annie gently shook her head and smiled before taking one of her sister's hands and sandwiching it between her own rough two.

"I know what you're goin' to say, but there's no need, honest, it was all strange that day and we didn't get to chat as we normally do, but in the end I think it's worked out for the best." Sarah felt herself pulled gently across the room to sit on the patchwork cover of the bed, her sister never letting go of her hand. "Thomas is always off working with his father now. They both like it that way and I'm told to tell the Attendance Officer that school makes 'im pale and weak so 'e's 'elping 'is Dad for 'ealth reasons. Maybe James could have benefited from a bit more learnin' but I'm not sure you'd 'ave managed to get 'im to stick at it. I can't get 'im to the schoolroom more than three days in seven and that's with the threat of a rod behind 'im," she said grinning wryly, "and our Dorothy looks so beautiful. Really looks the part she does. It's made my 'eart right glad just seeing 'er today."

"I know she misses you ..." Sarah began, feeling as if it was something she should say to a mother.

"Misses all this! You 'ave to be jokin'!"

Sarah had forgotten how disarmingly frank Annie could be and she felt foolish for even trying to hoodwink her with insincere platitudes.

"She's 'appy with you, anyone can see that, and I'm grateful for it. One look at 'er and you can see she'll never be back down rotten row, and good luck to 'er."

Sarah lowered her eyes feeling shamed by her sister's brutal honesty. Her gaze rested on the waistband of Annie's skirt and she was dismayed to see it stretched tight above an unmistakable lump.

"That's not another one is it?" she queried nodding her head at the protrusion and hoping Annie would say she was just getting heavier with the years.

"Yes, I thought I was past all that, but then this one crept up on me. Still, I'm 'ealthy enough and maybe it'll be a brother for James." She smoothed the skirt over the bump in a tender, stroking motion. "Things aren't as bad as when we asked for your 'elp, Flo's been made Assistant Cook and is doing really well for 'erself. Charles's work seems steady. Peggy's 'appy with 'er employers and Nora 'as got work with a dressmaker. Even Thomas gets given a few pennies now and then from the foreman."

They returned to the main room where Annie drew Dorothy onto her lap, kissing the top of her head and listening to all the children chatter, filling each other in on their lives with no more reticence than if Dorothy had only been gone a week. Sarah was relieved that the reunion did not feel forced or awkward and that Dorothy seemed able to slip back into her family without noticing the widening difference between her appearance and theirs, still happy to be rocked on her mother's knee, resting her thick red locks on Annie's shoulder.

* * *

Dorothy was cuddled into her mother, and a comforting thumb had crept into her mouth even though she continued to answer the ocean of questions James swamped her with, when the room became suddenly quiet. At first she snuggled further into Annie's ample chest enjoying the silence as a restful hiatus to the chatter, but slowly the feeling that the others were holding their breath crept into her stomach and she looked up to see her father and Thomas silhouetted in the doorway. Removing her thumb she slipped off her mother's knee, pushing through the atmosphere as she walked towards them. Father and son seemed to be joined in some way, united and solid in front of her, an impenetrable border of maleness which didn't soften at the approach of her faltering smile. The ease she had felt with her mother and sisters evaporated as she stood before her father and debated whether she should embrace him or shake hands. There was a throbbing between her temples as she wished he would make a move and take away the squirmy feeling by giving her a signal that this silence was from joy at seeing her rather than something more sinister.

"It's lovely to see you Father, Thomas," she tried as the mood fell around the room like a sopping blanket.

"I wouldn't 'ave recognised you, all done up as you are," her father muttered striding into the room. "Afternoon Sarah. Is there some lunch 'ere for the workers?"

Unfreezing at the command, the rest of the family began bringing bread, dripping, cold slices of beef and a jar of jam which Aunt Sarah had brought together with some fine strong cheese. The activity tranquilised the petulance which had landed on the room with the latest arrivals, but it was only replaced by a tense politeness which spread around the table with the passing of food and drink. Dorothy avoided her father's eyes which seemed disapproving if not actually scornful. She busied herself feverishly with asking Thomas about his work and showing unbounded admiration for every terse piece of information about his life she managed to tease out of him. Her chest felt tight and she struggled to swallow anything during the meal, alternately wishing that the room would revert to how it had been before, and then feeling guilty as she acknowledged that the thought entailed removing her father and elder brother. Confused and unhappy she probed further for subjects that would bring the happiness back into the day, but every touch of her voice seemed to cause father and son to flinch and with each rebuff the muscles up the back of her neck became more taut until it seemed as if they were pulling her eyebrows up through her scalp. The more she tried, the more Thomas seemed emboldened at belittling her, making comments behind his hand to James, ridiculing the lace around the cuffs of her dress and her unaccented voice.

Finding she had no answers to the petty criticisms, Dorothy felt the telltale sting at the back of her nose, she stared fixedly at the oilcloth on the table confused by James's sudden flip-flop from friend to foe, her stomach was churning with questions and frustration about why none of the adults, who had seemed so happy with her visit such a short time previously, were prepared to help. Without an explanation they silently accepted her misery, offering no light hearted escape route from the viperous atmosphere surrounding her.

* * *

Dorothy sat looking out of the window throughout the journey home allowing her small hand to rest in her Aunt's while Sarah stroked the back of it with her thumb as the train rocked them back and forth clattering rhythmically away from Wembley. As the carriage slowed and they drew into the station Dorothy said in little more than a whisper, "I don't think the boys like me any more," before lapsing into silence again.

Sarah tried to soften her eyes while looking down on her niece, willing the child to stop brooding on adult problems and hoping she would be mother enough to obliterate Dorothy's obvious pain. "Time may change things," she offered.

"I don't think it will," came the innocently simple reply, slicing straight through her own trite remark to a harsh uncomfortable truth.

Steph Mason

CHAPTER THREE

1912
(Nora: 21, Peggy: 24, Flo: 26, James: 16, Annie: 46)
Nora was the only Terrill still left in Wembley where she had developed into a competent dressmaker's assistant although the long hours and the need to live above the shop were beginning to chafe at her patience. Now that she had come of age she began to view Peggy's life in London with greedy eyes, she felt restless and recognised it was a mood that was unlikely to shift whilst she continued to spend most of her time bending over yards of material with a mouthful of pins listening to impassioned gossip above her head. The recent antics of the suffragettes had lessened the hours of boredom a little by providing her with a rich fantasy life. Regular acts of vandalism and increasing militancy had enlivened the clients' chatter, banishing much of the banal local tittle tattle in favour of the strident opinion each customer had on the latest illegal exploit or passive arrest. Nora kept her eyes down and her thoughts silent but her imagination was working overtime as she pictured herself walking down Bonds Street, where the shop fronts were so charmingly decorated with the most elaborate clothing or choicest foods, each beckoning the fashionable buyer inside. She saw herself promenading in one of the long silk dresses and matching bonnets she spent her days stitching: Nora Terrill walking daintily and in perfect harmony with her wealthy fellow shoppers until suddenly she whipped out a hammer from her colour coordinated handbag and smashed as many shop windows as she could, jumping back from the lethal rain of crystal shrapnel that exploded around her as she rampaged from men's tailors to jewellers and booksellers, stopping only as the sound of police whistles gave the signal that it was time to hitch up her elegant skirts and leg it as fast as possible. This, and the day dream about being

one of the suffragette arsonists, was Nora's favourite way of passing the working day. As fresh details of the unladylike crimes dropped from the mouths of patrons while she hemmed and pinned at their ankles, every snippet of information was stored away in her head to provide additional embellishments to her elaborate musings. If forced to choose between her two main fantasies she thought she preferred the arsonist as although it didn't involve the delicious shock value of pulling out a hammer in the midst of a crowd of London's elite, she relished the full bodied tingle of excitement she experienced when she imagined herself sneaking across dark fields with a can of petrol, and watching the uncontrollable burst of orange eating the night sky before she melted into the blackness again to present a respectable day face the following morning. Over and over again she would picture herself emerging from the shadows to ignite the glowing tongues of dissent that consumed churches and government buildings making pompous parliamentarians sticky with nerves that they might be forced to bow to her petticoat power. Nora had not actually met anyone who had invited her to become part of the cause, but the thought that she, young Miss Terrill, could take action and create headlines was almost as fulfilling as actually going out, matches in hand, maybe more so, it made her quite shivery just to think about it.

Consequently, when she was invited up to London to help her sisters finish the spring cleaning of the Lane's apartment she was hoping they would furnish her with the latest militant titbits that had not yet reached the shop in Wembley, but also, on this particular visit, she was bursting to confide the latest family gossip about which she had been unable to speak to anyone at work, forcing her to swallow it within herself until she could gain relief by splurging it all over Peggy and Dorothy.

Nora's family now spread itself from North London down to the South Coast, after a decade in Wembley the Terrill parents and younger charges had moved to Bexhill-on-Sea. Flo had been the instigator of the Bexhill move when she was taken on at Madeley House as cook. Nora suspected her sister was enamoured with a rather staid part-time gardener who always seemed to be calling at the house when she went down there and whom young James had become so familiar with he called him "Walter" instead of "Mr. Mitten" without being rebuked. However, both Flo and Walter seemed so shy of anything that could be deemed 'frivolous' that Nora reckoned they would both be old and grey before they made it to the altar. However, she was fairly certain it was Walter's presence that had made Flo unusually stubborn about remaining in Sussex when her mother began making it clear she missed her presence and her help considerably in Wembley.

Thomas had left home to work on a farm in northern England, and with Peggy gone to join Dorothy at Aunt Sarah's and Nora forced to live above the shop with the other girls, their mother had begun to struggle with the youngest siblings. Sybil had been born soon after Sarah and Dorothy's uneasy visit to Wembley, but five years later Vera had arrived and this pregnancy, at forty-three, seemed to have left Annie exhausted in a way Nora had not seen her before. She had always thought of her mother like a friendly carthorse, able to manage a baby on each hip, toddlers at her feet and still carry the groceries home from market, but by the time the family moved to Bexhill Annie was stooped and appeared to have lived many more years than her elder sister. Never one to complain, Nora had become worried when her mother regularly admitted to suffering from a headache, and her father grumbled continuously that his rest was disturbed by Annie abruptly throwing off the bed covers and walking around the room fanning herself with the hem of her nightie.

"She can't let a man sleep," he growled, "if it's not a baby yellin', it's 'er acting as if she's turned into a bleedin' volcano."

Certainly Nora had been concerned, but not quite enough to ask her employer if she could leave the camaraderie of the dormitory. Life at the dressmakers wasn't full of music halls, big parks and shops as Peggy's now was, but it was still a step up from Gladstone V Tenement and Nora wasn't about to lose the sliver of autonomy she'd obtained. She imagined Flo must have felt much the same, but as ever her elder sister had managed to be proactive in her resistance claiming it would be better for their mother's health to move to the south coast and persuading her father to accept a job in a local dairy despite it being a slight demotion from the post he had held in Wembley.

"The Head Dairyman will be retiring in a couple of years," Flo cajoled, "and the sea air will be good for mother and the children," she concluded briskly as she announced there was a cottage in Sandhurst Lane that would suit them, neatly bulldozing her father down south and removing the problem from Nora's doorstep, for which she was duly grateful even if she never quite managed to say so.

* * *

James finished his final year at school in Bexhill and at fourteen became the oldest Terrill scholar apart from Dorothy. He had managed to avoid the angry young man aspect of adolescence and had developed his role as family charmer. Even when his mother was drooping with fatigue James could always drag a laugh out of her. He adored the response he got when he brought home flowers he'd picked from the roadside for her, or when he forced her to sit down while he made her a cup of tea, settling a cushion behind her head and paying her extravagant compliments which she drank in and which seemed to restore her even more than the brew.

Two days after he left school James answered an advertisement in the local paper for a photographer's assistant, and began work straight away when the astute studio proprietor recognised the lad's ability to put any customer at their ease. Since the construction of the Sackville Hotel and the De La Warr Parade, Bexhill had burgeoned into a Mecca for well-heeled tourists who believed in the health benefits of the sun and sea. Innumerable wealthy widows patronised the area and James was so adept at flattering these ladies that, once through the door, they would often return for a second or even a third photo session to enjoy the gentle fussing and gallant ego-massage the photographer's assistant could be guaranteed to provide.

Arriving home when the shop finally closed up its shutters, James would regale his mother with stories of stout elderly ladies sporting hairy faces who had expected to be made to look like luscious stage stars and how much trouble he had gone to with lighting and strategically placed pot plants and feathers to cover up their most unsavoury aspects, all the time telling his mother she was a queen by comparison with these well-shod sows, but, as the clientele tipped more handsomely with every fresh compliment she must forgive him for his constant flattery of ladies so much less worthy than she, and think only of the food it put on the table. James luxuriated in the smile he could draw onto his mother's face, his mum was worth every trinket and treat he could bring home for her. His father, by contrast, was superfluous to requirements. He wouldn't antagonise the man by saying so out loud, but James couldn't help thinking the house always felt lighter when his father wasn't there.

* * *

Maddox Street, London W1
(Aunt Sarah: 48, Dorothy: 17, Uncle Edward: 62)
The apartment was in chaos, the curtains were down, the contents of drawers were emptied out onto beds and floors, the rugs were up on the roof terrace whilst Sarah and her nieces were dressed in long white aprons with turbans around their hair, as they scrubbed, dusted and sewed from first thing in the morning until dusk crept into the corners and it was time to light the lamps. Katherine Jones had left two years before to spend her twilight years in Clacton with her cousin, and Peggy had moved into the back bedroom, so she could divide her time between being a companion for Dorothy and keeping house for Lewis Rendell, a middle aged solicitor who lived alone on the floor above and who was jealous of his solitude.

Mr. Rendell insisted that Peggy confine her hours of work to when he was at his office, ensuring she was clear of his living space, leaving the apartment clean and his dinner prepared, well before he set foot in Maddox Street every evening. Anything he wished to say to her, or her to him, was done via notes and had it not been for her initial interview she would have had no idea what her employer even looked like. Sarah believed this to be an ideal arrangement as it allowed Peggy to dedicate most of her time to spring cleaning the Lane's apartment in the knowledge she could make up the hours for Mr. Rendell the following week without any explanations being required. Under Sarah's command the spring clean was run with military efficiency, no corner or crevice was safe from scouring, no piece of worn fabric could remain unpatched and certainly no living creature, however small, would continue to be provided with accommodation. As usual Edward had been instructed to remain at his club until the process was complete, and that morning Sarah had finally sent word to him that they were putting the finishing touches to the annual effort and would expect him back in the evening. To help with the final push to restore order Nora was coming to help Dorothy complete the new curtains being made for Edward's study. In fact, that must be her now, Sarah thought, hearing the heavy front door close and light footsteps begin up the stairs before a commotion of "hellos" as Nora met Peggy coming down from Mr. Rendell's apartment.

"The phantom domestic has escaped in time again!" Nora's voice echoed up the wide stairwell. "What's wrong with the man, does he think you've got three heads or a horrible disease catchable on sight?"

"Maybe 'e just doesn't like women," came Peggy's voice as the two sets of footsteps joined together moving towards the apartment.

"Maybe 'e likes boys ..." Nora's voice laughed as the girls appeared through the open doorway where their aunt was rubbing beeswax into the heavy wooden dresser which stood in the hallway.

"That sort of rumour mongering can destroy good men," Sarah snapped polishing the top with sufficient vigour to gain a cardio vascular workout, "lovely to see you Nora, even if I would prefer your tongue to be more controlled," she continued in a slightly softer tone and with a look calculated to demonstrate both the earnestness of her first statement and the real affection she held for her niece.

Bending to kiss her aunt's cheek, Nora mumbled "Sorry" before going in search of Dorothy.

***

"What's rattled Auntie's cage this morning?" Nora asked when she found her younger sister.

"Nothing as far as I know, thank goodness you're arrived I'm getting into a terrible mess with the pleats on this tie-back." Dorothy unwound her body from the big armchair she was sitting in, passing the fiddly bits of material to Nora. She had turned seventeen a month before and as Nora looked at her she recognised with a mixture of fear and envy that there was now a woman in front of her rather than a mere girl, and the woman was recklessly attractive.

Dorothy had written several times recently to ask Nora to come up to town as soon as possible for her birthday celebration. Peggy had been unable to stop talking about the music halls ever since she had seen Marie Lloyd perform at Drury Lane, and completely ignoring Aunt Sarah's frosty opinion of the popular acts and songs, she had persisted in giving regular performances of *"My old man said follow the van"* complete with knee slapping and jigs, in front of Uncle Edward until he had finally capitulated and agreed to buy tickets for the three sisters next time they were all in town as a birthday gift for his ward. Nora knew Dorothy had been in a fever of excitement ever since, particularly as Aunt Sarah appeared to believe that even a single outing to such a place could undo all the years of grooming lavished on Dorothy at the opera and the ballet.

Nora looked at her beautiful willowy sister, who seemed to have no notion her appearance was any different to her sisters', the men at the music halls weren't likely to be watching the stage much tonight. Dorothy spoke as if she was in for a night of wondrously outrageous debauchery; but her clothes were of the latest fashion, her hands were soft pink, the nails filed and unjagged despite the current cleaning frenzy, her teeth were white and even, her deportment was faultless, neither too stiff nor too sloppy, her body and hair looked just as if she belonged to the upper echelons of society but had somehow avoided inheriting the sneer. Chaperoning Dorothy anywhere was likely to be challenging.

Although Nora was filled with admiration for her little sister's appearance she still didn't want to swap places with her, not even for a minute. Nora was fiercely proud of making her own way in the world, she felt as though she had clawed her way out of Gladstone V and was in control of her own destiny, or at least as much as a girl could be, but Dorothy seemed to be stuck in an ivory cage from which Nora could not imagine how she could ever fly free. Looking down at the amateurish work on the tie-backs, Nora knew that for all her grace Dorothy was not trained for anything, she would never be fully accepted in Uncle Edward's social circle but nor could she easily fit back into Nora and Peggy's world, her separation from the rest of the family had left her in limbo, although she suspected it was a fact her sister had never even considered.

As she settled herself in Dorothy's chair, pulling out her sister's clumsy stitches and nimbly teasing the fabric into perfect folds, Nora was finally able to unleash her explosion of family gossip.

"'ave you 'eard about Thomas?" she said in a voice loud enough to carry to Peggy who was cleaning lampshades in the next room.

"Peggy said he was working on a farm in Cheadle," Dorothy replied in a distinctly uninterested tone

"Well 'e's back down in Eltham now," Nora said, attempting to work her sisters into the appropriate state of curiosity and managing to be sufficiently intriguing to prompt Peggy into putting down her duster and come to the doorway, allowing Nora the pleasure of watching her face as she ejaculated the final juiciest titbit, "'e's got a girl into trouble from there and 'er father went all the way up north and told Farmer Bentley 'e wanted Thomas back down south to make an honest woman of her."

"'ow's he going to look after a wife and child?" Peggy cried, "Does mother know?" she asked now fully in the room and giving Nora her undivided attention in a way that made Nora want to grin, although the subject demanded an expression of muted outrage.

"She knows 'e's marryin' and she's pretendin' to 'erself and everyone else that it's the force of true love rather than irate fathers! Thomas's goin' to be fine though, Elizabeth is a few years older than 'im but 'er father's got a successful house painting business and it's in 'is grandchild's interest to give Thomas a secure job ain't it."

"'ave you met 'er?"

"Last Sunday. I'd 'eard all about it from one of the girls at the bakery 'oose sister works at the same house Elizabeth does, so I pretended I was longin' to see my little brother…"

"… you were just itching to see 'er!" Peggy interjected, now seated at Nora's feet slurping up every syllable.

"Well, yes. She's pretty, although a little plump right now! The wedding's next week and no, we haven't been invited."

"Why not?"

"'Er parents say they want to keep it small and our family is very large."

"Nonsense! It's just that they're angry with Thomas because their daughter's about to pop."

"I know, but I think it's going to be good for 'im, 'e seemed happy enough anyway."

"I'm going to be an aunt," said Dorothy in a dreamy way, "Not that I'm ever likely to see the baby, it's ten years since I saw Thomas."

Nora looked up sharply about to contradict her sister before realising it was true, Dorothy had only paid one visit to Gladstone V, since then their mother had always taken them up to London, but she never brought the boys, or even their father if memory served her correctly. "That was a bit odd," Nora thought, "it would 'ave been cheaper and easier for Aunt Sarah and Dorothy to do the travellin', she won't even recognise the boys now, though I don't suppose it really matters."

* * *

Edward Lane had enjoyed the few days spent at his club. Spring cleaning gave him and his cousin, the respected seascape artist George Cochrane Kerr, a legitimate excuse to abandon their substantial numbers of womenfolk. George had four daughters, and was always as insistent on seizing the opportunity to escape and recreate their childhood bond, as Edward was.

They had spent their youngest years first at Moor Park and then at Sudbrook Park, both rambling properties that Edward's father and maternal uncles had turned into chic hydrotherapy clinics attracting a wealth of high society, interesting foreigners and renowned intellectuals including the illustrious Charles Darwin. Together with Edward's elder brother Campbell, they had formed a rebellious trio to withstand the buffeting of the endless social philosophising which occurred at every meal. Edward's childhood household oozed male respectability and maturity; even the women were faultless in their reasoned speech and dedication to aiding those who were sick or down trodden. King of this pride of altruistic lions, was Edward's father, larger and more knowing than all the rest within the extensive ménage, bursting with an intelligence that left no room for childish flippancy. One unguarded remark in front of Dr. Lane was always certain to bring forth devastating quiet logic guaranteed to leave the recipient both irked at being made to feel so completely mentally degenerate, and anxious that the feeling might be an expression of a deeper truth.

Campbell had been the first of the three boys to escape from the expectation that he would merge into the medical clan and be forever happy to sit below his father and uncles in the family pecking order. He opted to return to Edinburgh, where they had been born, to study medicine before swiftly changing to law, becoming a judge and then fleeing half way around the world to Montreal.

George had followed suit, slipping the yoke of being endlessly groomed into a worthy cub to continue the family medical legacy, by leaving to study in France where he honed both his prodigious artistic talent and his affable personality to make him a successful painter in his own lifetime.

Edward had been left abandoned and trapped. With the flight of Campbell and George, his father was rigid in his determination that Edward would become a doctor, and not just any doctor but a pioneer, a medic of great renown, the fulfilment of a father's ambitious dreams. Unfortunately, Edward had always suffered from a deep dislike of all bodily fluids, which was an inauspicious start in the profession, but from his earliest days, of the three of them, Edward had been the most diligent in his efforts to please his parents. He sought his father's approval constantly, whilst suspecting it was something that had been earned instead by Campbell just because he had displayed the guts to stand against parental demands and leave, and that bowing meekly to them would somehow never be quite good enough. It was an enigma that Edward could only understand in terms of the biblical story of the prodigal son, yet even then it didn't seem properly rational, and certainly it didn't feel fair. It was not until after his father's death, when Edward had been trudging through life as a doctor for more than two decades, that his mother discovered that her love for the ever struggling Edward was sufficient to back his sudden defiance of his uncles and give her blessing to her son's desire to abandon the life of blood and gore in favour of the cleaner profession of stock broking.

For each of the boys their escape from the tyranny of ancestral good intentions had eventually resulted in enjoyable and successful careers, whilst parents and uncles had long since been silenced by age, infirmity and death. The mass breakout from the prison of others' expectations had left an unshakeable friendship between the Lane brothers and their cousin, so spending the male domestic holiday of spring cleaning week with George always left Edward feeling revitalised and deeply content. They had chosen their club carefully, opting for The Constitutional whose membership boasted more intellectuals and men from a wide variety of nationalities than gentry or colonial types. Listening to the talk of people from diverse backgrounds was a passion of Edward's providing him with plenty of stories to take home to his ladies. Broadening their human education was one of his goals as although his spirit had striven so hard to haul itself away from his father's clinics, if he had never experienced them he would have missed time spent with many great men and women, among whom Mr. Darwin had made the most profound impression. He was a man who never left Edward in any doubt that when they spoke he was addressing Edward alone, giving his complete attention to the task. His dark, kind eyes, like one of the apes he claimed man was descended from, were deep, compassionate and almost unbearably sad. Frank conversations with the scientist at a young age had left Edward idolising him, hanging on his every word as a sacred truth. The wisest of these truths, in Edward's opinion, was the proclamation that human sympathy was the noblest part of man's nature, and it was this that had led Edward to search out different cultures, nationalities, political viewpoints and religions just so he could return home and explain their logic to his womenfolk, in his crusade to stamp out bigotry within his personal microcosm.

However, Edward was also a practical man and recognised the need to return home after his annual break armed with an impressive treat for his toiling females; a gift of a more substantial nature than the mere wealth of his conversation. He had ordered a special spring cake to be produced and he swung his cane jauntily as he left his club and walked towards the bakery in the glow of the afternoon sunshine. A tinge of excitement warmed his chest as he thought of the pleasure he would receive from watching his ladies' faces when the box was opened.

Edward loved giving presents, he received more childlike joy from watching Sarah or Dorothy unwrap his gifts than they did from receiving them. This was not to say that they were unappreciative, far from it, they praised Edward's choice in clothes and jewellery as never short of impeccable, and openly marvelled at how he could hold the colour of one of their outfits in his head and match it exactly with a scarf, gloves or ribbon, delighting them every time with trinkets which could appear quite ordinary, but when put with the clothes he had visualised would transform the overall effect into something stunning. This year however there would be no jewellery, civil unrest and strikes had made stocks jumpier than usual leaving Edward conscious of the need to economise, at least a little.

Entering the bakery and raising his hat to Mrs Alexander standing behind the long wooden counter, he made his way to the back room quickly becoming enveloped in the comforting smell of bread and cakes. As Edward approached, the confectioner's concentration was so rapt that he failed to hear the elder man and Edward was able to observe the final touches being put to the edible creation in silence. The cake was a triumph, certain to draw gasps from all who saw it and cause the person who made the first incision to grit their teeth against an overpowering feeling they were defiling something sacred, ruining a perfection of colour and texture so vibrant it satisfied the eye even more than the stomach.

Jean Nicolas Nicolai had first covered the square fruit cake in marzipan and a thick white icing, then he had written the names of Sarah, Dorothy, Peggy and Nora on the four sides in soft colours before building up filigree walls of sugar around the edges creating a basket effect into which he had placed the brightest nasturtium blooms, their reds, yellows and oranges varnished into hardened brilliance by layers of sugar water until they glistened, a crystal flower bed of nature, temporarily preserved at it's very finest moment.

"Extraordinary!" exclaimed Edward, "I request a spring cake for my ladies and you produce the gardens of Babylon." He moved forward to shake Jean's hand noticing again how peculiarly soft it was, not just smooth the way his mother's had been, but spongy like a young child's. He wondered how the fingers managed to tease the petals into exactly the right position and whether he worked with dozens of flowers to get just one perfect result. Edward didn't think so, the intensity he had observed as Jean worked spoke of a man who was too careful to make mistakes into a habit. A meticulous craftsman, it had always seemed strange to Edward that he was dedicated to producing perfection whilst knowing insatiable mouths would be unable to restrain themselves from annihilating his masterpiece within minutes of seeing it.

Thanking Mr Nicolai enthusiastically as he was handed the cake box, Edward promised to tell his many friends and business acquaintances of the man's unbelievable talent, and then hurried home to astound Sarah and the young nieces.

When Edward arrived, every surface in the apartment was polished to a mirror shine. He stood in the doorway breathing in the scent of rose water mingled with bees wax and soap, before being cajoled inside to view the rest of the handiwork. Once he had admired the new curtains and approved the movement of various pieces of furniture he was ushered towards his chair. Placing the cake box on the small table beside it he removed three tickets from his waistcoat pocket, presenting them to Dorothy with a small bow before seating himself. Squealing with excitement she gave him an enthusiastic hug which left Edward a little breathless and Sarah with an even straighter back than usual as she curtly told the girls to go and make a pot of tea.

"I had promised that they should go," Edward explained in response to Sarah's raised eyebrow.

"I'm just not certain such places are suitable for Dorothy," Sarah said tightly.

"They make up part of the culture enjoyed by her own sisters," he said gently, "you've sometime hinted I'm ignorant of the normal lives of other people and you're probably right, I'm trying to ensure Dorothy isn't being given the same handicap," but the logic couldn't soften the grim line of Sarah's mouth.

The beauty of the cake lightened the atmosphere when the tea arrived and very soon it had been fully admired and demolished, although Peggy insisted on keeping her flower, claiming it was just too beautiful to eat.

* * *

Later, as the three sisters settled into their seats in front of the small raised stage, Dorothy dared to voice that she had not been madly impressed by her nasturtium, "I thought the peppery taste clashed with the sugar," she announced.

"Maybe a bit," Nora agreed, "but I've never seen anything like that cake, it was amazing."

"Not as amazing as Uncle Edward getting us these seats, I've only ever sat bunched up on benches in the gallery before," said Peggy.

"Ahh," Dorothy cried triumphantly, "I knew the wonder of the cake would pale once we got here. I'm going to learn every song they sing tonight and play them loudly all day long until Aunt Sarah agrees what fun they are!"

"You might convince Uncle Edward," Peggy said with a grin," "but I reckon Aunt Sarah would rather burn in 'ell than lift up 'er skirts and give in to a bit of a knees up!"

CHAPTER FOUR

1914.
(James: 18, Dorothy: 19, Nora: 23, Peggy: 26, Uncle Edward: 64)
By the second half of September the summer boom time had quietened sufficiently in Bexhill to enable James' employer to be generous and allow the lad a few days of holiday in recompense for the past months of working seven full days every week. Endless hours filled with flattery and primping had resulted in James overflowing with an almost painful desire to escape. With each profile he praised or lighting adjustment made to disguise minor beauty blemishes, the eighteen-year-old had outwardly been all smiles and proper concern while in his belly there bubbled the dangerous urge to make loud coarse jokes about the number of chins one stuck up spinster had or the unmistakable body odour of another. James had promised himself that the minute the season was over he would head away from the delicate pleasures of the seaside, back to his mates in Wembley for a healthy dose of beer drinking, back slapping and thoroughly macho zone conversation.

As the train drew into his old hometown station James spotted Henry Rickman on the platform, smartly uniformed beside the handcart that was ready to wheel any luggage or post bags from the carriages. Waiting until the crowd had cleared and Henry's tasks were completed, James shook hands heartily with his friend. Henry confirmed that Henry Reed and several others who used to roam around the tenements were still doing much the same, and sent James off on a mission to round up as many of the former Pinner Road urchins as could be found before six o'clock to meet at the Black Horse when Henry's shift ended.

By the second jug of ale word had got around that James was back and all those whom he hadn't located during the afternoon naturally gravitated towards the inn. Exaggerated story telling was already progressing through the usual stages, every tale becoming more incredible or amusing than the one before. Talk turned to those who had left to train for the British Expeditionary Force or who had joined the navy or, most glamorous of all, the Royal Flying Corps. There seemed to be as much testosterone as beer entering the young men's gullets as they each span yarns about troops of women going weak-kneed at the sight of a military uniform when the chap in it promised to fight for the girl's freedom, and as the third jug emptied itself around the rough wooden table, cluttered by the glasses of the teenage crowd, the race was on to demonstrate courage and intent to do one's bit. The excuse of being under nineteen or of parents needing help with their market stalls or their building businesses were wearing thin in the scramble to prove strength, nerve and grit. Valiant protestations continued to increase in volume as James imagined his father's pride and his mother's tears should he take the decision to join up. Stumbling out of the door into the arresting blast of chill air, the band of braves remained stout hearted and resolute in their intention to present themselves at Harrow recruiting office the following day. Roughly a quarter of them acted upon the spiral of alcohol fuelled one-upmanship, joining the queue of other seemingly fearless fit males eager to sign up to serve King and country. James Terrill was among them, keeping up his steady stream of banter and jokes all the way to the front desk.

* * *

Dorothy was grumpy and Peggy's singing was making her grumpiness increase. Peggy used to do fun song and dance routines around the apartment while getting Dorothy to thump out jazzy tunes on the piano to the gratifying chagrin of Aunt Sarah who maintained the neighbours would be disturbed; now Aunt Sarah was perfectly tranquil as Peggy worked, leisurely drifting from room to room, warbling soppy love songs and greeting all of Dorothy's attempts to ignite a spark of normality in her with a serene, if slightly condescending, smile. Grinding her molars together as her sister hung on to a long note of yearning for an additional beat so as to extract maximum emotional effect, Dorothy prepared some colourful mental curses for Wilfred Greenslade whom she blamed entirely for Peggy's mental decomposition. To Dorothy's way of thinking he wasn't even particularly handsome being not quite tall enough, having ears that stuck out a fraction too far and with darkened skin around his eyes which she felt was highly unattractive. Peggy, by contrast, spoke only of his a strong physique, chiselled square chin and high cheekbones plus, most importantly, his kindness towards her, or as Peggy put it, "'e's a real gent to me."

To make things worse Dorothy could feel her 'bah humbug' attitude having even less effect now that Nora had affected the same slushy transformation over a young man called Arthur Fry, so that whenever Nora came up to London the two elder sisters would closet themselves in Peggy's room talking in low voices scattered with occasional giggles, or go off on long walks together leaving Dorothy both annoyed and lonely. Privately Dorothy admitted Arthur was tolerable, at least he wasn't as cow eyed with Nora as Wilfred was with Peggy, and he did have a boyish sense of humour, although Aunt Sarah called it "earthy" in a disparaging kind of way. Thinking about it Dorothy realised that Aunt Sarah's hint of disapproval over Arthur might be why she saw him as the more appealing suitor of the two.

At present there was nothing at Maddox Street that alleviated Dorothy's feeling that life was dull, dull, dull and at nineteen years old she demanded the right to excitement and entertainment. Of course she could never say such a thing, it would be tantamount to asking for a lengthy lecture from Aunt Sarah on prudence in the face of adversity terminating with the instruction that if she would only take proper care over knitting more socks for the troops she would no longer be bored.

Dorothy stared at the tubular object in her lap, her annoyance rising with the realisation that once again she had failed to construct the heel properly and her Aunt would insist she unravel it and knit it again. All arguments that it was better to knit socks without heels as then they would fit any foot, admittedly with a few baggy bits, were wasted words on Aunt Sarah who lived by the maxim that if a job was worth doing, it was worth doing well.

The only member of the household who didn't continuously irritate Dorothy was her Uncle who seemed to sympathise, at least a little, with her crabby mood and frustrations. He had brought home a gramophone a couple of weeks before together with five wax records and for a while she had managed to abandon herself to dancing around the living room, but when Peggy had gone for a walk with Wilfred and Uncle Edward had tired of being whirled around after three songs, so she had been forced to deposit him in an armchair like a living doll, perspiring and in need of a whisky, she soon felt her own loneliness even more keenly as she danced by herself. Strange how easy it was to feel completely isolated in a house full of people.

Aunt Sarah's response to Dorothy's restlessness was to find more tasks for her niece. She seemed to believe endless tiresome jobs would somehow provide interest and purpose in life, yet the only flicker of interest Dorothy derived was in quietly thwarting her Aunt's daily designs at filling each twenty-four hours constructively.

As Dorothy pulled the stitches out of the brown wool with more force and speed than was sensible, Peggy glided past stopping briefly to announce there had been a note from Nora to say she was coming to visit on Saturday and would stay overnight. Dorothy didn't bother to look up and acknowledge what would be a further dose of closet gossip to which she wasn't invited.

* * *

As it was, the weekend's events led to a worsening of Dorothy's situation. Arthur had decided to take the King's shilling and after scant reflection Wilfred had displayed a paternalistic whim to keep an eye on the younger man and had declared he would accompany Arthur to the same recruiting office so the two Terrill suitors could be dispatched to a training camp together and would hopefully remain with each other until the conclusion of the war. Now even her uncle was being annoying as he greeted the lads' call to arms with praise, urging fortitude in Nora and Peggy. Uncle Edward's nephew in Canada had recently written expressing his intention to join the McGill military training school as soon as his sixteenth birthday arrived and with Arthur and Wilfred's announcement Dorothy's uncle appeared swelled by the news that so much tenacity emanated from his own kith and kin in the face of tyranny.

Ever since Christmas the talk around the dinner table seemed to be unerringly about the war and the men known to them who were heading for it, and whereas Dorothy was passably interested in some of the uniformed chaps she saw strolling around the street, she felt left out now that all conversations turned towards Wilfred, Arthur or Campbell's son, Alfred, half a world away. Since the young Canadian had pledged his future to the great struggle, her uncle had written to him every week with the latest news from Europe, leaving the lad in no doubt that if the war continued there would be a heroic part for Alfred to play. Each missive was duly read out to the family before it was sent and it appeared Uncle Edward saw the teenager as some kind of avenging demigod even though he'd only met him once when Alfred was no more than ten.

When it was first announced, Dorothy had hoped that the departure of Wilfred and Arthur would bring some normality back to life at Maddox Street and her sisters would stop acting as a duo so the three of them could have some fun once again, but the calls for women to help in the war effort with slogans such as "shells made by a wife may save a husband's life" did not fall on deaf ears, and her sisters promptly ditched their jobs in favour of becoming munitionettes leaving to work and live together just as their beaus had done. Although Dorothy was unable to openly criticise such noble actions, her spirits hit the floor as she contemplated months on end of being shut up with her uncle and aunt, expected to gain excitement from knitting innumerable thick brown socks. It seemed so unfair, she wasn't allowed to go and do factory work or get a job on a farm, Aunt Sarah had said she might train as a nurse if the war was still going on when she turned twenty-one but that was years away and she'd only agreed to that idea because the training was in London and so Dorothy would remain under her guardians' watchful eyes, there seemed no way she was ever going to get any pleasure or freedom at all.

* * *

The conversations in the shop were audible in the back room even when voices were deliberately lowered.
    "Mr. Nicolai finished your cake half an hour ago, I'll just fetch it for you," came the tones of Mrs. Alexander.
    "'Nicolai', what nationality's he then?"
    "Russian I think, like the Czar."
    "That's all right then, you can't be too careful nowadays, if he'd been from the other side I'd have covered his face with his own icing."
    The nerve by the corner of Jean's left eye began to twitch, it was doing it almost constantly at the moment, a further little annoyance which added to the agitation he felt building inside him daily. Jean was grateful for Mrs. Alexander's ignorance of his origins, to be Russian was to be an ally, but to be Romanian would be a dangerous unknown quantity. His homeland was a traditional friend of the Austrian Hungarian Empire and although the nation was currently neutral, Jean lived in terror of receiving the news that they had thrown in their lot with the enemy. Since Christmas suspicion had swept through London in torrents, families with Germanic names who had lived in England for generations had suffered at the hands of righteous mobs who looted their homes and half lynched them before handing them to the police to be interned in camps. Many of those who had been persecuted couldn't even speak German and were probably as English as the King – with whose ancestors their families had possibly arrived on British shores many years before, yet decades of peaceful living had not saved them from the accusation of being enemy spies. What hope would there be for a Romanian, with a strong foreign accent, Jean thought, if his country were to capitulate to pressure from its former allies?
    Jean held no flirting fascination with violence, the bravado of many young men in the recruiting queues had always passed him by. He was acutely aware of his fear of pain, in all its forms, and its increasing threat made his chest constrict and the urge rise in him to run to the protective arms of his mother, or the reassuring figure of his friend Edward whose staid philosophies might take away the images of pain being horribly enacted upon his personal physical form, it was his greatest nightmare and

now it was brutally thrust in front of him on a daily basis in newspapers where most editorials reflected the view that performing grievous bodily harm on anyone of suspect nationality was closer to an heroic act than a criminal one. He'd always thought the British more reasoned and reserved than many of their European cousins but right now they appeared to be behaving like sharks in a feeding frenzy, leaving Jean spending most of his waking hours devising schemes for self-preservation if the worst occurred.

He had briefly considered returning to Galati, but the carrot of bodily safety was outweighed by the knowledge that his mother would see his reappearance as failure and even if she were magnanimous about the necessity for him to remove himself from a foreign arena of war, his presence would deprive her of her greatest pleasure, to boast about her hugely successful and artistic son. How, after he had spent years dishing up titbits to satiate her voracious appetite for fresh triumphs in his weekly letters home, could he turn up on her doorstep, travelling bag in hand, but minus any crock of gold, wife descended from royal stock or other trapping that would save her from the accusation of having been a fraud in the continuous filial bragging he knew she indulged in with all her friends and acquaintances. He couldn't do that to her, she was, and always had been, his goddess. Jean suspected other people probably found his devotion curious since his mother was not obviously demonstrative in her affection for her sole offspring. Their existence together throughout his childhood had frequently rested precariously on the continuing infatuation of one man or another for his mother's simpering carnal abilities and he had learned quickly to become invisible to both her and her friends unless there was something praiseworthy he could present to her. Jean craved those moments of praise and soon nothing was too much for him to sacrifice at the altar of maternal affection and he would go to any lengths to glean even one second of believing that she felt for him the adoration that he was consumed with when he thought of her.

His artistic abilities, it was claimed, came from her, and it was she who had swept him from their home town, which was too small for both of them, she felt, and directed him towards Paris where she was certain his masterpieces would gain him celebrity among the world's most fastidious palettes. But Jean had discovered France was a nation where culinary genius only succeeded when coupled with an expansive character – a quality he could neither disassemble and study, nor emulate. The dour reserved personality of the English was considerably easier to cater to, until now it had allowed Jean to thrive and in his letters he had been able to bury any part of himself he feared might earn his mother's disapproval, whilst building up every facet that could elicit her smile.

The burning desire to hold his head high and command her respect had led him to become intimate with duplicity before he even knew what the word meant. By 1914 he knew his outer shell had been remorselessly groomed in his quest to get others to think well of him, whilst his natural emotions and tendencies which failed to fit into this standardised picture of perfection were suppressed with a deep sense of shame that could explode into anger towards those who were not, he felt, worthy of judging him. The perennial internal struggle had burgeoned into a full time occupation to keep those whose opinion he valued in a permanent state of awe. Even in his leisure hours when he was alone with himself he could not proclaim "this is me" and be in any way satisfied with it, there did not seem to be a moment when he could relax his guard against his imperfections, they were best left bound and gagged in the deepest recesses of his mind where he strove to be unable to find them. It never really worked though.

To go home was unthinkable.

* * *

Edward was a regular visitor at the bakery. He would frequently drop in for a loaf of bread on his return to Maddox Street from his office in the late afternoon, often wandering into the back room and propping up the door frame to watch Jean work. He was fascinated by the delicacy of the decorations the man made and was never shy of voicing his admiration which prompted Jean to preen his professional feathers, telling Edward of the increasing numbers of important orders he was receiving from hotels, fancy shops and genteel families all over London.

"I would have taken on Beatrice full time, but the war makes business too uncertain," Jean confided, he paused seeming to concentrate furiously on his work before adding, "the uncertainty of my personal position in England is harder to bear."

"You mean if your country joins the other side?" Edward said as gently as possible.

"Exactly."

"But you have good relations with many important customers who would surely vouch for you."

"There was an excellent haberdashery on Regent's Street run by an Austrian, it had many important patrons, but they didn't save him from being beaten up by a mob before he was interned," Jean replied, without taking his eyes from the cake in front of him.

"Yes, I knew him," Edward said quietly, then almost as an afterthought, "it was brutal ... shocking." He continued to watch the younger man work while the silence swirled around the room making it harder to break with each second until with slow enunciation Edward pushed his thoughts out, "Do you think it would aid your position if you took an English wife?"

Turning his face away from the table to look directly at Edward, Jean replied, "Perhaps, but I have never wanted to marry if you understand me."

"Indeed, but there are such things as marriages of convenience which can work very well if both parties stand to gain something from the union. Perhaps this Beatrice who helps you might be interested."

Jean visibly shuddered before going to the sink, "I will think about it," he said, scrubbing viciously at his nails as the freezing water turned his hands puce. Awkwardness invaded the room as the confectioner wrestled with his obvious distress and Edward felt a heavy duty to talk of mundane things while his friend collected himself.

"This war is indeed a trial on so many levels," he began forcing a hearty edge into his voice, "stocks go up and down like yo yos, a man doesn't know from one day to the next if he's a prince or a pauper, and at home my niece appears to be afflicted with terminal boredom now that her sisters have left to do war work, so she's continually badgering my wife to allow her to go and find employment in factories and on farms which, of course, is not going to happen, although she's pretending she doesn't understand the reasons why. There seems to be war on every front of my life at the moment," he concluded with a slightly forced laugh.

"Perhaps you should bring her here with you one afternoon and I can teach her how to work with icing; you're very welcome to do so if you think she might find it diverting."

Edward looked closely at Jean, studying his features to determine if the kindly offer was genuine or just a throw away remark, a guileless round face smiled back at him. Edward was charmed, he was certain Dorothy would be delighted.

* * *

Dorothy and Edward arrived at the bakery the following afternoon; Edward took up his lounging position against the door frame while the confectioner bustled around finding a chair for the female visitor, all perfect smiles and perfect manners. Dorothy had embraced the idea of a few hours of icing practice enthusiastically, especially as it was with her uncle and so was likely to have more to do with pure entertainment than her aunt's favoured activities which seemed to be chosen because they would be "good for her" or "educational".

Mr Nicolai was producing a four-tier wedding cake for a reception taking place at Claridges on Saturday. He explained how each section was to be decorated and constructed separately as he showed her the drawings of his own elaborate designs. They were masterpieces, technical drawings of great beauty which Dorothy blurted out must be impossible to transfer into a three dimensional form. The little man laughed in a slightly self-effacing manner as Uncle Edward earnestly assured her that the eventual product would be quite as magnificent as the etchings. The largest section was to sit on a silver tray which itself would be full of the preserved flowers that were Mr Nicolai's trademark. Balanced above it were two cakes of diminishing sizes festooned with rosebuds, and from here the final piece was supported above the third tier by lattice-worked icing and was itself shaped as one perfect bud with writing running around the base announcing 'Life and Love' in a flourish of calligraphy.

"It would be a crime to eat it," Dorothy offered as her short host appeared to visibly balloon in stature in the light of her admiration. He really was a funny shape, she thought, though clearly hugely talented at what he did.

"Normally they keep the top part for the first christening, so maybe it won't all be destroyed on Saturday," Mr Nicolai said smiling at her in a very relaxed way despite the enormity of the task in front of him.

"Do you buy tiny rose buds from Covent Garden?" she asked, genuinely interested in how this creation was going to be accomplished.

"No indeed, look in the drawer behind you," he said. Neat rows of perfectly formed rosebuds made from delicately coloured rice paper, with miniature stems of crystallised angelica lay before her and she gasped audibly, they were flawlessly exquisite. Her uncle crossed the room to inspect the edible artwork as she held one out towards him.

"My goodness Mr. Nicolai, the work in that is unimaginable. Where do you get them from?"

"It's a little hobby of mine to make them in the evenings," he admitted in a tone both proud and slightly embarrassed. "I began by preserving edible flowers in sugar water, allowing each misting to dry and harden until the beauty of the bloom was preserved inside a sweet transparent prison. The method was fine for lavender, violet, nasturtiums and even sweet pea, but many of the loveliest blooms cannot be captured in this way so I would dissect them and transfer each part onto rice paper until I could rebuild them in edible form and then I had to find dyes that would not cause the rice paper to become soggy, it takes many hours, but, as I say, it is a hobby. I'm sorry, I must be boring you."

"Not at all," Dorothy replied "I'm quite amazed at the patience you must have to hone such a talent."

Brushing off her compliment by bending to his work again he smiled up at Uncle Edward saying "Come now Miss Terrill, would you be good enough to help me construct the lattice work?" as he demonstrated with deft efficiency how to squeeze the icing out to make precise tiny fences before handing the nozzled bag to Dorothy.

Although she attempted to copy his movements exactly, Dorothy's efforts had a tendency towards large blobs followed by thin stringy bits before being interrupted by a further blob. Laughing and turning pink she put down the bag announcing she clearly had less artistic ability in her entire body than Mr. Nicolai had in his little finger. With much hilarity the two men tried to offer tips on how to produce a smoother effect until finally Jean placed his hands over Dorothy's to guide her towards her only acceptable example.

Easy-going laughter tinted the entire afternoon and Dorothy found it hard to understand why her uncle had painted Mr Nicolai as so serious and intense about his work, she had been initially concerned that her pitiful attempts would draw a mild rebuke but instead he had encouraged her to continue trying and she quickly became as sticky as a child who had been playing with glue while both men bombarded her with well meant advice which had no visible impact upon her icing abilities.

Two hours later while thanking Mr Nicolai profusely for a very pleasant experience, Dorothy and Edward prepared to leave him to his monumental workload with many apologies for having taken up so much of his time.

"It was most pleasant for me also," the correct little man said clicking his heels and gently raising Dorothy's tacky fingers to his lips with a mock bow of gallantry, as they all smiled at his chivalrous charade. "If you would like to see the finished product please drop in on Friday morning," he said shaking Edward's hand warmly and ushering them out of the door.

* * *

Dinner was a light hearted affair with Aunt Sarah asking for all the details of their time at the bakery and being regaled by tales of Dorothy's dire icing efforts.

"It was very kind of Mr. Nicolai to take so much trouble, what's he like?" she asked.

"He's an artistic fellow, not much given to company usually I would imagine," Edward explained, "probably in his thirties, maybe older, it's so difficult to tell when a chap has a round face."

"Yes, it is rather like a full moon," Dorothy laughed, "and he's terribly foreign, and corrects himself so seriously whenever he mispronounces something. He's very precise and neat, I'm sure I caused more chaos in that back room than it's ever seen before!"

Later on in the evening as she sat on the box seat of the bay window Dorothy admitted to herself that the interlude had done her good, she felt happier and more relaxed than she had done in weeks. A dense fog had rolled in with the darkness leaving her glad she was inside with a fire watching the frigid dampness through the glass as zephyrs of wind shifted the sodden banks so first one area of the street became dimly visible, then another. The gas lamps produced a muddy radiance and she watched shop fronts and doorways appear in a ghostly gleam before being enveloped by the murk once more. The miasma slowly swirled again before clearing in the patch of pavement just below the streetlamp directly opposite Dorothy's window. A man's figure was momentarily stripped of its eerie cloak and for a second Dorothy stared directly into the unsmiling eyes of Jean Nicolas Nicolai before the mist rewrapped him again. Startled, Dorothy swung her legs off the seat, taking immediate refuge in the chair furthest away from the window. To see him looking up at her, so serious and intent, was weird.

Feelings of apprehension and confusion ran through her as she sat close to the fire idly flicking through her book, seeing nothing on the page and wondering if in fact there were other things that had been in front of her face all day that she had also failed to see. Curiosity, uneasiness and an almost fearful excitement jostled around her head as she replayed the emergence of Mr. Nicolai from the gloom over and over again, never quite grasping why he was standing there.

Steph Mason

CHAPTER FIVE

Early 1915.
(Dorothy:19, Aunt Sarah:50)
When Jean Nicolas Nicolai made a decision to acquire something he became single-minded in the pursuit of his quarry and he had now decided he urgently needed a quality English wife, as security against his country's continuing indecisiveness. Dorothy Terrill, backed by her illustrious uncle, was certainly the best he could hope for. Every morning an exquisitely decorated individual cake would arrive at Maddox Street in time for Dorothy's breakfast and in the evening there would be a further delivery of a long stemmed rose, or perfect budding lily only hours away from opening and revealing its dark centre and compelling fragrance, none of the gifts pandered to the austerity demanded by the war as every ribbon and frippery was carefully evaluated in its power to entrance a bored, unworldly teenager.

Jean was adept at avoiding intimate examination of his feelings for Edward Lane but he did admit to himself that the elder man was his vision of how he would like to become with the passing of years. The kind, tranquil eyes, aquiline nose, erect bearing, immaculately dressed form with top hat and shoes always polished to a mirror shine, all exuded the quiet refinement of a gentleman of the city, a person of substance and moral worth. In Jean's opinion it was impossible to be in Edward's presence without experiencing deep respect, almost veneration for the man. He too could aspire to this benevolent aloofness, and although Dorothy seemed rather excitable now, that was surely from the flippancy of youth and, having been trained from early childhood in Edward Lane's household she must undoubtedly have a calm and philosophical core beneath the currently exuberant exterior. Jean truly believed himself to be doing Edward a favour by wooing his ward, having gleaned in the course of their conversations that Dorothy's social background was not sufficiently robust to enable her to marry one of Edward's class yet her upbringing had left her unfit to wed with the sort of men her sisters were now courting. It was a conundrum Edward had mentioned more than once, leading Jean to be convinced that an offer of marriage from a successful tradesman such as himself, would be gratefully received by his friend who was so graceful in his complete lack of xenophobia which, in the current political climate, was a rare and precious commodity. Jean persuaded himself quite easily that a marriage would be to everyone's advantage, and that what he had previously viewed as an unpleasant encumbrance, namely a wife, could in Dorothy be moulded into a gorgeously serene and undemonstrative partner who would show her gratitude at being rescued from the English social quicksand by becoming a helpful, but hopefully largely invisible, part of his life.

* * *

Sarah watched from the window as Jean hurried away from the front door having delivered a perfect posy of crocuses to the housekeeper which would now be on its way upstairs to be greeted by a deliciously flattered Dorothy. Sarah acknowledged her lack of experience in the ways of modern courtship but this relationship still seemed uncomfortably wrong to her. There were plenty of presents and extravagantly worded notes yet the emotion she would have expected to accompany them seemed absent. Sarah was certainly not inclined to encourage open displays of passion and she had frequently been concerned by the obvious interest Dorothy's appearance regularly aroused in young men when they were out, but nevertheless she did expect a couple to want to spend some time together, yet the gifts and trinkets continued to arrive punctually twice a day but Jean would rarely come up and visit the person he was so earnestly trying to impress. If he did call it would usually be because he had met Edward on the way and the two men would converse over a glass of wine with interludes of polite enquiry aimed in Dorothy's direction before they reverted to talk of art and business. Sarah didn't quite understand why she felt such a deep sense of unease, after all Dorothy herself seemed happy and penned thank-you notes daily for her gifts while showing neighbours and friends the offerings, but she too appeared completely unconcerned whether or not she actually met up physically with her admirer.

As she watched his back finally retreat around the corner, Sarah was seized with the need to talk to Edward. Grabbing her coat, gloves and hat before hurriedly changing into her outdoor boots she slipped out of the house into an evening already lit by a bright moon at six o'clock. A sugary snow had fallen and the chill air stung her throat as she walked as quickly as her balance allowed on the slippery pavement, she nipped across the road, scuttling past Jean on the opposite side, pretending she had not seen him. When, after a few hundred metres, she turned her head slightly to look at a newsboy's placards, she was relieved to see that Jean had disappeared down a side street. Sarah slowed her pace, while searching both pavements for Edward's familiar silhouette, when she finally spotted him a layer of concern spread itself across his face as he recognised she was looking for him.

"Is anything wrong," he asked as they met and she fell into step beside him.

"Not exactly, I just felt the need to ask your advice away from the house."

"I would suggest we sit in the park, but it's so cold we might never get home, are you happy to continue walking?"

"Of course, the exercise calms my worries a little," and so, as reasonably as possible, she confided her anxieties to Edward.

"I confess, I was considerably surprised when he began taking such an intense interest in Dorothy, I had not believed he had any inclination to form any personal attachments," Edward replied, "but I now believe I must have read things incorrectly and although the relationship between the two of them does seem dry, maybe cultural differences have been at the root of the strange approach. Dorothy seems content?"

"Yes, she does," Sarah replied, hesitating for only a fraction of a second before giving vent to her true worries, no longer concerned if Edward saw them as indelicate or unjust. "I hope it is as you say and the constant gifts actually illustrate some deep feeling for her and are not purchased ivy designed to bind her, and us, to him with enforced gratefulness rather than genuine affection."

Edward stopped walking and turned to face her directly, his eyes fixed on hers as he said with deliberate calmness, "The question is does Dorothy believe she would be happy with him?"

"She seems to think so."

Sometimes Edward's very reasonableness could be extremely irritating, not that she could ever say so without seeming even more unreasonable herself.

"Have you spoken to her about what marriage entails?"

"No more than to tell her that a wife's aim is to always please her husband, which at the moment she's convinced she'd do, but" Sarah paused before adding in a rush, "she's quite headstrong. I'd be far less surprised if she ran off with Mrs Pankhurst than if she sat demurely at Jean's side for the rest of her life."

"Maybe I should drop in at the bakery tomorrow and have a word with Jean, explain how young she is and things like that."

"Perhaps," she agreed, unconvinced that such subtlety would work, as they turned their steps back towards Maddox Street.

* * *

An April wedding is always dodgy but the morning dawned full of spring promise. Jean had been buzzing since the small hours, visiting Covent Garden and producing beautiful nosegays for Sybil and Vera who were to stand behind Dorothy at Marylebone Registry Office. He had chosen a single iris to present to Annie as Dorothy had mentioned her mother's eyes were an unusually deep blue and were her most attractive feature. It was to be the first time he had met his fiancée's closest family and Jean was eager to make a favourable impression. Although her real parents appeared to have played little part in her upbringing and seemed to have no influence over her actions, their presence was bothering him and the previous night Jean had been tormented by a dream in which Dorothy's father had taken an intense dislike towards him; in his nightmare Charles Terrill was a rough, rather dirty farmer who overpowered the avuncular protestations of Edward, stopping the ceremony on the pretext that his daughter would not be marrying a foreigner from a country that continued to sit on the fence. He had woken up sweating copiously. Normally he rarely perspired and to wake up damp and clammy revolted him sufficiently for him to leave a note for the maid to change the sheets.

Once washed and properly dressed, Jean placed his own wedding cake and flowers into a cab before climbing in himself. He methodically ticked off the necessary preparations but found he remained plagued by the apprehension that things were going far too smoothly and he was sure to hit a brick wall horribly fast, horribly soon.

As he was of the Orthodox Church it had been decided it would be less alien for both parties if they were to stick to a civil service. Edward had privately admitted to him that he was particularly relieved by this decision as it removed the diplomatic problem of who should walk Dorothy down the aisle. Both Dorothy and Edward would wish it to be her uncle, yet her father would technically have the right to the honour and might have wished to press the point. Wherever they married, Jean had been wracked by nerves that the Registrar or priest would demand a full translation of his Romanian travel papers, he banked on the probability that no one would know an independent person who could do the job, so that he would be able to create an 'edited' version of the document which, in its original, gave such unnecessary details as his true date of birth and the fact that there was some doubt that his mother, Leonida Nicolai, had in fact ever been married to the soldier she claimed was his father and who had been conveniently killed before he was born.

By the time he and Edward presented themselves at the Registrar's Office, a week before the nuptials, Jean's stomach was churning so badly he had been unable to eat for forty-eight hours. Yet the presence of the quintessentially British Mr. Lane had allowed Jean to bypass the official process so that the moment Edward affirmed he had known the groom for several years prior to the war and provided a glowing character reference, the Registrar dropped his previously stern expression and gave only a very cursory glance at Jean's documentation. The incomprehensible language coupled with Edward's calming presence seemed to have led the registrar to decide the papers must be full of legitimate information that it was completely unnecessary for him to know, but, on the strength of the two official stamps carefully affixed to the bottom of the sheet, it was clearly all in order.

Pushing the thinning hair on his scalp firmly into the hackney cab's cushions at his back, Jean sent up a silent prayer that his luck would last a few hours longer.

* * *

Dorothy arrived at Marylebone flanked by her uncle and aunt, she was aware she presented a striking figure in a tailored cream suit, matching high heels and a small hat perched on top of her pile of strawberry blonde waves. She had spent some time looking at herself in the mirror before leaving the apartment and was surprised how the elegance of the colour seemed to transfer itself, making her appear poised and tranquil. She had practiced wearing just the ghost of a smile which, when she got it right, seemed to give her a knowing air of maturity.

As they entered the Registrar's office Jean hurried over and Dorothy realised her image of statuesque composure was being shattered by a groom who seemed Lilliputian beside her. He was a good inch shorter than her when she was barefoot, so her lofty heels left them both at a distinct disadvantage, a point not lost on Dorothy whose resolve wobbled a little as she sandwiched herself more firmly between her non-vertically challenged relatives. She hadn't thought about how they would look as a couple and she suddenly wondered if she was attaching herself to someone who might make her appear like a long red cartoon giantess. A small frown wrinkled her serenity, this was something she should have considered before, perhaps everything was happening a little too fast and there were more things to be thought out in a partnership than a good job and a home of one's own to tinker with. Surely it would be all right, it had to be, her uncle would have ensured it was all for the best.

The arrival of her parents with Sybil and Vera prompted Jean to move away from his lanky bride and lavish his attention on the little girls who squealed at the neat bows he made to each of them as he presented their posies and complimented them on their dresses and hair. Six-year-old Vera seemed particularly captivated by the man about to become her brother-in-law, Dorothy watched her, giggling nervously the little girl kept her eyes fixed upon Jean's round head with the thin lips that where smiling so encouragingly. Presenting an iris to the mother of the bride, Jean graciously told her that her eyes were quite as beautiful as her daughter had said they were, a double compliment that Dorothy could see left her mother bubbling with gratification as she came over to hug her daughter heartily and congratulate her on landing such a "gallant gent".

"Quite the charmer, ain't 'e!" she gushed. "I can't imagine why Sarah's looking so grim with a chap like 'im about!".

* * *

So, they were bound together 'til death them did part, Sarah thought as she watched the couple prepare to board the train to Salisbury for their brief honeymoon weekend. Annie appeared to be transported by the chivalrous attention she'd seen Jean spooning all over her and her younger daughters like thick custard throughout the proceedings, and Sarah had been forced to look hard at the floor concentrating on not allowing a snort of laughter to escape when she heard Charles growl to Flo that he couldn't understand why Annie was going all gooey over a load of blarney from a short foreign bloke who seemed more girly than his own daughters.

"I said it would end up like this with 'er marryin' someone we would 'ave nothin' in common wiv," he'd said peevishly and none too quietly. "At least your Walter 'as a bit of belly about 'im."

Certainly there wasn't much in Jean that would appeal to Sarah's brother-in-law, but now the couple was about to leave and Dorothy would no longer be under her protection. Charles Terrill might joke but this marriage was for real and now that the time to part had come Sarah found herself in danger of losing her usual air of a strict governess and being gripped by emotions sufficiently strong to punch a tunnel through her rigid outer casing in their anguish to be seen. Holding Dorothy by the shoulders and meeting the placid eyes with Sarah's own watery ones, she discovered her voice was so faint it was barely audible above the clanking and hissing of the train.

"If there's anything at all that you ever need, no matter what it is, you must come to me," she said laying her cheek briefly against Dorothy's one more time before hurriedly turning away and walking off the platform and straight out of the station with Edward trailing behind.

* * *

It was only 10 o'clock in the morning but Nora had already left her bag at Aunt Sarah's and was walking towards Dorothy's home on a bright Saturday morning, the thin gold band flashed in the sunlight, she still wasn't used to seeing it there and for a moment she held her hand out in front of herself to admire it whilst she continued on her way. Peggy and Nora had accepted a quickie double wedding the week before and the young women had spent many of the night hours in the three days beforehand stitching and bleaching their clothes to be properly attired on their big day. Two days later Arthur had left for the front but Wilfred earned a week's reprieve by virtue of having toothache which needed to be treated before he was dispatched to the trenches. Due to this Nora had vacated the sisters' shared room for the weekend to give the newlyweds a few more hours together.

Nora was glad to be back in Mayfair it seemed fresh and untouched by the bombs which had landed on her area, she paused on the outskirts of a huge crowd as she crossed Hyde Park and strained to hear the suffragettes' speeches, pamphlets were strewn around the grass urging women to take up job vacancies left by men who had gone to France, to fight for Britain rather than themselves, to beware the "Hun in the Home" and to "Eat less food". No more arson raids now that the Zeppelins were doing the job, Nora thought, strange how things changed but at least she knew she was already doing her bit in the munitions factory.

Dorothy threw open the front door before Nora had even reached the top step, "I saw you from the sitting room window. You look wonderful, and you're married!" her sister said hugging her enthusiastically. Nora wasn't certain she would ever look "wonderful" with her chipped front tooth and old coat but she allowed herself the small vanity of believing that the hour at the hairdresser she had indulged in before her wedding had been worth it and the chic bob gave her a more fashionable look than she'd ever enjoyed before.

"We've got the whole day to do whatever we like together," Dorothy said taking Nora's hat and gloves.

"Won't Jean be 'ome for lunch?"

"No, he's gone into floristry as well as more basic cake making, says the price hikes mean he has to look at other ways to keep business going. Tea?" Nora nodded following Dorothy into the kitchen. "He leaves for the market hours before it gets light and only returns late in the evening, eats a bowl of soup and goes to bed, I hardly see him."

"You'll get to see 'im more than we see Arthur and Wilfred."

"That's true. I reckon he'd almost like to be able to go to the front though, he gets terribly jumpy when anyone asks him what side his country's on or why he's not in uniform."

"Father and Thomas 'aven't joined up, you just need to produce some babies to stop the questions, they're not sendin' men with young families."

Dorothy spooned tea into the pot filling it to the brim, "Did you see Uncle Edward this morning?"

"'E'd already left for the office, but Aunt Sarah sent 'er love and said to come over tomorrow."

"When you see him you'll have to bite your tongue as he goes on and on about Alfred. Apparently he graduated with distinction from McGill and is now at the Royal Military College in Kingston, uncle's awfully proud of him it's as if it's his son rather than his nephew! He never stops holding forth about how much better qualified the Canadian troops will be when they arrive than our lads who have been shipped over after just a few weeks' training."

"Thanks for the warning," Nora replied as she sipped her tea from a translucent china cup, she couldn't help thinking that mugs were far more satisfying when you had a bit of a thirst, "it's not the sort of thing I want to 'ear right now with Arthur away. I keep seein' all the women clustered round the lists every morning when I walk to work and I know that soon Peggy and I are goin' to be lookin' at them too and prayin' we get past "F" and "G" without findin' their names. The women who don't see a name move away almost guiltily, they can't look at the others it's as if they think it might be catchin'."

"If Romania joins the wrong side I'll probably have to move back to Aunt Sarah's, they're bound to take Jean away. It might be better if they did it sooner than later, so many of the Hungarians and Austrians were lynched before they ever got to the camps. I can't believe they were *all* spies."

"You can't be too careful though," Nora replied slowly, wondering how much they really knew about Jean Nicolas Nicolai.

* * *

If 1915 had been testing for Jean the first half of 1916 had undoubtedly been worse but now, as the trees in their wide shady avenue were losing their leaves, he wondered if he would have survived intact without the elaborate strategies he had undertaken. No one could have been more surprised than he was when his country suddenly gave itself a fighting front of one thousand two hundred kilometres. Whether it was viewed as courageous or suicidal everyone must see it as mentally unhinged, he thought, and what of the king who had been such good pals with the Kaiser? The scant information that filtered its way through to London spoke of his kinsmen in terms of unimaginable bravery and gave Jean the pleasing experience of being able to hold his head high and accept acclaim for his country's heroics, it certainly boosted trade even in these taxing times.

Suspicion, which he had felt dogged his every move in the past twelve months, transformed overnight into concern. Jean became uncharacteristically chatty about his home town which formed part of the Siret Line holding the advance. His mother was under siege and he had not heard from her since August. Every time he recounted the story his customers seemed to order a few extra items and business was creeping closer to pre-war levels.

Jean was realistic about his chances of helping his mother. They were zero. He took a conscious decision to stop thinking about it, there was always a chance that she would emerge radiant and unscathed at the end of the conflict and if that was the case her appetite for fresh triumphs from her son would be even keener following years of postal starvation. He must build his business into a pinnacle of perfection and the problem of his wife needed to be urgently addressed.

While his position as a foreigner had been dubious Jean had been able to almost convince himself that the wedding hadn't happened. It had been such a quick dowdy affair compared to the staggeringly elaborate preparations essential for any marriage in Romania, in fact had it not been for the presence of the girl who ate her dinner with him every evening before curling herself into an armchair like a long sleek alley cat and settling down with a book, he could pretend he did not have a wife. When she left an hour later, gliding upstairs to her bedroom, he would let out a long deep sigh of frustration that he had held in throughout the time he was forced to share his space with her. Before she had been part of a safety strategy, now she was becoming an irritating encumbrance.

He had agreed to be shackled for better or worse til one of them died, the time for indulgence was over, she must be moulded into something acceptable, something helpful for his business, he wouldn't accept a silly young girl any more, she must become Edward, he would brook no compromise.

He would observe her until he had worked out exactly what needed to be changed then he could recreate her faultlessly just as he did with his rice paper flowers.

* * *

Late 1916.
(Dorothy:21)
Dorothy could not avoid noticing the sudden coldness in Jean's manner towards her, but at a time when the entire nation seemed to be fighting a series of millions of individual battles and when every day thousands of buff War Office envelopes and black rimmed telegrams rained down on families all over the country and her sisters and mother lived in fear of receiving one, to ask what fate held for the next week was sufficiently uncertain to make questions about the prospects for a long and happy marriage seem almost nit-picking. Dorothy decided it was her duty to expend all her energies on trying to please her husband, after all his beloved mother was unaccounted for, most of his country was in enemy hands and, Dorothy reasoned, he was probably frustrated at having to stay in a foreign land making cakes because he had a wife to provide for. She had never noticed any yen in Jean to hasten into armed conflict, but she supposed that it was impossible to know how one would react to a testing situation until it actually occurred and that Jean might be experiencing all manner of ambivalent emotions tearing him between the calls of wife and mother.

At the same time she wished her sisters had lived their married lives for more than a week and she had been able to prise information from them about what it was like. Perhaps it was just a class thing, but when she'd seen them together with their boyfriends there had seemed much more touching and larking about, although Jean was nine years older than her and naturally serious, Dorothy did wonder if she was failing to do something vital that her sisters somehow automatically knew about. However, whenever she had attempted a bit of light hearted fun her efforts had been met with stony silence or the instruction to pull herself together.

She knew Jean valued women who were demure and respectful, quiet and neat, whenever he employed staff he consistently offered the job to that type and, she noticed with a jolt of surprise, they were all considerably older than her. As they were all petite rather nervous characters forced to look upwards to meet their employer's eye she hadn't thought of them as older before, she had always felt more worldly than them in some way, but now she recognised it was just that they were so quiet she had thought of them as immature as she could not imagine them having an opinion. His choice of workers was about as far removed from her character as it was possible to be, she had always found it incredibly difficult to stop herself from saying exactly what popped into her head, a trait Aunt Sarah had made strenuous efforts to curb but which Uncle Edward had called "honesty"; as for her height there was nothing she could do about that.

For all her desire to please him, Dorothy seemed to be constantly one step behind. It was particularly bad when they were out together, at such times she seemed to be running an impossible conversational obstacle race in which whatever answer she gave ended up being blameworthy. There had been a time recently when Jean had pointed out a man who was consulting a particularly impressive pocket watch and she had believed the expected response was for her to admire it, but when she had done so Jean had instantly accused her of looking directly at men with intent to attract them and before she knew it she was saying "yes" and "no" in the wrong places so that whatever reply she gave dragged her further into his incriminating nets. He had once hauled her off a bus forcing her to walk more than a mile in the rain because he believed she had been making eyes at one of the other passengers. However much she protested she had merely been staring out of the window day dreaming and had not even focused on the man who was sitting beside it, her cries only seemed to make him more enraged with her "lies". After that she had claimed, out of respect for the losses and hardships of others, it would be best to stop going out more than was necessary. This saved her from further public embarrassment but didn't seem to make Jean any more impressed with her as a wife.

She would have to keep trying until the war was over, then perhaps things would change or if not she could ask her sisters for some hints.

* * *

In April 1918 Edward received a letter from Campbell saying that Alfred had graduated from military college and was a commissioned officer with the Prince of Wales Leinster Regiment. He was to set sail from Canada for England shortly and had already arranged ten days' leave on his arrival in Britain. Edward was in a fever of excitement at finally meeting the nephew with whom he had enjoyed such intense correspondence over the past three years. The news added to Edward's growing feeling of optimism, the previous year had been rather bleak with Wilfred returned to Peggy suffering from serious lung damage after being gassed at the Battle of Lys. Information about Arthur and James was sporadic and usually so delayed that the most the family knew was that the men had been alive the previous month, but since the arrival of the Americans Edward had begun to believe that the tide was turning in their favour.

By the time Alfred marched down the gangplank and onto his native soil for the first time, Edward was almost bursting with pride, cauterized only by a deep sense of responsibility to care for his brother's child. He guided Alfred around the places of historical interest to the Lane clan and invited George Cochrane Kerr to join them on a visit to Sudbrook Park, and one evening they all strolled down to 4 Harley Street where Alfred's grandfather had run another of his famed clinics. Everywhere they went Edward basked in the aura of standing beside his nephew's pristine uniform resplendent with the Prince of Wales feathers on cap and collar, bordered ironically by the German motto "Ich Dien" on either side. The mark of his rank as Second Lieutenant was affixed to his jacket in defiance of the facial evidence that the body within it was just a boy. Yet the excitement and expeditions were so frenetic that it was not until Edward and Sarah stood on the platform and Alfred had stepped onto the running board of the Southampton train, that his uncle was engulfed by a moment when his heart seemed to pause in its beats as a desperate clarity of thought gripped him and he lent forward towards the slowly moving carriage, recognising the teenager's smooth cleft chin, full lips and quiet eyes for the first time as better fitted for the schoolroom than the trenches, too idealistic for the task of leading men onto fields of death, and he almost shouted to Alfred to jump down, to remain in London, that the valour and heroics were a mere charade not meant for someone so fresh that his cheek was still soft and his flesh as untested by love as his mind was unsullied by torture. But at Alfred's raised hand, Edward's desperate grapple changed into a wave of farewell; within seconds his nephew was no more than a blur among a sea of uniforms moving inexorably where fate pushed them.

The close-typed lists of dead and missing still graced the news boards but the summer sun continued to warm hope into Edward as he read of the British smashing through the German lines at Amiens in early August before storming across the Canal du Nord in late September, the selfless heroics of his family seemed certain to end in victory and rejoicing, so when a slim package arrived at Maddox Street in the final week of October he opened it without trepidation. Initially confused as to why Regimental Chaplain Orr was communicating with him and what it was he enclosed, the comforting words gave way to unbounded horror as he held a second letter between his thumb and index finger, his hand shaking too hard to open the paper he now knew to have been penned by Alfred for his parents in the event of his death, but which had, in the confusion of war, been sent to his uncle instead.

Hours later Edward was shocked to feel Sarah's touch, he was still sitting at his desk, Alfred's letter held in one hand, his head resting in the other as he read the penultimate paragraph over and over again.

"Remember 'Dulce et decorum est pro patria mori', and I ask for no better death than to die fighting our country's enemies."

It ended in a single perfectly round red spot.

CHAPTER SIX

11 November 1918
(Dorothy: 23, Aunt Sarah: 54, Uncle Edward: 68)
Aunt Sarah was on the doorstep pleading with her to come out and join in the celebrations, Dorothy looked back down the hallway a birdlike nervousness in her glance. Jean appeared from the living room and was persuaded that indeed they should don hats and coats and venture out.

"Will Edward be accompanying us?" he asked as he closed the front door behind them.

"He has hardly left his study since Alfred's death, he blames himself for the considerable correspondence he had with the lad, claims he persuaded him to sacrifice himself to the caprices of war, that he mistook agony for glory, he feels there is nothing for him to celebrate. I only hope it will pass and he will realise he was not to blame, but I cannot seem to reach him at the moment."

"Oh poor Uncle Edward, perhaps we should just go back to the apartment and try to cheer him up," Dorothy said, but they had reached the end of the road to find the square in front of them packed with a heaving sea of bodies, a band was playing and the street lamps illuminated the thousands of moving heads like fields of wild flowers swaying and turning in the dark evening breeze. As they stood watching a uniformed man detached himself from the edge of the mass grabbing Dorothy's hand and dragging her into the dance. She laughed in surprise at his enthusiasm to grab her round the waist and tried to catch Jean's hand to pull him into the party with her, as the unknown soldier twirled her into the rhythm of the crowd. She saw her aunt was also moving to the sound of the music, a little like a wind-battered oak tree, but moving nevertheless. Jean, however, was standing rigid, no sign that the eruption of euphoria was touching him at all, the expression on his face was one of slight contempt, or perhaps, revulsion. As she danced back towards him, Dorothy again attempted to take his hand and ease him into the fray but he swatted first at her and then at the soldier beside her with a peevishness that could not dent her partner's happiness but which sucked out the lightness and joy that had begun to surround Dorothy.

They walked further, different bands inhabited every square but the picture was the same, an endless pirouetting populous, not gyrating with abandon, they had all lost too much for that, but expressing a majestic relief that it was over, a relief which should have engulfed them all. The British reserve seemed to have vanished as people hugged, kissed and danced, and in every square the crowd would try to include them. She wanted so badly to go, to become part of the collective relief, to drown within the good-will that was rippling out from every London heart, and there were queues of men, young and old, who pulled at her to join the celebration but every time she allowed herself to be eased into the mass Dorothy would turn and see the pale anger mounting in her husband, whether she was encouraging him to join in or she was being induced to dance herself, his eyes dripped with withering scorn and the expression of someone unhappily witnessing another embarrassing themselves horribly.

A desperation tightened within her throat to prevent Aunt Sarah from witnessing the character assassination she knew was waiting to project itself from the wings onto centre stage. "Not in front of my Aunt," she thought, "not tonight". She wriggled away from the laughing man who was jigging in front of her, holding out his hands, tempting her to join his laughter.

"I have a terrible headache, I think it's the music and the crowds, would you mind awfully if we tried to find somewhere quiet for a while," she asked, gently touching Jean's sleeve, an imploring look in her eyes.

Shaking her hand off roughly, before noticing Aunt Sarah's look of shock at his gesture and turning it into a smoothing of the coat fabric, he reluctantly inched away from the glorious wrath that he had been preparing when Aunt Sarah said it might be helpful for Edward if the three of them went back to Maddox Street and they shared a quiet glass of wine together.

"So many people have lost so much, but it's over now and Edward needs to stop torturing himself, a little company might help him to do so," she said, so reasonably that Jean's internal firestorm seemed almost doused, and Dorothy sent up a silent prayer of thanks that she had sidestepped the latest verbal grenade blast and a further plea that after an hour with her uncle and a glass of good wine her husband might have mellowed sufficiently for the walk back home to be uneventful.

* * *

In early December Arthur Fry stepped off the boat at Southampton and back into Nora's arms, one of the luckier soldiers who had secured a speedy passage home in time for the festive season. Five hours later he had been demobbed, which transformed him, as he put it, "from one of the newspaper's returnin' 'eroes into another unemployed bod, fully trained in the art of fillin' shells and preventin' outbreaks of frostbite in the toes, but not much else."

For the first few days Nora was so delighted he had returned miraculously intact that nothing could blight her horizon. However, it didn't take long before necessity forced real life to creep back into the Fry household and Nora could see Arthur shrink every time she began sewing or a customer called to take her away from him. Sending him on useful errands made her juggling act between caring spouse and sole breadwinner even worse as Arthur would return morose with tales of the servicemen he had seen on every street corner busking with penny whistles or selling matches yet decorated to the nines with medals, rows of useless metal pulling down the fabric of their demob issue suits by their collective weight.

"If men like that can't get a job, what 'ope is there for me!" he raged, "Land fit for 'eroes they say, what land needs a million men 'oo are experts at removin' lice from the seams of their clothes and dab 'ands at the best way to kill with a bayonet?" Nora would watch him, waiting for the frustration and anger to pass, impotent to say anything that would give her back the sunny confident lad she had waved off to war four years previously.

By Christmas Day when Peggy, Nora, Dorothy and their men folk were to spend the day at Maddox Street, a deep melancholy had settled on Arthur. He was only ignited into speech by his contempt for the members of the male population who had remained at home, building up their businesses while the rest of them had been to hell and back. Nora was more than a little worried about how he might behave at her uncle's house but had been unable to see any way of avoiding the meal without irritating her husband even further.

Wilfred's health remained poor and he too railed against a country where the women were working and the men were unable to find employment. Peggy was taking any work she could find to keep them from toppling into hunger and homelessness, and Nora knew that even with Arthur's struggles her lot was not nearly as bad as her sister's.

At the gaily decorated dinner table Arthur remained subdued, making only the occasional jibe at tradesmen with booming businesses and anointing those who had steered companies through wartime austerity with a lightly veiled contempt that even Jean's faltering proficiency in the English language could not fail to comprehend. As the meal teetered on the edge of open conflict and Nora inwardly battled with the question of how to stop Christmas Day ending in such ferocious antagonism between the brothers-in-law that Dorothy became completely cut off her family, Uncle Edward attempted a rescue mission by mentioning a piece he had seen in *The Times* about former officers who were making their living by hiring themselves out as dancing partners to well-to-do ladies at the fashionable London venues and dance halls which had mushroomed across the country the minute the ink had dried on the Armistice.

"Arthur could do that," Nora immediately piped up, "'e's always been an amazin' dancer," she said smiling encouragingly at her husband.

"You seem to have missed the small fact that I'm not some posh officer, so no rich Deb would give a farthin' to dance with me!" Arthur countered in a spiky tone. But the idea had given Nora something positive to seize on for the first time since her husband returned and, feeling as if this was probably the only lifebelt she was going to be thrown at the dinner table, she was not about to let it go. She'd heard of many men coming back and not speaking, staying mute and angry day after day their minds left in the mud of Gallipoli or Ypres with no way of getting home, she wouldn't have that, not for her Arthur, she'd fight to the last breath in her body to avoid that, as far as Nora was concerned there had been enough suffering, now was the time to forget and start enjoying life, to make up for all the time they had already lost, and dancing to earn a crust might be the perfect way of doing it.

"Desperate times require desperate measures Arthur Fry, I'm goin' to make you an officer by New Year," she announced with a flourish that instantly drew all those around the table towards her bandwagon which they leapt aboard ready to ride recklessly away from the heavy storm clouds that had been set to burst their cold water over the first peaceful Yuletide in years.

"I took elocution and deportment lessons years ago," Aunt Sarah chipped in, "it would be a great pleasure to teach Arthur how to imitate the accent of a gentleman officer; and Edward has a good suit which is far too tight for him that Nora could easily adjust for Arthur, I'm sure."

"Indeed I have," Edward said relaxing into a smile now that the threat of traded insults over the cranberry sauce was receding, "and I have spare white gloves and shoes. If I remember the gift of the gab you displayed while courting Nora I'd wager you can concoct some heroic tales that will have the ladies queuing up to dance with you."

Nora could see a guttering flame of hope flickering weakly at the corners of Arthur's lips, it was definitely there although the slightest zephyr of cool headedness would be sufficient to snuff it out. She had no intention of allowing it to be extinguished.

"No excuses Arthur! Edward and I will sort out clothin', Aunt Sarah will 'ave you walkin' and talkin' like landed gentry, Peggy can give you a classy 'aircut and you can start off at the Plaza's New Year Tea Dance, I know the under 'ousekeeper there, she's a good sort who's bound to 'elp. Dorothy and I will come along and pretend to be regular patrons to give you Dutch courage and make sure none of your partners get too frisky," she concluded with a wink before belatedly turning to Jean and asking, "You don't mind Dorothy comin' with me to chaperon Arthur do you? Only I'll feel a bit of a gooseberry sittin' there by myself."

Jean's round eyes seemed to bulge out of his round head and he paused long enough for Nora to know she had upset him far more than she would have dared to do deliberately. The silence at first unnerved her, then irritated her so that she knew there would be two tell-tale spots of colour showing on her cheeks. Who was he to stop the flow of enthusiasm around the table that might rescue her Arthur from falling into the madness of despair, how dare this unfriendly foreigner, who hadn't fought for anyone, hesitate in giving his consent to so small a favour, she looked directly at him, not dropping her gaze until she received a curt nod.

"Fantastic!" she cried, "It's all set then, Mr and Mrs Fry will be social climbin' by New Year!"

"It would be inappropriate for Dorothy to dance in these places," Jean began, "she is to sit beside you throughout, and perhaps sometimes it will be possible for Peggy or Mrs Lane to accompany you instead," he concluded, his thin lips set in a straight line.

"Yes, of course, so long as I 'ave someone with me I'll be quite 'appy," Nora said ignoring Jean's obvious irritation as she noticed the great crescent of a smile that had sliced itself across Dorothy's face which, even though she hung her head in an attempt to hide it, her sister was incapable of suppressing.

* * *

In the spring of 1919 James Terrill finally reached England again, but the carefree boy who had left with a jaunty salute and a wink after falsifying his age, had died. Four years of wading through sludge regularly punctuated by random bloated limbs led to James becoming infected by the decay and barbarity which surrounded him. Every body part that squelched beneath his boots or popped out from a trench wall was not merely an object in his mind, however deformed it was for James it remained a tangible reminder of a man, a person who, irrespective of his nationality, would be the usual jumble of qualities and faults, dreams and disappointments, small kindnesses and petty cruelties, who would have a family that would cry for him and whose flesh had been no different from James's own in the pain that it felt and the transformation it would undergo when the heart stopped and life's animation abruptly vanished leaving just the mannequin. James had seen it happen time and again, once when he was half way through his breakfast biscuit the tall bloke next to him had stretched himself a little too far from his crouching position and the remaining mouthful of James's meal, which had been clenched between his thumb and index finger, was instantly adorned with bits of bone and brain. He could not recall the person he had been before, how had he laughed and why, what had enabled him to primp and flatter silly old cows so filled with piddling vanities, or a time when sunshine on his back was sufficient to make him believe all was right with the world, a time when the image of his dead friends didn't haunt his dreams with their jaws showing where their cheeks had been blown away or their guts spewing out from the front of their jackets.

The returning Terrill was automated in the way he now viewed humanity; the soldiers who had fought beside him commanded imperishable loyalty, but the staff officers whom he had witnessed executing their own men when confusion and horror caused them to run the wrong way, earned his contempt. The top brass and politicians whom he felt had viewed the vast collection of individuals as no more than a black swarm on their strategic maps, to be pitched against an ant hill on the opposing general's chart, where the spray of bullets, shells and gas would wipe out hundreds of thousands and allow the bigwigs to move their markers quarter of an inch further on, towards them James awarded his intense hatred.

The hollow-cheeked, taciturn relic who stepped from the train at Bexhill knew he was coming home to a land of people whose authority he despised, and a family to whom he no longer knew how to respond. The man who had previously been the first to organise a party, rounding up all stray friends in a youthful stream of gregarious enjoyment, had failed to even send word that he was back in Britain, and as he walked up Sandhurst Lane towards his parents' cottage, he was unsure if he felt relief or regret that he was no longer sliding over wet duckboards and crawling out of shell holes, every second aware he could be extinguished without effort, and that his survival was based upon a lottery that he was not even certain he wanted to win.

The click of the latch drew his mother out into the cramped hallway where she halted, looking at him in silence.

"James?" she whispered, her nose becoming pink as her eyes brimmed with tears. At the slight lift of his chin in she catapulted herself to him, hugging his body as he stiffened at her touch. Looking down at her he seemed very far away, observing her from a distance as she stretched up and stroked his matted hair which stuck out from beneath his cap, reaching her lips upwards to graze them on his stubbly cheek, she appeared to want him to do something but he could not remember what. Caressing his back and murmuring loving words she seemed to take an age to release him. The contact with her flesh had been uncomfortable and he felt relieved when it finished, much longer and he would have had to push her away and leave.

"I'll put the kettle on and then I'll get Mr Brown's lad to go and tell your Father and sisters you're 'ome," she was prattling but he recognised he was thirsty although water would do as well as tea, "Vera will be over the moon to come in from school and find you 'ere, I can't tell you 'ow much we've missed you," she said hoarsely before dissolving into a fit of coughing. He could barely remember Vera so he didn't credit that she would remember him.

"Are you ill?" he asked.

"No, no, 'ow could I possibly be ill when you've come 'ome to me, it's just a sore throat and a bit of a funny mouth, but it will all be fine now, there couldn't be a better tonic than to 'ave you back with me. Everything's going to be just dandy!"

But the house he had left only four years before seemed too small to contain him now. It shut out the stars at night, trapping him with the ghosts that stalked his mind whenever he relaxed his guard against them, and he would be dragged from sleep by the shrieks he slowly recognised as his own. They forced him out into the cold darkness to walk away from his demons for hour after endless hour in the isolated company of all the other troubled silent spectres like himself who could only find rest once physical exhaustion made it impossible for them to remain upright.

* * *

Arthur walked through the lobby, a perfectly groomed gentleman; the slight trembling of his hands was fortunately disguised by the gloves all men had to wear to stop them from touching a lady's bare skin if she were wearing a low-backed dress, and the occasional twitch of the nerve in his neck could be excused as a minor legacy of the war. He stood straight attempting to exude the air of upper class confidence which was supposed to be his birth right. A young girl in starched hotel uniform spoke to him nervously in a low voice, in an exchange that any onlooker would view as deference to his status rather than collusion in Nora's risky plan.

"Here's the cards of two of our regular ladies. They've agreed to divide your services this afternoon so you'll be dancing every dance," she instructed him, "I said you were from the North of England but don't be specific. I don't know why I'm doing this, I'll lose my job if you can't act right."

"I know, I'm sorry, I won't let you down," he replied with every outward mannerism of giving her an order regarding his requirements.

Arthur strode through to the main ballroom, pausing in the doorway as he let his practiced arrogant gaze rest on his wife and Dorothy before sweeping over to his afternoon's bosses, performing a gracious bow and taking the hand of the more wrinkly of the two, leading her to the dance floor as if she were a pearl of the greatest beauty and value. As the fever of gaiety began and the band struck up the first waltz a tangible ripple of excitement ran around the excess members of the female population as the handsome stranger began acting his part. The music took hold of Arthur and his body began to move with the easy rhythm he had almost forgotten he possessed. His limbs gently guided his partner through the rise and fall of the dance dragging his mind with them. Like a pied piper, his outer form strove to force his brain to run from the past and immerse itself in the froth and frivolity that the musicians were urging him towards. He looked over at his wife, acknowledging to himself that it was the force of her belief in him that had pulled him from a vortex of desolation, allowing him to whirl dangerously around the edge but never slip over. The beat drummed through his veins as he held himself ever more erect, staring down his nose as he began to remember some of the more ridiculous officers he had been ordered to obey, and to quietly enjoy lampooning them.

The third dance brought a hiccup in his reverie when his partner began making polite enquiries about where he had been during the war. To tell the truth was to totter too close to the abyss and risk his mind descending onto topics he had been using all his strength to avoid thinking about. Pressing them down into the furthest depths of his soul and locking them securely out of sight, he managed to retain his benign smile, gluing it to his face as his feet never faltered but the mental turmoil left him mute. It was fortunate that the lady in his arms interpreted his silence correctly for the intense emotion it was and had the sensitivity to change the subject to the cut of the band master's coat, although he noticed she lost no time afterwards in telling every one of her girlfriends that Arthur Fry had clearly been engaged in many heroic deeds which had left him scarred but sexily stoical, a Chinese whisper which eventually reached Nora and Dorothy's table.

Afterwards it was once again his wife who rescued things from the jaws of defeatism by coaching him through several possible courageous tales that contained neither people nor places that he actually knew, but would furnish Arthur with sufficient ammunition to satisfy dance floor curiosity.

Arthur's luck held as his impeccable footwork and unfailing attention to every lady who hired him ensured he never had to sit out a dance and indulge in small talk. His reputation grew as a strong but silent type, which only added to the ladies' intrigue and his increasing popularity, both of which contributed to lining his pockets and keeping him clear of awkward questions and romantic advances under the watchful eye of his wife.

* * *

For Dorothy, Arthur's job was a godsend, it quickly became apparent that either Nora or she would have to dance, at least occasionally, or else arouse suspicion. Nora was solidly opposed to anything which threatened to unstick her from a seat in the corner, claiming it might put Arthur off if she were to glide past him on some other man's arm. She began to feign an injured ankle, stating to all enquirers that she was married and merely accompanying her younger sister to the dances as propriety demanded, thus throwing all attention onto Dorothy who lapped it up gratefully and was soon dancing almost as much as Arthur.

Every song the band played had her itching to get out of her chair and surrender herself to the steps which she now made so expertly. Her open smile and the cheeky twinkle she could not keep out of her grey eyes when she entered the dance halls seemed to put potential partners at ease, wiping out any fear of a cruel rebuff to their advances so that Dorothy returned home several afternoons a week with aching limbs having managed no more than a couple of swigs of tea between spates on the floor.

She became adept at her new life as a chameleon; at home she wore a suitably downcast expression, sighing lightly as she told Jean of the next dance Arthur needed her to attend, yet carefully admitting she enjoyed listening to the music and keeping Nora company. She frequently made disparaging comments about the cakes served and how commonplace they were when compared to her husband's creations. Inside her house she still wore a slightly superior air and an unhappy coldness in her manner when dealing with any staff or tradesmen, careful to demonstrate to Jean that she gave no one, man or woman, cause to believe they could be informal with her. To her husband she was consistently deferential, unsmiling and cautious, even when massaging his ego, careful that she did not overdo things and spark his suspicion. She stuck to accompanying Nora to tea dances only, leaving Peggy to go to the few evening engagements Arthur was booked for, arguing volubly in front of Jean that when her husband returned from his working day she wished to be at home for him, hoping her performance would pacify him and stopple the fountain of mistrust about her behaviour that she could feel, barely dammed, ready to flood from him. Her salvation was Jean's immovable work ethic which entailed she was quite safe at the tea dances to waltz and foxtrot, quickstep and polka with as many partners as she pleased, secure in the knowledge he would never leave his business premises before the stroke of six o'clock.

As she stepped out in the direction of the Palais or the Plaza some subtle changes took place. By the end of the road her forehead had relaxed and her eyebrows were no longer disappearing under her curls, as she crossed the park her arms swung more freely and her hips and back shook off the pose of walking with a broom handle down her spine. By the time she reached the far side of the park she was offering an open smile to walkers coming in the opposite direction. The short distance had transformed her face with a few minor muscle movements back into a vivacious young woman, excited by life. Dorothy on the dance floor was swept along in the euphoria of her ever changing partners, lack of men had led to the rule that it was impolite to monopolise a single female for more than two dances, but her easy grace and deep crests of red-blonde hair that were softly pinned into place at the nape of her slender neck, led every hopeful Romeo to insist upon his quota of her attention. She was particularly enthusiastic about the chic faster dances that were coming into vogue. The five piece bands had to adapt quickly to the new music that was filtering across the Atlantic or lose their young clientele. The elderly musicians in tight morning coats with perspiring foreheads seemed to Dorothy to regain some of their youth with every bit of ragtime and jazz they mastered. The more stately ballroom dances were still employed to allow the dancers to catch their breath, but increasingly something faster and more desperate and discordant was taking over her afternoons.

It was following a particularly energetic few hours that Dorothy skipped up the steps to her house, flinging open the front door to find Jean already home and looking through the mail on the hall dresser. The happy ease with which the door had been treated was still visible her face and Jean's reaction was superhuman in its speed. Slamming closed the heavy piece of oak so the knocker brasses cracked together, he pinned Dorothy by her forearms against the hall wall, crushing the brim of her hat into the paisley patterned cream paper.

"Where have you been?" he snarled at her, his thin lips moving whilst his teeth remained clenched together.

"To watch Arthur at the Plaza with Nora," Dorothy stammered instantly aware she had made a deadly error. "I'm sure I told you …"

"Who did you meet?"

"Nobody, I just kept Nora company," she replied attempting not to meet his eyes in case any traces of her former happiness remained.

"You think I'm a fool? You expect me to believe you've spent all these months behaving like a nun?" he screamed, gripping her arms harder and squeezing his stout fingers so her flesh bulged between them. "A woman like you who's hardly better than a Whitechapel whore, panting for men's attention ..." his anger was touching the level where he reverted into his native tongue confident that the spittle hitting her face and hair plus the noise of his spiralling ecstasy of fury made his meaning unmistakable as she felt him push all his strength into bruising the muscles beneath his grasp.

An orgy of resentment urged her to push him off and flee upstairs, locking herself inside her bedroom. Pain shot between her temples as self-preservation compelled her hurricane of indignation to be compressed back down inside her. Life before Jean had never contained violence in any form and she was unsure how far the blinding red mist would lead him or what his next move would be. All she knew was that anything other than complete submission would result in her never being allowed out with her sister again. If she could only contain the storm of frustration and injustice that was trying to burst out of her, then Nora or her uncle might be able to persuade Jean he had scant grounds to stop her from helping Arthur to make a living, but the slightest eye contact or resistance would convince him that all punishments of her were rightfully deserved. She hung her head and let her body go limp, but only when there were finally hot angry tears cascading off her face smudging into the rug did he throw her aside to slide down the wall into a confused heap littering the hallway.

* * *

By the summer of 1919 Annie's sore throat had become so acute she found it difficult to swallow and the constant mouth ulcers she suffered plus the strange lump on her tongue made it easier to use cigarettes than food to ease hunger pangs. As the pounds dropped off her, Flo began bringing round nutritious soups every day which she would set down on the table and then wait, watching her mother spoon down every drop while instructing Sybil and Vera to help more in the house so their mother could rest. Annie appreciated the backup but it did not solve what she considered to be her greatest problem, the intense tension between James and his father.

Soon after he returned home she had persuaded James to make an attempt to be rehired at the photographic studio. It had been a disaster with the proprietor not even letting the haunted face through the front door before telling him there were no vacancies. It was the same wherever he went and the more rejections James received the more embittered he became with his own family.

Charles was still working as a dairyman but there were no openings for his son at his work place, so in desperation he struck upon the idea of contacting Thomas and urging him to find work for his brother in the house-painting company he ran with his father-in-law. Although having James around was undoubtedly awkward for all the family, Annie was unenthusiastic about her husband's plan believing that her son might suddenly become himself again if he enjoyed sufficient quantities of mother love and home kindness, but Charles refused to listen to her and announced his scheme with paternalistic pride.

James's reaction was swift and violent, "An 'and out job under my brother's thumb, 'im what's too lily livered to fight for 'is country! That yellow pansy what hid behind 'is children and beneath his wife's skirts while the men I was with 'ad the balls to leave it all behind," he spat striding up and down the tiny front room, filling it with the energy of his derision before stopping in front of his father's armchair and leaning down until his face was no more than an inch away. The bloodshot eyes stared hard at Charles and Annie could see white foam flecks at the corners of her son's mouth, "I'd rather starve than work for my weaklin' brother that you seem to value so much," he hissed before stalking out to the hallway and slamming the front door behind him.

From the moment James raised his voice Annie had stood immobilised in the corner of the room, tea tray in hand, frightened that any movement by her would cause his eruption to intensify further. She had felt the simmering resentment towards all of them threatening to burst from him for months and she had been terrified that any argument would escalate to the point where James's contempt for his father would be vomited out with such force that Charles's pride would be incapable of doing anything other than throwing him out, depriving Annie of her boy once again.

Still standing in the corner as the thin walls ceased juddering from the force of James's exit, tears coursed down Annie's thin cheeks in an unstoppable stream, running off her jaw bone and splashing onto her wasted breasts where the water seeped down her thin cotton dress that hung from her emaciated shoulder bones.

* * *

By late November the lump on Annie's tongue was so pronounced that it was hard for her to close her lips normally and she finally allowed Flo to call the doctor. He was a kindly middle aged man who chatted quietly to Annie as he examined her but shut the door carefully afterwards so that she could only hear his murmured voice and Flo's higher one on the landing.

Flo's head appeared round the door, her face unusually pale as she squatted down next to her mother. "The doctor says 'e'll 'ave to operate, oh mum I feel so bad we didn't get 'im in sooner."

Annie squeezed her daughter's hand, "probably wouldn't 'ave made no difference," she tried to say although the sound came out as if she had a whole potato lodged in her mouth.

"It will be best if you and Vera come and live with Walter and me until you're well again," Flo said, in her usual practical way, but Annie tried to protest that she should remain to care for Charles and James. "Rubbish, Sybil's more than capable of looking after those two, in fact she can run over to father now and get 'im to beg a piece of prime beef off Farmer Eliot before 'e leaves work so I can make a big batch of tea to make you well again."

The following day Annie was moved into a pristine sick room in Flo's cottage, Vera was to sleep in the main room so that her mother could have complete peace, and Flo had put a little bell by the bed so that she could ring for anything she needed, not that she ever did as Flo appeared with a fresh cup of beef tea almost every half hour so that by the end of the day Annie was beginning to feel it was running through her veins. For those twenty-four hours she felt like a Queen, she couldn't remember ever having spent a whole day in bed when she had to do absolutely nothing for anyone else, it almost seemed blasphemous to enjoy it. Although she was worried about the operation which was set for Thursday, Annie was hoping that if she avoided thinking about it and asked no direct questions of any of her family, who she was sure knew what procedure the doctor was intending to perform, then perhaps it would not be too bad. In this she discovered she was completely wrong.

Annie was cruelly silenced, yet after she became conscious of the brutally hacked stump, bloody and swollen beneath her nasal passage, the next awareness, which sliced through the grating agony enveloping her head, was of a rough hand holding hers. Fevered effort transmitted weak power to her thumb and she moved it slowly rubbing up against coarse hairs on the fingers which clasped her own. She lay there, blankets pulled up to her neck, hardly daring to open her eyes. For a full ten minutes hope battled against curiosity as her tired brain strove to avoid having its dream shattered by discovering it was the doctor or Walter by her side, but as she heaved her eyelids open a slit her inquisitiveness was rewarded with a massive burst of joy which leaked down through her aching head and settled on her heart comforting it in a way that nothing other than the tenderness of James could do.

From the moment of her operation onwards he stayed by her side, dozing in the upright wooden chair beside the bed only to be fully alert once again when he felt her stir. If she came to when he was asleep she would try not to wake him, just moving her eyes to check he was in his customary position, but he seemed able to sense her consciousness however hard she worked to leave his scant rest undisturbed. His forbidding wordless figure with its intense gaze left even Flo no option but to leave the nursing duties to him and although she handed him her puréed concoctions every meal time with an air of slight reluctance, she did not argue once she had watched how gently he spooned sustenance into Annie's dribbling mouth. His eyes softened now when he looked at his mother and the tenderness with which he performed every one of her requirements, apart from the most intimate, let Annie know she had been correct in hanging onto the belief that part of her son's soul still survived. His distance from the rest of the family appeared unchanged but her own painful muteness created a mutual silence that rejuvenated their bond as no conversation had managed to do, and she began to feel almost lucky that her illness had allowed her to discover how to reach him again.

* * *

After James had poured each bitter dose of Laudanum down his mother's inflamed throat he would sit looking into the eyes he had loved so much throughout his vaguely remembered childhood, until the medicine took effect and her lids drooped allowing her an hour or so free from pain. He watched her as she slept, the sharp cheekbones and scraggy neck bore little resemblance to the woman he cherished in his memories when he managed to think back to his time at the photographic studio. Now she had stopped talking he could feel her far more clearly than when all the fuss and chatter had been going on around him, and when he could feel her, he could begin to absorb some of her love, although the fog in his mind remained, being with her silent form allowed him to relax as he had not been able to do since he came home, and the deep silence left him able to sleep without screaming, his hand resting in hers on the patched bedspread.

Two weeks after the operation James awoke with an aching neck. Moving his shoulders to stretch he felt stickiness on his wrist which caused him to open his eyes and see the bedclothes dyed red, blood haemorrhaging from his mother's unconscious mouth. A gravely shout erupted from him, his voice rasping from lack of use, as he leapt to the doorway calling urgently for Flo.

She took the steep wooden stairs like a hurdler calling to Walter to get the doctor, working with him to stop the crimson flood pumping over their mother's lips. After ten minutes James stepped away from the bed, he observed his sister with curiosity unable to understand why she was still tending to the body on the bed so feverishly. He had seen life depart too often in his twenty-two years not to know the instant it occurred, when the time for physical effort had passed. It shocked him to realise his elder sister still possessed hope when everything was over. Straightening his back he quietly left the room, pausing only briefly to collect his kit bag from his father's empty cottage, before beginning a marathon silent tramp to Southampton where he boarded a ship for New Zealand.

* * *

"I received a letter from Sybil today," Dorothy announced, trying to keep her voice light and sooth Jean's hackles which she knew would rise the moment any of her sisters were mentioned. "Father's decided to move back to Wiltshire and Flo's already got Vera, so Sybil was wondering if she could come and live with us for a while."

He didn't move his head to look at her, his stillness ached at her, forcing her to talk even though she knew that bearing the atmosphere was part of the game. "Peggy has Wilfred to care for and Nora and Arthur aren't exactly back on their feet yet, it wouldn't be forever…"

"And when something else goes wrong will I be expected to take in more of your family's strays like Edward was?"

"That's not fair," she cried her heart constricting in her chest against the manipulation of what she knew to be the truth, "Uncle Edward wanted Peggy to stay after Miss Jones left."

"Dorothy, there are eight of you, your father is still alive Sybil should go with him, I can't be made responsible for some young girl who hails from a family who appear completely incapable of not living off the charity of others, first it would be her and then there would be more of them."

"She's never been to Wiltshire, she doesn't know anyone there, all she's asking for is one of our rooms until she's got a job."

"And if she doesn't I'll be expected not just to house her but to feed and clothe her too. You must write back and instruct her to go with her father."

"He doesn't want her, he hasn't even got a job himself yet."

"If he doesn't want her why should I put up with another silly woman in my household, it's a ridiculous idea, once again your family is just trying to take advantage of others. She can go with her father or make her own way, it's nothing to do with us."

Dorothy clenched her teeth together to keep in the explosion of words that were clamouring to splurge themselves all over him, why did they have three completely empty bedrooms that nobody had ever stayed in? Why was he punishing Sybil, who had just lost her mother, for having a father who had no great interest in any of them? Why couldn't he be kind just for once? She could slap him with the argument that his precious Edward would never have turned Sybil away, but there was a sudden edge when his annoyance would transform itself into a frightening level of anger and she was never sure where it was which made her wary of driving him towards that precipice. She was meeting Nora at the Palais that afternoon, she could let rip about how inconsiderate her husband was then and see what ideas her sister put forward.

She was surprised to find Nora's face wearing a huge grin when they met in the grand entrance. It was easy to tell when her sister was truly ecstatic as her cheeks would tug so hard on her lips that she could not avoid showing the chipped right incisor which gave her an unmistakeably roguish appearance. Nora hated her shortened tooth and had perfected a smile which generally hid it, but today the full toothy show was on display.

"Whatever's happened to you?" Dorothy said giving her a hug, "On Tuesday you were quite normal and now you look as if you've found a hundred pounds."

"Arthur's been offered a job, a real one," she bubbled "and we're moving into the sweetest basement flat in Sinclair Road."

"A job?" said Dorothy attempting an emotional gymkhana which would result in her sporting a pleased expression for her sister.

"As caretaker at the Sacred 'eart, it couldn't be better, Arthur can fix anythin' and 'e'll enjoy being surrounded by all the children, don't look so worried we'll still be able to see each other, it will be fine," she said encouragingly.

"No, it won't be," Dorothy countered the tight desperation in her chest making her forthright in her determination to make her sister understand, "Jean only agreed to the dances because he had no other option without seeming inhumane in front of Uncle Edward, he thinks all my family apart from Uncle Edward are bad influences and he'd much rather I never saw any of you. He's even refused to take in Sybil so I'm going to have to ask Aunt Sarah ..."

"'E won't let Sybil stay?" Nora said slowly, aghast at her sister's torrent, "but you 'ave so many rooms."

"It's not the space, he just doesn't want anyone near me, even my family. As far as he's concerned life would be perfect if he could just take me out to talk to important clients once in a while and then shut me up in a drawer until he needs me again. It's awful going out with him, if he sees anyone looking at me or someone accidentally jostles me he explodes saying they're trying to touch me and I'm enticing them. He's the most jealous man I know and yet he doesn't really care for me like Arthur does for you, he seems to despise me."

"A lot of men act strangely since the war ..." Nora began soothingly.

"But he wasn't *in* the war! That's just it, he's become increasingly angry from the moment we married. There's no 'soft kind Jean' who's been bruised by battles, this *is* Jean, and dancing was the only way I began to feel alive again."

The sisters leant on the iron railings looking out at the street. "Sybil will come and live with me," Nora announced, "there's only a tiny second bedroom but it will be fine and she likes Arthur. It'll be better for 'er with us than Aunt Sarah, more lively and she could do with a bit of fun after Mum." Streams of eager dancers passed behind them into the cavernous building ready to abandon themselves to the music.

"Don't tell Jean about Arthur's job," Dorothy said almost to herself.

"What?"

"He only ever sees the family at Christmas and maybe I can avoid even that this year."

"Doesn't 'e see Uncle Edward?"

"Sometimes, but I'm sure they talk about more highbrow things than me and the family."

"It's an 'ell of a risk."

"I'll take Sybil with me. She'll love it."

"You must be out of your mind."

Steph Mason

PART TWO

Steph Mason

CHAPTER SEVEN

17 May 1908
233 West Green Road, South Tottenham, London
(Harold: 14, Charlie: 38, Harriett: 41)

The kitchen was warm and smelt of the usual mixture of cooking sausages and fresh bread, Harold sat at the table savouring the attention he was receiving from his mother and Fanny as they brought him tea and a plate of breakfast wishing him a "Happy Birthday" and ruffling his dark mop of hair. The scullery door banged open and Harold's father entered the room, rubbing his hands together briskly, whilst consuming the entire space with the full force of his character before slapping Harold on the back and announcing, "I've the best present for you son, no more school and book learning, today's the day you join the business."

Harold had been worried his parents were plotting to do this. He had hoped they would allow him to stay on at school until sixteen, giving him two more years to work out some avoidance strategy for his father's plans so that he could become apprenticed in one of the new sciences instead.

"Morning Dad, I was wondering if you'd let me study engineering for a couple of years first," he said, trying to make his voice light to disguise the desperation that was coursing through him to effect an immediate escape from being taken to the abattoir that morning.

"What's the use of that? No one's ever going to use that electricity you're always on about. There may be a few more motor cabs around at the moment but it's just a fashion, you'll see they'll be back to hansoms in a year or two. Eat up boy, we've got a couple of cows and a pig to do before nine o'clock."

Harold took a gulp of tea while looking up at his father with a half grimace, the left side of his compressed lips raised in a gesture of resignation. His mother stood behind him, hands placed on his shoulders.

"You'll be fine son," her affection and pride flowing all over him, "they'll be plenty of time for you to study all that clever stuff once you've got a handle on the business."

"Don't pet him Harriett, once he's got the respect of the men he'll want to use his time expanding not chasing rainbows."

"Yes Charlie," she replied meekly, but not without giving a colluding squeeze to Harold's sagging shoulders.

Harold's parents had exhausted their youth in a vigorous quest to prove to Charlie's father that they could do better than him. The small family butchering business was earmarked to be handed down to the eldest son leaving nothing for Charlie and his nine other siblings. Charlie's relationship with his father had been strained, Harold's grandfather was a strict disciplinarian who was continually at odds with Charlie's natural high spirits and expansive ego. Frustration regularly led the old man to revert to shouting in his native German so young Harold was plunged into mystery at the nature of the insults being hurled at his father although there was no doubt they were highly uncomplimentary. On every occasion, rather than being stung, Charlie would just laugh and lead Harold away from his incensed relative, whispering "watch and learn" to his son and apparently in the best of humour. By the time Harold turned fourteen and was promised his first official day at work, his grandfather and father had inverse numbers of offspring and shops: Charlie, one child and eleven shops; his father, eleven children and still just one shop. The arrogance that had been visible in Charlie's youth had blossomed with every freshly painted Wieland outlet and Harold knew his father viewed today as the ultimate moment of jubilation, the time to present his empire to the fruit of his loins, and he expected his son to stand in awe and appreciation of what had been created for him. There was just one problem, Harold wanted to be an engineer.

During his childhood Harold had frequently helped out at one or other of the shops, and had often been put in charge of a handcart to do deliveries at busy times like Christmas, but he hadn't worked at the abattoir and it was here Charlie was intending to take him as his "birthday treat".

"You need to learn every job from the very bottom to the top if you're to get the men's respect," Charlie lectured as they strode towards the slaughter house. "You're a clever lad, it won't take long, I'll soon be able to take a well earned rest and pay a bit more attention to your mother."

Two hours later Harold bolted from the slaughterhouse into the courtyard losing his breakfast on the way. Packaging up slabs of rump steak and pork chops in the shop had never bothered him and he was far too much of a city lad to go all sentimental over animals, but something in the soft brown eyes and long lashes of the cow had got to him. As the eyes lost their trust, showing their whites, and the velvety nostrils flared in terror, every muscle of the gentle beast's body strained to prove the strength of the life within it, and yet its engine was abruptly stopped by Harold's first lesson of the day. His mind had been managing to cope with the visual evidence of what he had done but the warm gooey feel around his hands and the stickiness of the floor left him grappling to retain any composure at all in front of his father's stern gaze, and when the stench rose up washing over him, engulfing his mouth and lungs until they were full of the smell of blood and excrement, Harold ditched the final vestiges of control, lurching for the door as the red river grabbed at his boots attempting to glue him to his post.

As Harold drew deeply on the cigarette he had clamped between his still quivering lips, his father sauntered towards him, a look of mild disdain on his face as he carefully avoided the pile of fresh vomit.

"Get back in there," he ordered, "you'll get used to it. Your mother's never been squeamish over chopping up a few beasts so I don't see why you can't stomach it." Harold lifted his eyes to look at his father unsure whether he should employ pleading or blather, but Charlie appeared to be in no mood for a discussion.

"You should be thankful to have a job laid on for you when there's thousands loosing their work and relying on handouts. You've had a full belly of meat all your life so there's no excuse for going soft over the production process," he growled, striding back inside.

* * *

Harold knew from his first hour in the abattoir that he would never take over his father's business, but he was also aware that his father was just as stubborn as he was, so the struggle was likely to be a long one. Harold could not refuse to work but he could conduct a campaign of irritating and embarrassing his father so much that he would be 'punished' by being given the lowliest jobs. He ensured swift demotion onto the handcart delivery rounds, where he was paid a pittance and made to do extra hours in the worst of weathers. From the moment this sentence was pronounced, Harold announced he was now content and would not be accepting any offers of promotion.

George Weiss, Harold's good friend who ran the chemist next to the main butcher's shop, confided that Charlie was telling the staff that with a good hard winter he'd have Harold begging to be let back into the abattoir before New Year, he had even started a small book with bets on which day the weather would break his son. Harold smiled and raised an eyebrow confident that Goliath had met his David.

Time was on his side and even in the most appalling weather when his glaciated hands stuck to the cart handles, Harold was careful to appear continually jovial to customers and staff alike, determined his father would hear of no chink in his resolve to avoid becoming a fully fledged master butcher. As torrential rain and tearing winds clawed their way through his layers of clothing he took to doing his rounds at a run, joking with customers that they were receiving their meat ready tenderised as he clattered around the streets faster than the horse drawn carriages. By the time spring came to sooth his chapped knuckles and frozen toes, Harold had become a huge favourite with everyone who had anything to do with Wieland's butchers. His cheeriness when performing whatever demeaning job his father demanded left Charlie apoplectic with frustration and his staff turning away from every confrontation to mask their smiles at seeing the old man so thoroughly outwitted. Harold whistled as he cleaned the shops to a sparkling perfection; he sang jaunty songs on his rounds, and never failed to raise his cap with a chirpy "Good morning" to everyone he met. It was a charm offensive calculated to annoy Charlie so thoroughly that his unwilling heir was referred to as "your son", whenever Charlie discussed the problem with Harriett, which was never less than once a day, and always in front of their contented offspring who would look on at his raging parent with a soft benign smile and a concerned kindness shining out of his eyes which he knew infuriated his father to combustion point.

* * *

George and Alma Weiss were twenty, they watched the daily battles of the Wielands with the knowing air of sages observing a heavily maned old lion, accustomed to being chief of the savannah, having his ears pulled by a lively cub, quick enough to dart away from every cuffing. Although the couple were six years older than Harold and twenty years younger than Charlie, both Wielands were so naturally happy and hell bent on having a good time that it was completely unsurprising that George and Alma counted father and son as their very best friends. As Harold confided his passion for all forms of engineering to George, and Charlie vented his vexation over his son's avoidance of his empire, the Weiss's became the diplomatic service between the two sides, forever smashing into Wieland mulishness at each new mediation attempt.

* * *

Harold spent every hour he could prize himself away from under Charlie's thumb at Straker's motor agent where the resident engineers looked up expectantly from beneath car bonnets at the appearance of his floppy hair and laughing eyes rounding the garage door, ready to pitch in and pass them whatever spanners or parts they required. Always eager to squeeze his smaller hands into any awkward places to fasten troublesome connectors, Harold was adept at finding solutions for innumerable mechanical problems. Many of the cars at Straker's had been individually made so any engineer needed to be an inventor, draughtsman and metal worker as well as have a thorough understanding all the physics involved. Every time Harold designed a new gadget to solve one of the problems that was plaguing the professional engineers he felt a buzz of pure ecstasy. He was certain that mechanics and electricity weren't merely fads, as his father's generation contended, but would soon become an essential part of everyone's lives.

As his father took moving things and made them still, Harold spent his waking hours working out how to make inanimate objects move. Pushing handcarts and mopping floors provided him with far more thinking time than if he'd taken the generous pay rise and excellent working hours his father had proffered to lure his son back through the shops, abattoir and safely into overall butcher shop management.

* * *

"Did you hear about Charles Rolls?" Harold asked George as he entered the kitchen after work one day to find his friend and his father sharing a pot of tea.

"Yes, terrible wasn't it, but it's Henry Royce who's got the brains."

"He may not be able to continue without Rolls' backing though."

"My point exactly," Charlie interrupted, slapping his hand down hard on the table, "one accidental death and a whole business grinds to a halt, that doesn't happen in butchering. Everyone will always need meat, but motor carriages are just a fad, like balloonless airships, they're just toys for rich men. It's the nature of toys to be discarded when a new toy comes along and then you're left with nothing."

"That's the whole point Dad," Harold said with mock patience, "these 'toys' do revolutionary things for you like factory machines but smaller so that eventually everyone will own one."

"Stop dreaming son, where are thousands of Britons going to store balloonless airships? You'll always be able to make a living from the things people need," he explained in the laborious tone he usually employed when talking to a person of underdeveloped intelligence, "that's food, housing and clothing, not toys that crash out of the sky or carriages that stop in the middle of nowhere because they're not attached to four reliable legs and a hunk of horseflesh."

"You'll see," Harold replied smugly as he poured himself a cup of stewed tea from the pot and watched his father's irritation build.

"The only thing I see is that I want to retire soon and enjoy the fruits of the business I've built up for you, and you're being downright selfish in not allowing your own father to do that. Your mother's brought you up too soft," he ranted, scraping his chair back and jamming his hat onto his head as he grabbed his coat before taking his annoyance out on the doorframe.

* * *

At the age of nineteen Harold was rescued from a further freezing winter with his cart.

"All the men from Straker are being sent to work at the Bristol factory," Harold told his parents during dinner in early October 1914. "Mr. Grant said I should go too. He says the government is instructing all engineers to switch from building cars to aero engines and trucks, so his lads are being shipped off to the Fishponds works. He reckons I'm as good as any of them, and better than many at design, so he says it's my duty to go," Harold concluded, making a failed attempt to keep the delight out of his voice. The quiet smile on his mother's tired face told Harold he had her blessing, although she bowed her head in fervent concentration on her plate contents, leaving the official response to her husband.

Harold watched him and tried to gauge what ploy Charlie was cooking up this time to win the fight and bamboozle his son into butchering. Harold had seen his father and grandfather spar for too many years to have any illusion that Charlie might magnanimously capitulate, it wasn't in the Wieland nature, so the eventual reply left him wondering what the next round would be.

"It won't be difficult to fill the position of a delivery boy," chew, chew, swallow, "and a spell working for a real employer," gulp of water, "rather than your soft mum and dad," knife and fork cutting pork chop, "will soon make you come to your senses," munch, munch, swallow, "Capital idea. Let your mother know where you're staying."

* * *

Although his digs in Bristol were so cold that there was regularly frost on his blankets in the morning and food was in scant supply, Harold had never felt so alive. He spent every waking moment, and many of his dreaming ones, grappling with the problems of weight to lift ratios, manoeuvrability and how to substitute engine parts when the required bits became unavailable as the country was gripped by chronic shortages. The dark bags beneath Harold's eyes paid tribute to the number of hours he spent working to improve the planes which remained so flimsy and unpredictable that pilots were having to be replaced at a more alarming rate than regular soldiers. Whilst Harold put all his efforts into designing planes with more speed and improved firing arcs, there were few improvements being made to comfort and the extreme cold continued to steal pilots' limbs and lives through frostbite on a daily basis. Aware of this, and realising the iciness up in the sky must make his digs look like a tropical paradise, Harold concentrated his efforts on speed and accuracy in the hope his faceless flyers would then be able to spend less time in their frigid cockpits.

A year into the war he was transferred to Filton to work for the British and Colonial Aircraft Company. All the engineers working on the Bristol F2 were conscripted to remain there for the duration of the war, yet the government order did not prevent Harold from suffering nuggets of guilt at the huge enjoyment he was experiencing in his wartime role when so many millions of his contemporaries were suffering in the mud and carnage abroad. But Harold could live with his twinges leaving only one real blot on his landscape which, true to his practical nature, he intended to remove without delay.

Dear Mum and Dad,

I hope you are not suffering from too many shortages and Mum's headaches have improved and she is feeling less tired. In general everything here is fine now that the warmer weather has arrived, however there was an unpleasant occurrence on Tuesday last which has led me to take a decision I hope you will not find objectionable.

There is a general store at the end of Southmead Lane which I pass several times a day. The owner's son was rejected by the army due to his flat feet, but even before that he seems the sort of chap who would delight in being sour and argumentative. On one occasion he was looking so thunderous that I attempted to lighten him up a little with a well-intended joke, but instead he took things personally and has been making strenuous efforts to torment me ever since. Unfortunately when he discovered my name he decided I was an enemy of the crown which culminated in him throwing a brick at me whilst regaling the street with his opinion that I was a "Hun spy" sent to sabotage British planes.

Luckily his aim was poor and everyone here knows him for what he is, so it was nothing more than a nasty incident. However, since Prince Louis' resignation and the prolific Hun Hunts, which the newspapers appear to condone even in their most extreme form, I have become increasingly sure that our family name is turning into something of a liability.

> *In all other circumstances I would be proud and happy with my name, but I do not wish other, perhaps more believable, people to make mistakes about my trustworthiness based on the slender premise that one of my grandfathers was born in Germany, and so I have decided to alter just one letter in my surname in the belief that "Willand" sounds and looks fully English in the way "Wieland" never can. It is an alteration so slight that it hardly requires a new signature, yet the double consonant gives an air of respectability in today's political climate that is wholly absent from the double vowel.*
>
> *In hope that you do not regard this decision as in any way disrespectful.*
>
> *Your loving son,*
> *Harold.*

* * *

Once again Charlie employed the words "Capital idea!" and promptly made arrangements for all the signage on his shops and carts to be carefully altered. The subtraction of a vowel seemed to have a secondary effect of creating a new theatrical role for Charlie who, despite the austerities of war, began to take increasing care over his wardrobe ensuring that even when at work his attire, bearing and mannerisms demonstrated him to be British right through to his marrow.

Now that Charlie had settled into his new, even more flamboyant, persona he could happily disregard most of the incorrect statements he had made in his previous body without fear of even a whimper of hypocrisy, and he flourished as he boasted about his talented son whose engineering skills were invaluable to the Allies, and even substituted several of the business's horse-drawn carts for motorised vans, claiming to any customer who would listen, that petrol driven vehicles were the way of progress for any serious entrepreneur and that the horse would be largely retired within a decade.

* * *

December 1918
(Harold:24, Charlie:48, Harriett:51)

Charlie met Harold at Waterloo as he arrived back from Bristol, an uncharacteristically serious look upon his face. Even at a distance Harold felt a spasm of alarm, three possible explanations jostled in his brain. Top favourite was that Charlie was about to employ a new ruse to get him back into the business. However, as Harold drew closer he noticed an unmistakeable sag about his father which didn't fit with the theory of fresh manipulations and made him concerned that either the business itself was suffering or Charlie was ill.

"Great to see you, son."

"You too Dad," Harold said returning the back slapping embrace. "You look tired though, is everything all right?"

"Your mother's health got worse," his father replied. "There was no point in writing to you when you were due to arrive in a few days, but the doctor said she needed proper treatment and recommended a nursing home in Brighton."

"Has she left already?" Harold asked, upset at the idea of missing his mother when he had not been home in the past eighteen months.

"I took her down there yesterday. She's got a nice room with a sea view, I made sure she had the best," his father assured him, "I knew you'd be disappointed but the doctor said we could visit next weekend once she's settled in and they've got her problems under control."

The two men walked slowly through the station and out to the rank of motor cabs. A driver took Harold's suitcase and fixed it to the luggage rack while the two men settled themselves inside.

"She was a good worker, your mother, never stopped, rather like a clockwork mouse," Charlie mused.

The unusual praise worried Harold more than any other factor so far, although everybody else recognised that Harriett's tireless grafting had been as much the source of Charlie's business success as his own extravagant ideas, it was unheard of for any credit to be verbalised by Charlie himself.

Harriett had never been a big talker or joker the way her men were, yet without her quiet audience both of them seemed unsure how to behave at their meal that evening. Although there was plenty of conversation about his new position at Straker-Squire, Harold felt that the sparkiness between him and his father failed to ignite without his mother there, she was the completion of the triangle, the sole person who could tranquilise either of them with a raised eyebrow or the seemingly innocuous question, "Do you really think so?" A mild voice to their strident ones, but capable of stopping both of them from running on blindly in a direction they had not properly thought through.

The following day Harold went to find George knowing he would be more forthcoming about his mother's ailments than his father was being.

"The headaches and tiredness had been getting worse for some time and then she started getting pains in her right leg which made her limp," George explained. "A couple of weeks ago she lost the sight in one eye and kept feeling dizzy. The doctor thinks she has picked up a virus which has passed to her nervous system through her blood, I'm sorry Harold but it doesn't look good."

Although theirs had never been a whirling love match, with Harriett's departure it was suddenly clear that Charlie relied absolutely on having her around. Harold watched his father shrink further within himself with every day that passed. Although it had never occurred to him before, Harold suddenly recognised that Charlie was a man who needed a consort, without the constant attention of a wife he became confused, fearing he was no longer the grand man her continual grooming had made him believe himself to be. Pitiful loneliness seemed to gnaw at his very soul mere days after she left. If Harold had ever examined his parents' marriage, which until that point he never had, he would have thought Charlie valued Harriett for her thriftiness and her dedication to the business plus her ability to run a warm and comfortable home. He knew his father's substantial bank balance would hardly be dented by taking on a small army of housekeepers and accountants, but having these basic needs provided for didn't lift Charlie's dismal mood and it became obvious to Harold that his father did not enjoy his own company, he needed to be the sun around which others revolved and with his wife's absence he discovered it was not sufficient to have a host of random workers and friends magnetised to his personality, he needed more. As Harold put it when talking to George about the problem, "Without Mum as his planet Earth, Dad's wondering what he's shining at, in fact I think he's in danger of going out completely."

Moping and lethargy were so alien to Harold that George and Alma had to assure him the condition was not life threatening. Charlie's obvious unhappiness was beginning to invade Harold as all his efforts to lever his father from his depression were ineffective and he was becoming mildly panicked that Charlie might have permanently swapped exuberance for gloom. Eventually it was Harriet herself who provided the solution.

"Your father's not yet fifty and he's looking like a defeated old man," she said one day as Harold sat holding her hand in Brighton, the two of them looking forward out of the window across a grey rolling sea. Charlie had gone to find a nurse to get some tea and as Harold turned towards his mother he noticed how thin her hair had become so that patches of white scalp were visible at her temples where the comb had clumped strands together as it pulled them firmly up into the bun on top of her head. Harriet was only fifty-one herself but Harold thought most people would have been being generous if they guessed her to be fifteen years more than that.

"I've been trying to get him back to his usual self but he seems to have lost all his drive. Do you think he might be ill?" Harold replied, worried that both his parents might be disintegrating prematurely. His mother gave a wry smile, but weariness prevented it from lifting to her eyes.

"Goodness, no," she said gently squeezing her son's fingers, "he's just forgotten how to make an effort to get his regular fix of attention. You must take him to the dance halls, it won't do you any harm to get out too and it would be nice for George to take Alma out with you as well." Harold's eyebrows would have buried themselves in his hair had it not been so firmly slicked back.

"Dancing?"

"Yes indeed, dancing," she replied in a voice almost reminiscent of her giving 'orders-to-be-obeyed-immediately' tone Harold had heard her employ in the shops. "Your father has always been an excellent dancer although you may not know it as we seemed to be so busy working whilst you were small. Dancing makes him feel young, it lets him put on a bit of an exhibition. Take him to the dance halls, you and George can keep an eye on him."

"It's worth a try," Harold said as they lapsed into companiable silence again, gently hypnotised by the sea's endless movement.

* * *

On Saturday afternoon as Harold rounded the corner seeming to drag Charlie behind him, he saw George and Alma already waiting at the bus stop. Apologising for their lateness while rolling his eyes at George to demonstrate how much trouble he had experienced extracting his father from his armchair to come on this expedition, they set off for the Plaza.

"Not bothered to change your jacket for me then!" Alma said disapprovingly to Charlie.

"I know," Harold said sighing deeply, "Come on Dad, make an effort not to be a complete party pooper, if only for Mum."

As the four of them entered the hall, Harold noticed that Alma's slight, tight frame encased in its flowery print cotton dress seemed to relax itself a little, the easy beat seeping into her. George took her into his arms, whisking her onto the floor with a backward glance at the Willands.

"Find us a table and we'll see you in a minute," he called after a first, somewhat unsteady, twirl.

"It looks as if it's doing George and Alma some good already," Harold said as he settled his father into a seat facing out across the field of moving bodies in a prime position for observing most of the smaller tables where single young ladies sipped tea with their chaperones. A neat little blonde looked bored beside her matronly bespectacled companion directly opposite them and caught Harold's eye.

"Come on Dad, no time like the present, you get the one with the specs," he said hauling a still reluctant Charlie on to his feet.

* * *

By the time the band struck up a final waltz Charlie had begun to have a say in the pick of partners.

"No Harold, not the one in the green dress, her chaperone looks like a grumpy hippo. The one in the mauve on the right is far better," he instructed, more animated than Harold had seen him for months.

Dancing had indeed been the tonic Charlie required, and Harold was mildly astonished that his mother had been so astute. If he was honest the whole outing had been a wonderful eye opener to the excess numbers of highly presentable young ladies that were wandering around London. He had been aware there was an imbalance since the war but he'd never had its effects demonstrated so clearly as they had been that afternoon. It was slightly worrying that his father had discovered so quickly that it was unnecessary for him to dance with comely spinster aunts while Harold whirled around embracing firm young beauties, but at least Charlie's shoulders no longer slouched, there was a twinkle back in his eye and his booming laughter could be heard right across the dance floor.

* * *

By the third visit to the Plaza Harold was beginning to fret that his father was enjoying dancing slightly more than he thought was healthy. Charlie had begun taking inordinate care over his dress before leaving the house; his buttonhole was always fresh, his handkerchief colour agonised over, his shoes glinted. As George and Harold waited downstairs they regularly shouted up the stairs that it took Alma far less time to get ready.

Charlie's confidence had been completely restored to its previous levels and he began to irritate Harold considerably by cutting in on his most lithe and attractive partners employing the line, "I'm the one with the fortune not him, you're better off dancing with me."

"I wish I'd left him miserable," Harold grumbled to George, "I'm sure Mum didn't intend him to feel this much better!" But now that Charlie was once again robustly pursuing all the entertainment on offer in London, any fit of pique from his son passed largely unnoticed as he saddled up London's fittest fillies and whipped them up into joining his delighted gallop around the dance floor.

Several months later one of Charlie's vans was giving trouble and Harold's head was stuck beneath the bonnet at the time the group would usually leave for the Plaza. "You go on and I'll meet up with you later," Harold said, lifting his grease smeared face for a moment before returning his full concentration to the gearbox. His enjoyment at solving engine problems had not diminished during his years of butchering freedom, if anything he had become greedier to absorb all the new theories and discoveries from the world of electrics and mechanics. Harold had even managed to infect his father with his enthusiasm and Charlie had recently purchased a six cylinder, six litre, Humber motor vehicle with full moon headlamps and wide running board, a throbbing metal predator whose gleaming form drew awestruck glances from both pavements wherever it went. Father and son agreed it was the perfect male accessory.

By the time Harold had finished the van and removed the worst of the grease from beneath his fingernails it was debatable whether he would manage more than a couple of dances at the Plaza before it was time to head home. Harold decided to go anyway, it had been a solitary afternoon and he was in the mood for some company.

He spotted George and Alma moving across the floor in his direction and waited for them to whirl towards him before attracting their attention and asking where their table was. George jerked his head briskly to the left, his lips a grim line as he held a rigid Alma whose face was equally stony.

"They look as if they've had a hell of a row," Harold thought before turning to seek out Charlie in the direction they'd gestured.

Harold's face dropped. "Oh Christ," he said.

* * *

Charlie was in heaven. The slender young brunette who had been perched on his knee for the past half an hour clearly believed him to be the most fascinating and attractive bull in the room and he easily convinced himself that she was undoubtedly correct. He told her about his car, his business and his large house, emphasising that he now had little need to work and was hoping to begin travelling soon. True, he hadn't mentioned Harriett, but she hadn't been a natural topic of conversation, he felt.

The brunette had said she was staying with an aunt in London because she wanted to be closer to some of the theatres, museums and, of course, she added with a little tinkling laugh which Charlie was beginning to find irresistible, the dance halls. Bursting with chivalry, Charlie immediately offered to take her to all or any of the places on her list, which led the brunette to feign surprise and wild excitement, taking his hand in hers and gleefully kissing the back of it to seal the bargain.

"Good afternoon, Dad," Harold said loudly, placing his chair in a position which almost made him the ham in the sandwich and which could, Charlie felt, cramp his progression somewhat.

"Hello there Harold," Charlie bellowed, his geniality not noticeably dented by the appearance of his off-spring.

"What train do you want to take to visit Mum tomorrow," Harold asked, flicking his eyes at the brunette as he did so. She removed herself from Charlie's knee slipping onto a chair and leaving his lap to cool.

"The eleven o'clock," Charlie replied, slightly punctured, but feeling that the truth might rescue him from the imminent ruin of his fantasies. "Harold's mother is in a nursing home on the south coast. She's been there for some time and unfortunately her prognosis is not good," he said to the brunette while adopting a look of such wounded concern that his beseeching eyes would soften the heart of a convicted psychopath. The brunette moved forward stroking his face and assuring him of her very deepest sympathy. Harold clicked his teeth. It was, Charlie thought, a most unpleasant habit which his son employed whenever he was seriously irritated. He decided to ignore it.

"Aren't you going to introduce me to your young friend," Harold said, placing the emphasis firmly on the penultimate word.

"Yes, of course, Harold this is Miss Cecelia Long, known as Sis to her friends; Miss Long, my son Harold."

"Will you dance?" Harold asked as she leant forward daintily to offer him her hand in greeting.

"Oh no you don't son," Charlie cried jumping to his feet in mock agitation and grabbing Sis by the waist so she squealed prettily, "this one's mine, you get your own."

* * *

Harold's feelings about "The Sis Problem" were forthright from the outset. For once he could not agree with George's slightly dismissive attitude that it was just an old man's final harmless fling.

"He's just using her to massage his ego, he'll come to his senses soon enough," George would sooth, but with his mother weakening in Brighton, Harold saw Charlie's actions as almost criminally disloyal.

"She's a desperate hussy," Alma stated unequivocally. "Over twenty-five and afraid of being left on the shelf, so she'll even throw herself at a married man," she sniffed.

Yet despite the fierce disapproval tumbling out of Harold, Sis glued herself ever more firmly to Charlie's side, creating an exclusion zone for his friends and son by her endless gales of laughter at inexhaustible private jokes. Harold became morose on his visits to Brighton, unable to meet his mother's eye and only capable of parroting information about work and the weather leaving Charlie's expansive personality to fill in the awkward gaps.

"I don't know how you can do it," Harold growled as they walked away from the nursing home on King's Road one Sunday afternoon. "Don't you feel any guilt?"

"You're being over dramatic as usual," Charlie replied theatrically, "your mother is a very sick woman, whom we visit in order to cheer her up and try to ease her pain. How would we achieve that with a load of breast beating and church confessions? You need to get your priorities right and start acting normally," he said striding down the promenade as he hastened back to the soft, toned body of his lover, leaving Harold to grind his teeth together with such force he was in danger of doing permanent damage to his enamel.

* * *

1920
(Harold:26, Charlie:50, Harriett:53, Sis:25, Dorothy:25)
Hat boxes, trunks and a birdcage littered the hallway as Harold returned from work one Thursday lunchtime in December 1920. Taking one look at the evidence and hearing Sis's grating voice instructing a porter to "leave the birdcage in the living room," he hurried through the house, face dangerously flushed, to find his father whose arm he grabbed, forcing Charlie to turn and face him.

"What the hell is going on?" Harold demanded.

"Sorry? Ah yes, meant to tell you, Sis is moving into one of the lodger's old rooms. She's had an argument with her aunt and has nowhere else to go."

"You're moving that woman into our house with Mum still in Brighton?" Harold shouted, rage coursing through his body until he could feel the veins in his neck bulge around his tight shirt collar.

"Harold why are you having such a tantrum?" his father said, attempting to make his son's indignation melt in the face of his own dubious logic. "Throughout your childhood we always had two or three lodgers who helped in the shops, some male, some female, it's unreasonable to have all these rooms empty and not help a friend in need."

"She is not like the lodgers."

"Of course she is, it's no different at all."

"There's no way she's going to be stuffing sausage skins tomorrow morning!" Harold yelled at his father's back as the elder man retreated towards the hallway with a dismissive royal wave as he busied himself with the installation of his mistress.

* * *

Harold crashed out of the house and down the street, resentment and anger boiling inside him, his skin felt as if it would split open spurting all the explosive emotions out of him to hit passing pedestrians as he rampaged through the capital.

Taking buses and trains at random he journeyed anywhere he could that was away from his home, eventually halting outside the Hammersmith Palais where he realised he was desperately thirsty. On a normal day Harold would have searched out the nearest Lyons Corner House rather than go into a dance hall alone, but it wasn't a normal day and the Palais had a reputation for playing the jazziest, most modern dance music which Harold felt matched the abandoned wrath which still had him firmly in its grip.

Marching through the pillared entranceway, he installed himself at a corner table, drinking his tea as quickly as the heat would allow, his gaze trance-like as his whole mind was consumed by the events at home. Slowly, the warmth of the liquid and the frenetic energy of the music penetrated through to grab some of his attention and he looked round the hall at the dancers. He spotted the long-necked redhead he'd seen several times at the Plaza. He had been fascinated by her from the first moment she had appeared, it wasn't that she was startlingly pretty in a conventional way but rather that she had a languid grace not mired either by the guarded look of unavailability that wealthy attractive ladies tended to adopt, nor by any element of coarseness, she was the sort of woman a poet or painter would have as a muse, and yet when she danced she never failed to show how much she was enjoying herself and so there were always a succession of partners lined up upon whom Harold had never had the nerve to break in. Now she had sat down alone at her table directly across the floor from him. The band struck up a fast American beat; if anyone could do justice to that rhythm the redhead could, Harold thought as he got up and walked across the floor.

"Will you dance?" he asked with a slight bow, keeping his eyes on her face. She looked up at him calmly, a smile gently lifting her cheeks to reveal perfect white teeth. In spite of his wretched afternoon Harold found it impossible not to smile back, showing his own rather pointed incisors. Never lowering her gaze, she took his outstretched hand and allowed the friendly wolf to lead her to the dance floor.

CHAPTER EIGHT

Harold felt as if an insidious infection had invaded every part of his home. When he arrived each evening Sis would parade a succession of brightly coloured cocktails in front of him, her high voice urging him to choose one of that day's vile concoctions.

"Do you like it Harold? I'm calling it Green Eyed Monster," she trilled before dissolving into peels of repetitive giggles as he was left with no polite option but to swig down her latest excess with the Crème de Menthe bottle.

He hankered after the tranquil days when he would open the front door, still preoccupied by some interesting little engineering conundrum, sink into his habitual deep squashy chair with a drink and a full pipe of tobacco, to day dream quietly free from interruptions until Fanny called "Dinner". Now his chair had been placed in a corner and the fireplace was fronted by a chaise longue, so tightly stuffed that Harold thought it was like sitting on a pavement, plus a couple of powder blue arm chairs with narrow upright backs that Sis had insisted on purchasing because the colour was so much to her liking. The enveloping cracked brown leather which had provided Harold with so many evenings of relaxing comfort would have been banished from the house completely if Sis had acquired a ring on her left hand but until that time there were certain things that even she did not have the temerity to attempt.

Fluorescent drinks were followed by dinner where the conversation revolved around clothes, flowers and shopping. If Harold began to introduce interesting subjects such as motor shows, building wirelesses, the prevalence of strikes or the Bolshevik influence, the eyes beneath the brown bob would harden whilst the sweetest of smiles drew itself across her face and a hand reached beneath the table cloth to touch Charlie's thigh, instantly guaranteeing the return of his full attention, then cementing it with some risqué remembrance she whispered as he leant his ear towards her, so that a full stop was abruptly placed at the end of Harold's part of the conversation by the couple's delicate tittering. The tiny morsels of food that were placed into the reddened mouth, led Charlie to call her his "little pigeon".

"Look how daintily she eats Harold," Charlie said, attempting to get him to praise the woman who made his son feel like an outsider. Harold grunted.

"You should find yourself a beautiful woman, then you wouldn't be so surly," his father continued testily before transferring his full attention onto Sis's tales of new dresses and the urgent need to redecorate the hallway.

The habitual hour of peace Harold enjoyed with the newspaper after dinner was destroyed by a gyrating female, long strings of pearls swinging dangerously close to his face, as she danced around the living room to the sound of the gramophone whose arm regularly jumped during her more energetic phases causing her to collapse with laughter and begin the record all over again. Harold's bedroom became his only sanctuary, but even here the gaiety below drifted up through the floorboards, leaving him feeling like an imprisoned alien within the building he had lived in for most of his life.

Harold had stopped asking his father to join him at the dance halls knowing it would force him to spend more time with Sis. George and Alma had avoided going out with the Willands since Charlie's dalliance began as although Alma seemed in all respects slight and mousey, she was ferocious in her condemnation of the love match. Her heart remained loyal to Harold's mother, it was a trait that made him love her and feel he had at least one caste iron ally, Alma exhibited deep resentment at the circumstances that had caused her to stop visiting Harriett in Brighton, she was hopeless at keeping her emotions off her face, and her straight forward nature would have made it impossible for her to lie or prevaricate if Harriett had asked what was bothering her. Instead she wrote twice a week to her friend, confiding to Harold that her pen would not betray her churning rancour with his father the way her mouth definitely would. To Harriett Alma used the excuse of her pregnancy as the cause of both her abstinence from dances and any train travel to the south coast. George was in a continual frenzy over his wife's health since he had discovered he was to become a father and so it seemed understandable for the couple to draw away from the Willands at this time in their lives, however this left Harold feeling even more adrift in an ocean of Sis's tense frivolity. His response to this was to spend as much time as possible out of the house among acquaintances who had nothing to do with Willand's butchers or Miss Cecelia Long.

The months of Operation-cheer-up-Charlie had ensured that Harold was well known among the clientele at the Plaza and could be guaranteed a warm welcome and an attractive procession of willing partners. He began to spend several afternoons a week at the Palais and the Plaza, enjoying the slight deception he employed to persuade his father to loan him the impressive Humber.

"There's a bit of wear on the brake cable in one of the vans," he might say, "I need to get a part from across town, is it all right if I take your car?"

Charlie, forever eager to ingratiate himself with his son again, would invariably agree.

Although Harold's home life was massively irritating, his career seemed little short of perfect. Two days a week he would work at Straker-Squire and three mornings a week he would be employed as a consultant by Morris motors, in his spare afternoons he was paid to maintain Charlie's fleet of vans – the only role in the business that Harold had ever readily agreed to. The vans did not require huge amounts of attention leaving Harold free to haunt the dance halls whenever he fancied it.

There were plenty of young ladies whose pleasant company now filled Harold's afternoons; some of his favourites included the young Sybil Terrill and her sister Dorothy Nicolai. Sybil's easy chatter, broad grin and refusal to be impressed by any 'toff', as she called him, reminded Harold of some of the milkmaids he used to meet on his rounds when he was delivering meat. Every time Harold drew near to their cart the girls used to regale him with a hail of dirty stories aimed at embarrassing the butcher's boy, they then become ecstatic when far from cringing at their bawdy jokes, Harold proved he could be equally ribald back. A firm friendship had sprung up among the banter and Harold had been able to count on a free half pint and a chat to see him on his way throughout his teenage years.

Sybil worked in Covent Garden market sorting vegetables, and although she had only been there a year her speech was dotted with the Cockney rhyming slang she heard around her throughout the working day. She began work when the sky was still black even during the summer months, but by midday her job was completed, and so she explained to Harold, according to her bizarre working clock, the tea dances were her evening's entertainment and she was tucked up in bed again by the time Big Ben struck seven.

If Harold had been asked to compare Sybil to an object it would have been an India rubber ball; not that she was fat, in fact it was only her cheeks that were especially rounded, but she seemed to be constantly on springs. She would throw herself into the energetic new dances with a gusto that left the more demure girls wishing they had the balls to copy her. However, Sybil was unable to curb her need to bounce, and her waltz had more in common with a jack-in-the-box than with suave elegance; even when she walked she seemed incapable of attaching herself to the ground long enough to affect anything close to a feminine glide or a seductive saunter. In short, Sybil was as far removed from Sis as it was possible to be and Harold lapped up her company, hoping some of her 'normalness' would allow him to ignore the brittle hilarity that swamped him when he arrived home.

Yet as much as Harold relished Sybil's uncomplicated exuberance, it was Dorothy he thought about afterwards. The sisters were so startlingly different it was hard to believe they were related. Sybil's level of spring was matched by Dorothy's level of grace; although Sybil was not even twenty she was clearly used to the world of work but Harold could not imagine that the porcelain features and manicured hands of her elder sister had ever shared the same knowledge; Sybil would slap her lips in satisfaction after draining a cup of tea, Dorothy would sip it grasping the cup with index finger and thumb, the smallest finger often held a little separate, yet without ostentation.

A few weeks after they had met Harold's curiosity was so aroused he decided to risk being thought rude by asking direct questions. A Viennese waltz with Sybil provided the perfect opportunity. The slowness of the dance bored Sybil and created a need to chat.

"Why does Dorothy sound as if she comes from Mayfair and you don't?" Harold asked bluntly.

"'Cos she does, well, pretty close. She was brought up by my uncle and aunt near 'yde Park. I only got to know 'er properly after Mum died and I moved into Nora's flat near 'ammersmith," words bubbled out of her. "She's great though, not really stuck up, although she can act a bit weird at 'ome when 'er 'usband's around."

Harold suddenly discovered he had developed a desire for gossip which would have done Sis proud. "Why's she strange at home?" he asked, trying to make his tone sound politely interested rather than eagerly probing.

"Jean's foreign and I don't think 'e likes our family. Us sisters and Mum and Dad only met 'im first at the wedding. I thought 'e was all right then, but I was twelve so what did I know! Mum loved him. Dad and Flo didn't though," she paused to concentrate on her feet which had unfortunately begun to put four steps in where there should only have been three. "I've been to 'er 'ouse twice, but it's better if she comes to Nora or

Peggy's, cos we never feel comfy there. 'e's always watchin' you, it makes a person feel uneasy. 'e got all hoity toity with me when I bit into me cake, telling me I should cut it. Dorothy never says a word when 'e's there, it's like she's frightened to be 'erself and 'as to be this regal lady instead of just our sister."

"Is that so?" said Harold a wicked grin spreading across his face, "We can't have her acting the posh lady over you now can we?" he said leading Sybil back to their table.

"'ey Bill, come and 'av a knees up with me will yer."

"Are you addressing me Mr Willand?" Dorothy replied, her left eyebrow delicately arched as she employed every exaggerated vowel sound the years of elocution lessons had furnished her with.

"Yep Bill, me lovely, let's 'av a prance!"

She looked at him and paused, clearly unsure if he was ridiculing her. Harold grinned back holding out his hand.

* * *

Dorothy hadn't encountered anyone who treated her with such irreverence since Arthur used to take the Mickey out of her "airs and graces" before he went to the war. That seemed like such a very long time ago when everything was fresh and unspoilt. It would be wonderful to feel that way again, she thought, even if it were only for the duration of a couple of dances before this comedian bounded off to spread himself around all the other women she saw watching him hopefully.

"'Arry, me old china, are you 'avin an 'at an' scarf," she replied in Peggy's best music hall voice.

"Ha!" Harold shouted triumphantly, bundling her into his arms and flinging her around the floor until the two of them were gasping for air and paralysed by their laughter.

Dorothy felt slightly miffed when in the middle of their second dance one of her regular dancing partners cut in on Harold. He gave way with good humour and immediately started dancing with a rather attractive blonde in a turquoise dress. Dorothy's cheeks were aching from laughing her way through a quickstep and a foxtrot, but now she became more subdued watching Harold talk to the blonde who threw back her head and guffawed loudly at something he had said.

"He does it with everyone," she thought, a twinge of sadness rising in her throat when she realised that the connection she had felt with him moments earlier wasn't in fact evidence that he saw her as someone special. "Stop being an idiot," she scolded herself, "you're a married woman, and he's a single man free to do what he likes." Attempting to divert her attention from Harold and focus on her partner, she instructed herself to "pull herself together" in a tone which sounded in her head like Aunt Sarah at her most strident, yet she felt she was lumbering through the steps and a small childish voice seemed to rise from the pit of her stomach calling out to her rational, controlled brain, "it could have been me, surely he could have liked me best!"

***

Several times a week Harold blasted onto the same dance floors as Sybil and Dorothy. They would see him appear round the pillars and step into the main dancing area, a rakish grin on his face as he eagerly searched the tables for his first victim whom he would guarantee to corrupt with his chirpiness within five minutes; whenever he arrived Dorothy would consciously let her eyes rove around the rest of the floor, feigning she had not noticed him while hope squeezed at her heart that he would come over to their table first.

It was bad manners for a single man to dance more than two dances with the same woman unless he was engaged to her, and Dorothy began to find this rule irksome, she wished he would stay at their table for longer, the small child's internal voice battling with the reasonable adult in a way that made no sense, even to her. Although she was unhappy with Jean, it had never occurred to Dorothy that there was any way out of her predicament. She knew to her bone marrow that a woman could be single, married or widowed; any other label was too shameful to contemplate. But still, when Harold was at their table or dancing with her she could forget the constraints of her home life and for a few brief minutes be the carefree young woman whom she had believed died during the war. As the weeks folded into months she discovered her teenage ghost could be instantly resurrected whenever she heard the words, "Come on Bill, let's 'ave a prance."

***

September 1921
(Dorothy:26, Harold:27, Sybil:18, Harriett:52)
Just as Dorothy had arrived at the point when it was no longer the tea dances that made her feel free from Jean, but the presence of Harold at them, he disappeared.

During the first week of Harold's absence, Dorothy's eyes searched incessantly for him. Every man of a similar height or haircut was scrutinized and she remained looking happy and bright in case he should surprise her by appearing from a direction her darting gaze hadn't covered. Sybil danced, laughed and chatted as wildly as usual only mentioning on Thursday that they hadn't seen Harold in a while.

It was during the first weekend of his absence that Dorothy began to torment herself. Shut up in the house with Jean, she imagined Harold had found a fiancée. Her dreams throughout the day pictured him smiling at some gorgeously exotic woman as he held out her chair for her to sit down, or bent forward to light her cigarette. At night in her dreams Harold was always blithely happy, unaware of her own hankering to be near him, and the various images of the women who were luring him away were uniformly petite and needy in a way that her phantom Harold was only to delighted to attend to.

As the second week wore on she steeled herself to approach some of the other regular attendees; "you know the dark haired man, a little taller than me, I believe he's called Mr. Willand, we haven't seen him for a while and my sister was wondering if he was all right. Have you heard anything?"

But nobody had, and with every uninterested "No", Dorothy's abdomen felt queasier and there seemed to be a permanent lump in her throat and a couple of weights dragging down the corners of her lips. She began to refuse to dance, confusing partners who had always counted on her endless reserves of enthusiasm. She realised she was behaving like the army of very pretty girls who seemed to find sport in waving regular blokes away, unconcerned at the level of courage it had taken to ask them to dance in the first place and indifferent to any anguish their rejection caused. She didn't want to be like that but somehow she had lost the ability to just dance for dancing's sake and to laugh with anyone who wasn't Harold.

Sybil became embarrassed as the number of rebuffed young men increased.

"There's not much point in comin' if you're not goin' to dance."

"I'm a little tired that's all. Nora never danced and nobody complained about that," Dorothy retorted, a wave of misery crashing over her as she realised she was even being spiky with her own sister.

"But *you* always *have* danced, and now you're not," Sybil argued. "I don't see why you're tired when you don't work, are you ill or something?"

"No, I'm not," Dorothy said wearily. "Could we just leave it, I'll be better next time I promise." But as Friday afternoon drew to a close and there was still no sign of Harold her body felt leaden and she dreaded a further weekend with Jean when she knew tears were so close to spilling down her face. The snide comments she usually shrugged off by focusing her mind on the next dose of fun, now pierced her fragile membrane of happiness, their initial barbs stinging her before columns of questions trooped through her head, "was she as flighty or ignorant as Jean said?", "was her flightiness why Harold was clearly not bothered about her?", "why should he be bothered about her when she could offer him nothing?", "why was she bothered about him when her life belonged to Jean?" – til death us do part.

* * *

Wearing a shapeless brown dress she would usually change out of before going shopping, Dorothy arrived at Nora's flat with scuffed shoes, not having bothered to change her handbag to match her drab outfit.

"Are you all right?" Nora asked, concern brewing within her as she took in her sister's unkempt appearance.

"Fine," she replied as she walked through the door into the narrow hallway, "I just feel a bit bad as I need to tell Sybil I want to stop going to the dances. I can't run away from reality for ever, my life is with Jean and I must make the best of it," she shrugged off her coat. "The dances can be distracting and Jean would be furious if he found out, better to stop now before any damage is done."

"I see," Nora said, each syllable weighted with questions. "Will you go today? I know Sybil's almost ready."

"I don't know, maybe we could just have a cup of tea."

Her sister fell silent, putting on the kettle while Dorothy slumped into one of the hard wooden chairs in the minuscule kitchen. The idea of sitting there, hands wrapped around a warm mug, listening to Nora talk of everyday things felt comforting. The dances had meant so much to Dorothy, the gaiety, the movement, the succession of conversations with so many different people, even the adventure, the knowledge she was doing something so completely forbidden, then Harold had appeared mesmerizing her, seeming as perfect as one of the roses that topped Jean's cakes, and although she'd kept telling herself she meant nothing to him, beneath the surface she hadn't been able to resist being drawn in by his energy and his laughter, the way he always made her feel as if she were someone special so she would leave the dance hall walking tall, confident in her allure, and then on the trip home she would have to consciously stifle her new found boldness before she stepped through her own front door, yet the brief moments when she glowed in the knowledge she was desired had made her home sterility bearable, now that Harold had vanished it felt as if someone else had picked the rose and left her flailing around in the thorns.

Sybil entered just as Nora was handing Dorothy a mug. "Aren't we going?" she asked.

"Dorothy's been saying she thinks she should stop going to the dances," Nora said quietly.

"Fair enough, but you might as well come today now that I'm ready. I'll get Janet to come with me on Wednesday," Sybil said turning to Dorothy, "that colour doesn't really suit you, if you don't mind my saying so."

"All right, just one more time, but let me finish my tea first," she felt she owed Sybil a final effort and after that she could concentrate on trying to improve her relationship with Jean, although she didn't hold out much hope that things would ever become noticeably better. "It'll probably be more fun for you to go with Janet than your old married sister."

"Don't be daft, I'd go with you any day, especially as you always pay, but there's no point if you've gone off it, I'll meet you outside."

* * *

Sitting on the white slim-legged padded chair with its open oval back that offered so little comfort it almost forced patrons onto the dance floor, Dorothy seemed shrunken in her old brown dress. Even had she not been keeping her eyes down, few potential partners would have taken the plunge to approach her as every aspect of her body language screamed "leave me alone".

A long pair of men's legs clad in suit trousers, with roughly clean leather shoes on the feet appeared in front of her.

"Dance with me," he said as her eyes travelled from the toes of the shoes, up the legs to the bottom of the jacket, the hem of the waistcoat, the watch chain, tie, collar and finally to the face itself, at each stage the bubble of delight in her chest growing larger and larger until she felt it would burst upwards leaving the drab woollen dress on the floor, while the bubble transformed into a Tinkerbelle of twinkling happiness, but she was checked by Harold's eyes, they didn't match his smile.

"Please dance with me," he repeated as she stood up slowly, her gaze questioning what she found in his face.

They moved onto the dance floor yet this time she did not feel like half of the most glittering couple in the hall, all that seemed like a shallow show by comparison to this moment of union, both resplendent in their shabby clothes. She lay against him, without jewellery and, if she had put her hair in a turban, looking just as if she was about to clean the house, yet somehow she felt they were more connected than they had ever been when she had attempted to be perfect for him. The time apart had stripped her emotionally and she was too raw to redress in the trappings she had employed to sparkle, plus his expression cautioned her against the jokes and froth they had surrounded themselves with before.

"What happened?" she said into his chest.

"My mother died."

Her head snapped up to look at him. Of course, that was what she had seen in the eyes.

"Harold, I'm so sorry," she said still studying his face, feeling helpless and inept, unable to express herself and take away what was there, incapable of making it better. All the things that entered her head seemed trite and went no distance towards what she wanted him to feel; that she was there for him, that she would do anything to lessen the wounded child she could feel leaching out of him. She held herself closer to him and half mumbled, "What can I do?"

"Will you walk with me?" he asked haltingly, drawing back a little so he could judge her reaction to the question.

"Give me a moment to fetch my coat and talk to Sybil," she replied without hesitation.

* * *

The street was awash with dead leaves, their crispness ruined by the light drizzle that was falling but which gave them the intimacy of a shared umbrella as they began to stroll away from the Palais.

"How did it happen?" she asked gently.

"A heart attack, but Mum had been in a nursing home for years," he explained. "She had multiple sclerosis."

"How's your father taking it?"

A harsh angry laugh erupted from Harold, "He's relieved, now he can marry his mistress."

There were so many sides to him she'd never seen before. Nobody could play the jester all the time, she realised, but until that moment Dorothy had not considered how Harold might react in more serious situations.

"Will she be good for him?"

"God knows, I reckon she's only after a fat income, but he's been behaving like a spring chicken ever since she first plonked herself onto his knee," he said. "For god's sake she's younger than me! It was all so disrespectful to Mum, although I don't believe she'd have been surprised, she was the only one who knew the two of us so well she could predict every madcap move," a doleful smile blossomed on his face as he became engrossed in his thoughts.

"Do you have any brothers or sisters?"

"No, the closest thing to a brother I have is George who lives down the road, but his wife's just had their first baby and I don't want to go round there all gloomy when they're getting madly excited every time the tiny thing burps."

They walked on in silence, Dorothy feeling an inner desperation to say the right thing but completely uncertain what it would be.

"They were quite similar in a way," he said rescuing her from the need to speak, "quiet, hard workers, deeply loyal, both of them. She was very upset when it happened and I think George was concerned it might have harmed the baby because she arrived two days afterwards. They're understandably relieved everything's all right."

They had reached Brook Green, sparrows were picking up the crumbs that had fallen to the ground outside a bakery where the baker was slapping his hand against the back of the large square bun trays which would be needed again in the morning to hawk his wares around the streets.

"Will you answer me one question absolutely truthfully?" Harold asked, turning towards her. "Not with an answer you think I might wish to hear, or one that panders to my being unhappy at the moment, just the simple truth."

"Of course," she replied, unsure if she was properly prepared for what she had just agreed to.

"Do you love your husband?"

"No! not at all," she said before realising how ruthless it sounded and blushing deeply. She touched the hand he used to hold the umbrella, forcing him to look back at her, "it's not like that, it's not that sort of marriage. I can't really explain it. It's as if I agreed to a living arrangement seven years ago and now I can't quite remember why."

"So is he happy for you to lead a separate life?"

"Goodness no! I come here to escape for a few hours that's all. He'd go mad if he found out. I was going to stop coming, this was to be my last time," she said miserably, "I should get back to Sybil soon."

They turned their steps back towards the Palais, she found she couldn't speak any more, her mind was too roughened. Would she continue to go to the dances? Would he want her to after what she had just said? Shouldn't she stay strong and give her marriage another chance? Would she regret it if she didn't? Would she regret it more if she did?

"I was talking to Mum a couple of months ago and she told me that before she married Dad she used to go into the parks and draw squirrels and rabbits," he said abruptly breaking the silence. "She said she loved drawing and yet I had never seen her do it. She dedicated every minute of the rest of her healthy life to what Dad and I wanted. I wish she hadn't," he fell silent again.

"Go on."

"She thought that was what she had to do, that her life was somehow forfeit and she wasn't allowed to do what she really wanted to. It seems such a waste."

"Wasn't she happy?"

"Probably, in her own way, but there are so many people who aren't and are always waiting for 'tomorrow' for things to resolve themselves instead of realising how quickly it all passes and doing something about it today."

"What are you saying Harold?" her voice so soft and low it hardly sounded like her own. She waited for his answer trying not to breathe in case the movement should obscure what he wanted her to understand.

"I don't really know," he replied with a deep sigh. They had arrived back at the entrance to the dance hall and were standing awkwardly outside. She wanted to reach up to his forehead and ease out the lines that were running across it, then move her fingers to his temples before cupping his face in her hands and drinking in everything that was written there, but those things could only be done if she were sure what he meant, what he wanted, that she was truly special to him.

"Will you be here tomorrow?" he asked.

"Yes," she replied, deciding to put a tentative toe into the gulf of water between them to see how warm it was, "if you would like me to."

He raised one eyebrow and with a playful grin reminiscent of every other ambivalent encounter she'd ever had with him, just said, "See yer then, Bill."

CHAPTER NINE

October 1921
(Harold:27, George:33, Aunt Sarah:57)
Harold's head was looking up at the underside of a van as he lay on the workshop trolley, spanner in hand, preparing to renew a pipe in the exhaust system. Nothing was happening. His body was as immobile as if he had been laid out for burial, his eyes as unseeing. Even though the blackened pipes were only inches from his nose he was unaware of them. He had slid himself beneath the vehicle fully intent upon doing the task yet the sudden obscuring of his face liberated his thoughts and the afternoon seemed to drift into a siesta while Harold's internal soliloquy ran its course.

"I can't live without her. I can't imagine it. I've got to be with her. I need to wake up with her. Every day. I have to do something. Get her away. If I lose her there won't be any point to anything. I'll grow old and cranky like Mr. Andrews, she'll be trapped with a man she doesn't love.

"I wonder if he's kind to her. Maybe they do love each other and it's all some huge act I haven't caught onto which will leave everyone laughing at me. How can I know if she feels anything? Maybe I'm just a diversion from a boring home life. But that dress she was wearing, true sack cloth and ashes, she had missed me, I think, almost definitely, and those eyes they cared, I'm sure, those eyes don't lie. Ahh, but she was going to stop coming in case he found out, she was putting him first. But she said she'd come today, doesn't that means I'm more important to her?

"Christ, what am I doing? I despised Sis moving in on Dad when he was married, but I'm no better. A complete hypocrite; but Dorothy isn't Sis, she isn't brassy, she's soft, gorgeous. But Dorothy's husband is well and kicking, there's no excuse for me at all. Dad'll laugh himself hoarse, he'll see it as poetic justice for my months of sanctimonious indignation. Alma will give me the silent treatment.

"George will think I'm out of my mind for not choosing any of the pretty single girls we trip over at the dance halls.

"Why her? Why is she different? There are hundreds of beautiful women, there are plenty with a healthy sense of humour, there are even probably a few who seem well-bred but have a great dollop of earthiness underneath.

"If I found all those things in someone else, would it be enough? I'll imagine her. She's got all those qualities, she's slim, pretty, with an easy smile. Yes, very nice, but I only feel a pleasant liking for her. Now I've put her in Dorothy's clothes, with Dorothy's face, her hair, her voice, the way she lifts just her left eyebrow, her hands, she's lovely. Why can't I love the one who's not Dorothy? She's someone else's wife, dammit!"

A drop of oil that had been slowly forming above Harold's face fell precariously close to his lip. He turned his head to make it roll towards his ear.

"We'll have to go abroad; France, or maybe America. Get right away from the husband. Dad's happy with Sis and George and Alma have the baby, it will be good for us to start somewhere new.

"She may not come. It's not just him, there are all her sisters and her aunt, would she walk away from all that for me? Why would she do that? It's probably enough for her to see me a few times a week to break the monotony of life with him. She won't want to rock the boat, go charging half way around the world leaving everything behind her. She'll want to keep it secret, retain her reputation ..."

A hand roughly pulled the leg of his overalls.

"Harold are you asleep?" George's voice called from above him, "you lazy lump, you've been lying there ever since I came through the doorway doing absolutely nothing. I don't know what Charlie pays you for."

Rolling himself out from beneath the van, Harold felt faintly annoyed at having his reverie interrupted by a real person from the real world. "Afternoon George, what can I do for you?"

"Came to see how you were bearing up, let you know we hadn't forgotten about you. Make sure you're not avoiding us just because of Antonia, you know," he said pulling Harold to his feet as the trolley slid away from under him.

"Thanks George, very good of you, I'm fine. How are Antonia and Alma?" Harold wiped his hands on a grease splattered towel.

"Fine, great, sleeps a lot, usual baby stuff I imagine. Alma's besotted," George confirmed looking a little crest fallen.

"So she finds a smelly nappy more entrancing than you! Never mind old man, things will probably look up again soon."

"And you? How are you doing?" George asked, "Does taking a midday nap underneath a van mean your social life's picked up a bit?"

Harold felt himself redden.

"My god Harold, you sly dog, I thought you were staying away because of Harriett ..."

"Stop jumping to conclusions."

"Don't give me that, there's not much that makes you blush. When do we meet her? Does Charlie know?"

"It's not like that ..."

"Stop wriggling Harold!"

"It's complicated."

"How complicated? Oh lord, she's not married is she?"

Harold's lack of response and sudden energetic washing at the rust stained sink was enough to ensure even George shut up. The minutes of lathering and scrubbing stretched on with the only noise coming from the running water splashing into the deep porcelain tray.

"Losing a mother can make a fellow not think straight for a bit," George said gently as he moved towards the doorway Harold's back view firmly dismissing him. "Don't do anything hasty old chap, it will probably pass. Any time you want to come round, you know, don't be a stranger."

As Harold heard George's footsteps echo fainter through the cobbled courtyard he lent his forehead wearily against the rough wall above the sink letting out a long, deep sigh.

* * *

Sybil mashed the tinned sardines Nora had put on her plate before loading them onto the white bread she had spread liberally with marg.

"I think I've been an idiot," she said as Nora poured boiling water into the teapot to warm it.

"About what?"

"Dorothy."

"In what way?"

"I think she fancies 'arold Willand and I've only just realised it."

Nora sat down opposite her younger sister plonking the tea tray between them. "It's not a crime to fancy someone, even I fancy the chap on the Odeon cinema poster but it doesn't mean I'd do anything wrong."

"But what if it's more than that?" Sybil asked, "What if she does somethin' daft and Jean finds out?"

"What makes you think she's likely to?"

"There was all that stuff yesterday about not going any more, and 'er lookin' like a washerwoman and refusin' to dance for the last two weeks when 'e wasn't around; then 'e turns up again, dances only with 'er, they go for a walk and suddenly she's all eager to go back to the Palais today. There's got to be somethin' goin' on."

Nora munched slowly, swallowed and then used her tongue to clean around her gums before answering. "I can't believe she'd be so stupid as to throw away 'er marriage. Aunt Sarah and Uncle Edward would be 'orrified. What's this 'arold like?"

"'e's a great joker. A bit like your Arfur only 'e's a toff and drives a huge shiny motor."

"Sounds like a chancer. I used to see that sort all the time at the dance 'alls. There was one who got three different girls thinkin' 'e would marry 'em, then 'e knocked one of them up and 'ad to scarper, but someone said he was doing the same thing in Bristol a month later."

"What should I do?" Sybil wailed, it seemed as if there was a panicky snake slithering around her stomach, "imagine if 'e makes a fool of 'er and then Jean throws 'er out. I wish I'd never made 'er go yesterday."

"Maybe it's not as bad as you think," Nora soothed pouring tea into both cups, "Arthur gets off work at four, I'll meet 'im at the gates and we'll come along to the Palais and have a look see. If I think you're right I'll speak to Dorothy meself."

* * *

Taking their seats at a small table beside the dance floor at three-thirty, Sybil reckoned Dorothy was almost unrecognisable from the previous day. Dressed in an emerald green dress with a cream silk flower pinned just above her left breast, a cream cloche hat on her head with wisps of red hair escaping beneath it and the main bulk of her tresses pinned low on her neck; handbag, shoes and gloves all matched and an irrepressible smile flitted across her face, while her grey eyes shone as they had not done for weeks. Five minutes after their arrival Harold walked over to them, greeted the sisters with his customary nonchalance before attempting to lead Dorothy towards the floor.

"'old on there 'arold," Sybil said only half playfully, "You didn't dance with me at all yesterday, you can't favour my married chaperone every day you know!"

With a mock bow to both of them, and a "Nothing could be further from my thoughts," Harold took Sybil's arm, but although she felt a small flare of triumph at having won the first dance it was dampened as she noticed how Harold's eyes still held Dorothy's, as if they were humouring her, both secure that at a deeper level no matter who they partnered their souls would be dancing with each other. The feeling of being excluded from their alliance, a droll third extra who could never pierce their inner sanctum, irritated Sybil, yet whatever curt comments she made to Harold they seemed to merely amuse him, which increased her annoyance until by the time they left the floor she was bristling with resentment, convinced they perceived her as the innocent little sister who was of no consequence to their bond which appeared to inhabit a higher plane.

As the last notes of the quickstep faded Sybil found herself led back to her chair and once she had been deposited there Harold immediately fixed his attention back on Dorothy. She wanted to shout at them, to make a scene, yell she wasn't stupid and she could see what was going on, in fact do anything that might shake them away from melting into each other and separate them back into their individual characters with whom she could mess around, have a laugh and a joke without some big globule of sickly emotion landing in the middle and ruining everything, and yet, what if she'd got it wrong, if there was nothing there but friendship, then she'd make a right fool of herself. The indecision kept her quiet long enough for Dorothy and Harold to ease into a waltz, spiralling away as Sybil chomped angrily on a ridiculously small sandwich.

* * *

"What's eating Sybil today?" Harold asked as he finally obtained a dance with Dorothy.

"I don't know, is she snappy?"

"That's putting it mildly."

"Perhaps we've made her feel left out, I don't want to do that," Dorothy said even though every moment she wasn't Harold's partner left her uncomfortably impatient to get him back.

"Can't have that, I'll dance with her again later and see if I can cheer her up." But at that moment the waltz finished and the band struck up the first notes of a tango, sending the pulsing repetitive beats blasting through the building. Dorothy looked straight at Harold.

"Is this a good idea?" she said in an undertone, but his hold on her remained firm.

"There's a Tango Tea at the Odeon next Wednesday," he said. "Come with me."

She adopted the rigid pose demanded by the dance, torsos touching, neck held long, still unnerved that he would not allow her to break free from the smouldering Latin seductiveness that oozed out from the musicians sweeping across the floor to compel acres of reserved Londoners to entwine their restless bodies closer to one another as they bent to tell a story of barely restrained lust. For Dorothy the floor might have been empty of any other couples as she moved, the music dripping with intensity, saturated by the physical pain of longing. Harold seemed to be acting out the Argentinean tale of consummate infatuation while she was meant to remain aloof, but as the dance reached its climax and her lithe thigh muscles seemed to fuse with his, the heat of their passion liquefied them into a single form.

* * *

Nora and Arthur entered the hall, and watched the final thrusts of fervour while still in their overcoats. Nora murmured to Sybil, "I'm guessing that's Harold Willand."

The couple left the floor and smacked abruptly into Sybil's triumphant face as she dragged Harold towards introductions. Dorothy excused herself heading like an arrow for the Ladies in an exit that seemed unnecessarily hasty to Nora, but Harold remained to launch a charm offensive on Arthur. Nora stood quietly by her husband's side watching Harold Willand draw wry chuckles out of Arthur, he didn't seem like a true toff whatever Sybil said about him and his smart car, a real toff would make Arthur bristle whereas this man was having completely the opposite effect.

"Maybe he's a clever chancer who's leading Dorothy on," she thought, "although that type usually sticks to flattering the ladies and Arthur can spot them a mile off."

Ten minutes later when Dorothy still hadn't returned to the table, Harold grabbed Sybil's hand and began dancing recklessly with her to some American Jazz while Nora and Arthur interpreted the music more sedately.

"What do you think?" Nora asked her husband.

"'e seems a regular good bloke," Arthur replied.

"But is he a danger to Dorothy?" she persisted.

"'ow the 'ell am I meant to know that?" her husband laughed, swinging her round with a bit more spirit, "all I can say is I'd rather have a beer with 'im than 'er 'usband any day!"

* * *

As Dorothy bolted for the sanctuary of the loo she felt a fleeting stab of guilt at leaving Harold to cope single-handedly with her sisters. Seeing Nora observing her as she left the floor had been unnerving, her sister's eyes had neither lit up in greeting nor lowered from staring too hard, Nora had continued to look at her as if she were trying to decide something and Dorothy was instantly aware what the 'something' might be when Sybil appeared in front of them grinning like a hyena. It didn't take a genius to figure out that Sybil knew Nora and Arthur were coming but had somehow forgotten to mention it.

Other women came into the room jostling for position in front of the mirror, Dorothy realised she couldn't stay there much longer applying her make-up but she did not feel ready to take on Nora's prying eyes just yet; she headed for a cubical to gain some minutes of solitude and hopefully some greatly needed poise. Sitting on the seat, her head in her hands, she wrestled with her two-pronged dilemma: what answer should she give Harold about the Tango Tea and, with such a huge decision to make in the space of the next half an hour and all the implications of saying either 'yes' or 'no', how was she to behave 'normally' in front of Nora who had obviously been primed to look for inappropriate behaviour from her married sister and who had arrived at just the right time to witness the culmination of the world's most erotic dance. If Dorothy hadn't been concerned that one of her sisters might come in search of her, she would have happily sat in the cubical for the rest of the afternoon and avoided making any decision at all.

By the time she emerged, their table had been swelled by the arrival of several other tea dance regulars and Dorothy was able to calm herself by chatting with them as she watched her sisters' dance, but directly Harold led an exhausted Sybil back to her seat and squeezed his own chair in beside Dorothy she could feel a palpable frisson rise up from her toes to her cheeks so that it seemed unimaginable to her that the entire crowd around the table could not feel the atmosphere panting. Their bodies were behaving like attracting magnets, pulling together more strongly with every moment, every cake dish passed seemed to involve the brush of a hand, or their legs would meet when everyone shuffled chairs around to make room for dancers coming off the floor, there seemed no end of times when their bodies touched. Had they touched this often before and she had failed to realise? Each tiny unconscious contact made Dorothy jump away as if burned, her skin breaking out in harsh tingles while her breath caught deep in her throat. Harold also seemed to have become minutely aware of her, his usual stream of conversation stilled when the others were not at the table, leaving a silence obese with unspoken expectations. As the others danced again the two of them were left sitting mute, both staring forward into the undulating mass of moving couples. Dorothy had no idea what to do, feeling as if the eyes of the room were glued onto her every gesture, eventually Harold gently lifted her hand and led her to the floor for the final waltz.

"Will you come?" he asked as her eyes held his.

"Yes," she replied, feeling herself to be strapped to the front of a ship, sailing towards the horizon and uncertain if the Flat Earth Society was actually correct and she was about to plummet off the edge of the planet into the abyss.

"If you can get there by twelve we can learn the Ballroom Tango first," he said. It would mean leaving before lunch, forcing a confrontation with Jean, requiring a bigger excuse.

"I'll be there," she promised, embracing the abyss, dressing it in the blessed colours of being alone with him and a violent anticipation of relief.

* * *

As Arthur and the sisters walked home after Harold's offer of a lift had been politely refused and he had swept past them waving with dangerous exuberance, Nora fell behind to walk with Dorothy. Arm in arm they strolled towards Sinclair Road while Nora became more reluctant to speak with every step. She thought back to when Dorothy had lived with Peggy at Maddox Street, how her inner imp and quirkiness had made her the natural ring leader of the three of them even though she was the youngest. That confidence and sparkle had all but disappeared after her marriage, but at the time Nora had attributed the transformation to the calmness of new found wedded maturity. Now, she suspected Dorothy had been deeply unhappy, her self-assurance shattered by a man who would never see her eccentricities as comical but rather as evidence of unconventionality that needed to be squashed or surgically remodelled. The woman beside her was proof that the old Dorothy may have suffered grievous bodily harm, but she hadn't been slaughtered and now Nora wondered if to voice her worries about Harold and the dances would be to complete the destruction Jean had so ably begun.

"I thought you were intending to stop going with Sybil," she probed gently.

"Yes, I think for the most part that would be best," said Dorothy, so lightly that Nora's fears were smoothed away, there was clearly nothing to worry about at all.

* * *

From the moment the Tango Tea was mentioned the event became so massively important in her mind that Dorothy immediately knew she wasn't even going to tell her sisters. Nor was she going to use them or Arthur as excuses. There was little chance that Jean would see any of them and check his wife's alibi, but as she sat down to dinner with Jean that evening she had already decided upon her monumental gamble.

"I saw Aunt Sarah today, she's asked me to go up to town with her next Wednesday to choose some new material for winter dresses," she announced. "Would it be all right if I left you a cold lunch so that we could go before twelve?"

Jean looked up, dabbed at his pristine mouth with a starched white napkin and stared at her for a full ten seconds as she speared a small carrot before placing it delicately into her mouth. She knew he was checking her hands, neck, lips and face for signs of tension, but her expression remained as bored and bland as usual.

Dorothy's normality stemmed from earnestly thinking about the appearance, taste and smell of boiled cabbage. It was a trick she had perfected to stop her body from giving away any trace of enjoyment or enthusiasm about a subject so that she no longer shot her own plane down in flames by her eagerness to get Jean to agree to a request. Boiled cabbage was so intensely disagreeable that when she fully visualised it she could even stop the colour rising to her cheeks if someone mentioned Harold.

"Concentrate!" her mind screamed as she began to cut into her potato, "mounds of slimy, steaming leaves, putrid reeking vapours …" Jean's searchlights passed over her with their 'all clear' decision.

"I suppose if that's what she wants you to do; it's not too much to ask. Be sure you don't get more extravagant ideas whilst you're up there."

"That's hardly likely Jean," she said, a shadow of tenseness creeping into her tone, "and even if I did Aunt Sarah would be all too willing to treat me."

His eyes narrowed, "you're my wife. You're not provided for by your aunt and uncle," he stated, an edge of menace entering his voice, "If there's anything you need you have to ask me, not anyone else. Do you understand?"

"Yes, of course Jean, I apologise," she said hastily, realising that relief and nervousness had weakened her usual deference, "this wasn't meant to be something that caused a squabble, I was only seeking permission to accompany her." She lowered her eyes to the table cloth, waiting for the final sentence. He paused, chewing slowly, observing her minutely.

"I don't see the harm in it, but make sure you are back for the evening."

"Oh, I shall be, don't worry about that, how long can you take choosing dress material after all!"

"Quite long enough if you are with your aunt, and then it carries on into lunch and tea and bumping into old friends."

"Yes, of course, you're right, I'll make sure that she knows I have to be home in time for dinner, and then we can enjoy a quiet evening. I'll certainly need it after the rigors of walking round town and standing in endless fabric shops all day."

"You sound as if you won't even enjoy it."

She was trying so hard to get the pitch of the conversation right and realised she was teetering on the edge of sabotaging her own plans, "No, indeed, it's always lovely to look at the new things in town, every woman enjoys that, but it can get a little wearing on the feet after a few hours."

"Fair enough."

Employing Aunt Sarah as her pretext for leaving before lunch was the one lie Dorothy calculated she could get away with. Uncle Edward's office habits were precise, and he was unerring in his practice of never prying into how Aunt Sarah spent her days. They appeared to have a solid partnership based upon unshakable trust in the integrity of one another. Aunt Sarah herself was of such formidable stature that she was the sole family member who caused Jean to cower. Whereas he would not have hesitated to interrogate any of her sisters, should he believe he was being deceived, he was highly unlikely to tackle the Aunt about something so seemingly minor as asking her adopted daughter to help her choose material. Dorothy knew that Aunt Sarah had spent decades perfecting her outer shell which delivered the unmistakable message that this was an individual who would be intimidated by no one. Only those very close to her knew it to be a complete charade. Jean judged her to be a female force equal to his mother's and so had always avoided even the mildest confrontation with her.

Over the coming months the name of Aunt Sarah was likely to be rather useful, Dorothy thought. In fact, it was quite possible that the Aunt might become unusually demanding upon her niece's time.

CHAPTER TEN

For Dorothy, to maintain a cool, apathetic countenance became almost impossible when her heart seemed intent upon winning a championship for palpitations and the dimple where her neck met the collar bones felt as if it was housing a large walnut while her abdomen vacillated between intense excitement and the uncomfortable sensation that she required an urgent dose of dry toast to settle it. Dorothy's mind exploded with fantasies about the tango tea; how he would look? How they would behave away from the prying eyes of her family? What would she wear? How would they dance? The film show in her head went round and round, always omitting the final reel of how they would part and return to their normal lives afterwards. Even with her boiled cabbage ploy, the difficulty of sustaining a creditable mask in front of Jean, his staff and their joint acquaintances, had suddenly increased tenfold.

But it was not merely the problems of expunging the glint from her eye or the upward curl of her lips that troubled her, on a practical level she had decided she must have a pair of tango shoes with cross-lacing ribbons. She already had a skirt scarf that Nora had made for her from one of the patterns in *Queen* magazine the previous Christmas. It was black with embroidered red flowers and was fringed in a delicate grey; where Dorothy was dexterous with her fingers on the piano keys, her sister was a genius when you put a piece of material and a needle in her hands. The shoes, however, would have to come from money she still held in a private bank account. On her sixteenth birthday Uncle Edward had set up the account so he could give her a monthly allowance, "for the trinkets young ladies require," as he had put it. Somehow, upon her marriage, both the account and Uncle Edward's continued deposits into it had been overlooked and, after the event Dorothy never had the inclination to remember to mention it to Jean, and Uncle Edward suffered a similar lapse of memory when on the fifth of every month he settled all his accounts. Even throughout the war years when much of the family silver and jewellery was sold to make ends meet, Uncle Edward never failed to ensure the deposit was made. As Jean was voraciously precious on the subject of Dorothy being "under his care", she had ceased spending anything from this account in case Jean should note an expenditure he had not sanctioned. Consequently the balance had grown steadily.

Now, however, Dorothy was intent upon attire befitting a ravishing señorita, or perhaps a señorita intent upon being ravished. After all, she reasoned, a pair of clandestine shoes were a very minor sin in comparison to what society would condemn as the actions of an irredeemably wanton woman, and Jean would view as the worst treachery, namely her wish to spend an afternoon sutured to a man who was not her husband, re-enacting a dance born in the brothels of Argentina, moving together hip pressed against hip, two bodies orchestrated to react as one, interpreting a Latin desire which recognised no coyness, but painted sweat and tears, passion and yearning, every drop of which she felt when dancing with Harold. In comparison to this, buying a pair of shoes was of no consequence whatsoever.

Dorothy sat demurely for a full five minutes of concentrated clock watching after the front door closed behind Jean on Friday morning, then sprang to her feet, took the stairs two at a time, flung on her hat, coat and gloves before hurtling out into the watery sunlight and skidding to a dignified walk by the time she reached the corner as she headed for Oxford Street on her quest. As it turned out the forbidden footwear was not particularly expensive, nor anything like she had imagined. Although her mental picture had been of a black shoe with ribbons, directly she had seen the soft grey leather with delicately crossed ankle straps she had known to look no further. The colour complimented her eyes, the thin lines of the straps accentuated the drawn up muscles leading from heel to calf but looked less brutal than black ribbon. The heels were high enough to show off her legs but not so high that she would be too tall for Harold – her shoulder would still fit snugly beneath his arm, protected and in exactly the position she spent hours imagining it.

Once home again she stashed the shoes in her wardrobe wrapped in the shawl Nora had made, trying them on whenever Jean left the house until Wednesday morning dawned eons later.

* * *

Harold was pacing the Odeon lobby, chewing the stem of his pipe and regularly drawing his watch from his waistcoat pocket. It was clearly faulty as each minute was taking at least a quarter of an hour to pass. He tapped the front, anticipating the sudden pressure would cause the hands to jump forward several minutes like a barometre, proving he had been correct about the watch's inaccuracy, but they remained stubbornly showing ten minutes to twelve and Harold continued on his marathon walk around the entrance.

"Surely ten minutes beforehand is cutting it very fine if she intends to come," he thought. Perhaps he had offended her by suggesting a private meeting. She could have walked with him last week just because of his mother, to be kind, not because she intended seeing him alone regularly. What if she had told her husband and the elusive Mr Nicolai turned up in her place?

Harold stopped pacing and stood close to the wall, pretending to study a poster just in case the next single person to enter the lobby was an irate Romanian male, but keeping still was almost impossible, he fiddled with his watch again, giving it a shake before replacing it in his pocket; it undoubtedly needed to be taken to the menders. He wished he hadn't already checked in his hat and coat with the concierge feeling somehow naked standing in his best suit, unable to double back onto the street again and pretend he had just been there to have a look around the posters and glean information on forthcoming events. His whole appearance shouted to the world that he was meeting someone, yet the longer he stood there the more it looked as if Dorothy did not have the same idea. How did one diplomatically ask a married lady out on a date? He'd probably totally messed it up and would never get the opportunity to put it right. After all, she had been intending to stop going to tea dances and this was far more villainous than dancing when she was meant to be chaperoning her sister.

The sight of his smiling redhead being bowed through the entrance by the doorman at two minutes to twelve was such an immense relief to Harold that he was unable to stop grinning inanely for the first half of the class despite the teacher becoming increasingly exasperated by his inability to draw his chest back and entwine his legs more firmly as she was instructing. Attempting to stem his exuberance and follow the directions led him to beetle-crush Dorothy's metatarsi three times in as many minutes. The nervous stumbling stretched on throughout the class leaving him relieved when it ended and they could head for the light lunch provided before the main event began.

"I prefer the Argentinean version," Dorothy said as they walked across to the dining area, arm in arm for the first time.

"You get less personal injury!" Harold replied, a slight apology in his voice.

"I didn't mean that," she said squeezing his hand, "the ballroom version seems more controlled, less fiery somehow."

"Too tame for you!" he said laughing down at her as he interlocked his fingers with hers keeping her elbow firmly against his side until he had to release it to pull out her chair.

* * *

Enmeshed in a maze of stories told, or deliberately left unsaid, Dorothy was unable to fully relax into the role of a couple. By her silence she had lied to her sisters, and with her words and concentrated acting she was deceiving her husband. Her gamble was huge. The meeting at the Odeon seemed to change the unthinkable into the probable, yet it was only one more step in a direction where each alteration had been so small that on its own nobody would pin point that hour or minute as the instant a decision had been taken from which she could not turn back. It was impossible to say when things shifted from mild friendship to special interest, from strong attraction to obsession or infatuation. There had been no sudden catalyst, no theatrical revelation when her actions had become life changing. When was the precise moment the harmless flirtations Dorothy enjoyed at Arthur's tea dances turned into something unacceptable? Was there one tiny act that caused the chain reaction? Was it the first time she danced? Or when she began to take Sybil after Arthur got a job? Or when she first partnered Harold? Or when she walked with him after he told her about his mother? Or now, when they were sharing a table alone? Or was it still to happen and, if so, would she really know, at the time, when it had occurred?

As they moved into the dance hall where the Dixieland Jazz Band was playing its first number everything was bright and lively, the sea of smartly dressed dancers seemed to be spinning passed them in a separate orbit, one that was more carefree than hers, that she longed to join but her own tortured feelings of duplicity barred her more effectively than a national border post.

Harold led her to the floor for a rather slow tango, full of moody promise and incapable of lifting her away from the weight of her anxieties. Floundering without the humour that cemented them together and which could override the worries of where the next dance would leave her, Dorothy was rescued from morosity by Harold who after a couple of struts bent in towards her saying, "Does this remind you of *The Four Horsemen*?", relief flooded through her with the chance to revert back to gentle sparring,

"Does that make you Valentino then?"

"Of course!" he said, sweeping her into a deep backbend whilst leaning over her with an expression of absurdly exaggerated virility as the music grew.

With their gaucheness banished they moved to sit out the succeeding dance, she looked at him playfully, "Isn't this the part where you cast the woman aside and stride out with your grandfather?" she said, left eyebrow raised.

"Oh no," he replied touching her knee beneath the tablecloth, "I don't think I'm ever going to cast aside this particular dance partner," and her delight in the statement was tempered by the feeling that he might have said too much to shrug off the heavy mantle of 'what next?' and revert to enjoying the afternoon. When they danced the music seemed to feed her frenzied imagination leaving every fibre in her body aching to grab him and refuse to let go, but in the cold reality of tea with iced cup cakes fear invaded her, murmuring that she had relinquished all control over her life and had no idea what she was doing.

She agreed to be driven part of the way home, changing her shoes and removing her shawl as they drove. Miserably confused she bundled them together wondering if Harold's emotions had experienced the violent see-sawing that had plagued her throughout the last few hours, and whether he would wish to walk away, leaving her in favour of less complicated partners, women who could just be enjoyed without the fear of the 'what next?' question which seemed to reverberate throughout the car. The further they drove the more she panicked that she was about to be dumped on a pavement without the promise of a further fix of his rough jacket fabric touching her arm, his indescribable male scent when they were close, the easy smile that toppled out of his dark eyes, and the endless jokes and laughter that had gradually converted mild enjoyment of his company into a destructively serious need.

"There's a knees up at the Ally Pally tomorrow afternoon," he said as her hand hovered above the door handle. "I don't think your sisters venture that far north do they?"

"No, I'm sure they don't," she replied, happiness surging through her, making her knees unsteady as she stepped onto the street.

"Here at two thirty?"

She nodded. Half running along the narrow road she forced herself to slow to a brisk walk after Harold's Humber glided passed her and around the corner. Elation mixed with wretched uncertainty pulled at her as she entered the small park close to her home and in one swift action hid her incriminating clothing underneath the bushes. It would be a complete give away to walk through the front door with such items when the day was meant to have been filled with winter fabric shopping. Seven years of being minutely observed by Jean had taught her never to take chances. As she mounted the front steps her composite bored, aloof expression was plastered into place. Turning the door knob she took one last deep breath, realising the façade would have to stay on her face until the following afternoon.

* * *

Sometimes Dorothy would still accompany Sybil to the Palais or the Plaza but Harold was unfailingly cautious whenever any of her family was present, he would arrange to arrive at a different time to them and was careful to dance with a respectable quota of other partners before approaching the sisters' table, and he always ensured he had at least one more dance with Sybil than with Dorothy. The discretion appeared to be working as there were no further appearances of Nora, and Sybil's scowl had been banished.

In early November a dance with Sybil left Harold with a dynamite piece of information. It was whilst Harold was attempting to interest her in the reliability of some of the newest models of Morris cars that she said, "Uncle Edward says they'll never take over from trains where you've got room to move around and stretch your legs whilst you travel. 'e and Aunt Sarah are going all the way down to the West Country next week to visit my other aunt, all the way in First Class mind, that's the way to travel."

Later in the afternoon while Harold had Dorothy in his arms he mentioned the forthcoming trip.

"Yes, they're going for ten days, I'll go in and air the apartment on Wednesday as the maid has the same week off ..." Dorothy replied before falling silent, a deep crimson creeping up her neck as Harold looked at her before pulling her sharply closer to him and moving his hand just a little further down towards the base of her spine.

* * *

Dorothy was feverishly flicking dust off endless dustless surfaces when she heard the heavy footstep of the housekeeper stop outside the apartment and a knock was followed by the woman's voice calling out, "Mrs Nicolai, the plumber's here, says he's to sort out the siphonic system."

Harold in a flat cap, overalls and bicycle clips was holding a large bag of tools and treating the housekeeper to his best rendition of a broad north London accent. No "TH" was safe from slaughter as he "Fanked" her for "''er 'elp" before being ushered through the doorway by Dorothy.

He had gone to some trouble to ensure that if she wanted a way out she could claim there was a mistake and she did not require a plumber. Even as she welcomed him into the hallway, her reputation remained intact, and she was grateful for his attention to costume detail, she took in the jaunty angle of the blue cap as Harold put his tool bag on the floor and removed his bicycle clips. Beginning to lead him into the living room she hesitated in the doorway, stern black and white formal photographs of Aunt Sarah and Uncle Edward flanked the mantelpiece and she shrank from their all-seeing stare, turning instead towards the room she had inhabited from the first night she arrived in Maddox Street and which Aunt Sarah, in an uncharacteristically sentimental gesture, had never altered. Yet, once she opened the door she became even more flustered as the bed with its worn white bedspread and plump eiderdown seemed to dominate the room and she half backed away, her face burning as Harold followed her in, quietly closing the door.

Taking her hands and moving in front of her, he led her to the bed, sitting beside her, removing his cap and reaching to cup her face in his hands as he leant forward to kiss her.

"I'll never hurt you, Bill," he murmured as he began to remove the pins from her hair, studying her eyes. She knew she could halt him at any time, but her head was a turmoil of what she wanted and what she should want, what was genuine and what was prudent or acceptable. The dense strawberry blonde tresses began to uncoil in his hands and his gaze left her face as it continued to unravel past her waist, the ends curling up gently from the bedclothes as the full mane betrayed that it would hang down below her buttocks.

"It's magnificent," he breathed moving towards her, covering her with kisses as he leant her backwards to half lie on the bed, feet still attached to the floor but arms entwined as he began to unbutton her blouse. Was it here she should stop him? But every nerve ending was screaming out against wrapping the cloth back around herself. Suddenly he paused and she thought he had decided he should go no further. Leaping from the bed he began ripping at his overalls, looking like a stage comic attempting to get out of a sack that was hobbling him.

"Hang on a moment Bill. Please don't move," he implored, kicking off his shoes and fumbling to extricate himself from his disguise. She laughed at him a little nervously, but deftly slipped off her own shoes so he could lift her stockinged legs onto the bed and move beside her, unfettered at last. He smiled at her as he completed the blouse buttons, the fabric falling apart to reveal her silk lace-trimmed camisole through which there shone two dark red points. Stroking the material he inched towards the right one until a shudder ran through her body and her lips parted in an involuntary moan.

She worked her way down his waistcoat buttons to find his trousers stretched tight beneath. "I never realised there were so many ruddy buttons," she thought, urgency making her hands clumsy, as Harold's lips caressed her neck, one hand teasing her breast as the other found the hem of her skirt and moved up between her legs.

The first time was too fast for either of them to be properly undressed, but as they lay there holding hands in the silent aftermath, Dorothy felt a fierce sense of freedom. What she had done could not be undone and that single fact allowed her to seek answers to all the lesser questions she had spent so many hours attempting to stop herself thinking about, but failing every time. Propping herself up on one elbow she gently used her free hand to remove Harold's tie, dropping it beside the bed. Working the cuff links free she undid the shirt, shrugged him out of his remaining clothing and rested her cheek on his chest, she lay there feeling the rough hairs against the side of her face, breathing in his musky perfume whilst her hands traced the taut diagonal muscles of his abdomen leading her to his groin.

The second time left neither of them with any secrets. Afterwards he gathered up the splayed cape of red hair, winding it up like a sailor's deck coil, and placing it lightly below her collar bone. He kissed her forehead, her eyelids, the end of her nose, before whispering, "We have to sort this out."

* * *

The emptiness of the apartment when he had left gave her a window of stillness in which to adjust back to the life that buzzed in the street below before time dictated she had to open the door and rejoin it. She straightened her old room, taking great care to smooth each rumpled cover and remove every tell tale dark hair; small affirmations of what had occurred that made her smile slowly even while she felt so frightened and very alone. But after she had closed the front door behind her, entering the bustle of the city as she moved towards her habitual lunch at home with Jean, she began to panic, uncertain she could maintain the false front even though she knew her physical safety depended upon it. There was nothing about her that felt the same, she was convinced he would notice, and part of her was too elated to care.

* * *

Harold threw himself into his leather armchair feeling relieved that it had been placed in the corner behind the door during Sis's refurbishments. Hunkered down within its comforting depth he thought of the conversation he would have to go through with his father. Harold was determined to talk to him alone, there was no need for a third party to complicate things further, even if Sis was soon to be Mrs Willand she had no relationship to

Harold and he needed no appendages at this stage, there would be plenty of time for all the peripheries to air their opinions once his intentions were out in the open. That would be soon enough.

Entering with a handful of tinkling glasses, the appearance of the household cocktail maker left Harold's spirits at an all time low. It would have been such a relief if, just for once, Charlie had come in first and Harold had been given even a single minute alone with him to beg for a hiatus of privacy. It should, he felt, be his birth right to have time with his father without having to suffer Sis's pique or Charlie's uncomfortable squirming. The two men shared nearly thirty years of life before Sis had invaded their home, a past that could neither be wiped out nor expanded to suddenly include another person who had not been there. The history just *was*, and Harold was irritated that even his father seemed to be striving to subtly alter the facts.

Charlie's arrival in the room merely confirmed the double act and Harold groaned inwardly recognising that he would have to wait until at least the next morning before he could begin to remedy the unpleasant queasy sensation that had taken hold of his stomach more tightly every day for weeks until now it had become a tourniquet which he could only begin to release by splurging his messed emotions at his father's feet.

Escaping to his room as soon as dinner was completed, Harold spent the night perfecting his monologue. He had no intention of engaging in a discussion, there was no question of *if* he would be with Dorothy, Harold knew he had met his life's partner and he could see nothing more pointless than continuing to search for what he had already found. To remain on the treadmill of human existence: job, aspirations, dreams, without her beside him was to remove the purpose from all of them. Restless to begin arranging his future he left the house before it was light, walking to the abattoir where he waited for the appearance of his father's car, way-laying him before he had even stopped the engine.

"Harold! Don't tell me you want a job here!"

"Please Dad, just drive and park this great thing somewhere we can walk quietly."

"If you insist, but I can't see the point of walking when we've got this," Charlie said revving the accelerator.

* * *

"Well then, what's on your mind?" Charlie was becoming impatient and the puddles were in danger of staining his expensive shoes. Father and son had been walking for several minutes as Harold remained annoyingly silent whilst clearly bursting to say something. Charlie was trying to cultivate a look of serenity, but there were limits which he knew he was approaching fast.

"I'm moving to America, or perhaps France."

Charlie chewed over the announcement, "There's a couple of thousand miles between the two, so it's a good idea to decide which one's your destination," he offered wryly. "Could we begin with 'why'?"

"I've met someone …"

"Assuming this lady is not an American Frenchwoman, would I be correct in believing she's married?"

Harold's silence stretched on down the road as his father attempted to reign in his desire to lecture. "There are many wonderful ladies in London, surely this is a very hasty reaction over one who isn't even available."

"Just because I haven't chosen to speak to you about this before, doesn't mean it's hasty," Harold countered testily. "It's not a case of trying to find someone else. This is not a problem that I want miraculously dissolved away. It's my choice."

Charlie took his son's arm, turning Harold to face him. He noticed the glistening in the brown eyes and was shocked by the realisation that his son seemed bruised as he might have done after some cruel schoolboy incident twenty-five years before when Harriett would have been there to bundle him into her arms and make it all better. It surprised him that the girl was so clearly non-negotiable, but nevertheless Charlie believed the expression before him was not that of an individual so callous that he could easily leave his friends and family to relocate half a world away, however infatuated he was.

"Any problem can be tackled in several different ways, son," he said gently, "and sometimes two heads are better than one. What's her name, by the way?"

* * *

By "two heads" Charlie actually meant four or five and he wasted no time by going to work himself, instead he drove straight to George's chemist shop, turning the window sign to "Closed" before tapping the bell on the counter.

"Have you met this young lady Harold's intoxicated with?" he demanded as George emerged from the back room.

"Not yet."

"I think it's time we did."

CHAPTER ELEVEN

Seated in front of the small black grate in the living room-cum-kitchen of their compact Tottenham flat, George lowered his newspaper to watch the red embers brighten with each gentle down draught from the chimney. Alma's needles were making a comforting click as she fashioned an intricate pattern on a matinee jacket she was making for Antonia.

"Charlie came into the shop today, asked us to meet Harold's girl." The strangled snort from his wife and increased clicking speed indicated that the idea was being badly received.

"Harold's threatening to go to America and the old man's desperate to find a way round it."

"So, *he's* upset now is he?" she huffed, clicking faster than ever. "Didn't expect anyone to turn a hair though when he moved his young floozy in before poor Harriet was even in her grave."

"But this is about Harold. He could mess up his whole future."

"Like father, like son, both chasing women they shouldn't be. I'm not inclined to get involved."

George turned a page of the newspaper, shaking it out with a sharp crack before disappearing behind it as the knitting needles continued to clatter. He read the same paragraph three times before realising it was still merely a jumble of words made up from a jumble of letters, none of which his brain had ascribed any meaning to as it grappled with the problem of supporting his friends whilst incurring the least possible wrath from his wife.

"But you wouldn't want me to go alone to meet this lady, would you?" he asked quietly, anticipating that the spectre of a scarlet woman capable of luring men away from their reason would be sufficiently threatening to ensure he was accompanied. Alma's fingers worked furiously, her lips a compressed white line, a rosy pink rising up her neck that had not been there before, despite the warmth of the fire. Heavy silence sank into the space between their two wing-backed chairs as George imagined the various sentences his wife could be about to mete out.

"Don't expect me to be civil," she snapped, before viciously rolling up her ball of soft white babies' wool, stabbing it with the needles and marching into the bedroom to attend to the tiny bundle of innocence sleeping in the cot.

* * *

Harold was no longer Harold. The carefree, floppy-haired young man with permanent half-smile and playfully wicked eyes who seemed to be at ease in almost any situation, had been replaced by a body that exuded nervousness, his face was set in a stern expression and he gave out a bruskness of manner that deterred even long term acquaintances from making enquiries about his well being. He no longer felt he was inhabiting his own tall, athletic body but rather as if his head had grown into a massive crushing weight which the rest of him was staggering to support. During every conscious moment he was tormented by one of two images that, no matter how hard he tried, he could not wipe from the front of his brain. He seemed to be stuck in the middle of a long black tunnel where both directions looked as menacing as each other. If Dorothy was telling the truth and her husband only ever stared at her, never reaching out, never touching, just observing, then Harold could not comprehend what moved such a man and the picture in his mind became so sinister that he feared just leaving her in such an environment could be putting her in desperate physical peril. This Jean morphed into a monstrous manipulative being who had already discerned the subtle changes in his wife since the start of their affair, and was waiting to wreak some awful everlasting revenge on both of them. If, however, Dorothy was merely attempting to stem other worries by her tales of the taciturn watchful spouse, then Harold's imagination was battered by visions of a very different man, legally justified to take his carnal pleasures with her whenever he desired and, in Harold's experience, that was ninety-nine percent of the time. The graphic hallucinations of this lascivious wretch climbing onto Dorothy's flawless naked body left Harold continuously inflamed with jealousy, his temples throbbing as the grey matter within his skull seemed on the point of bursting out in an eruption of anger and hatred towards an individual he'd never even seen.

As an engineer Harold was accustomed to dissecting any problem into its logical parts, finding the trouble spot and reassembling it to provide a perfect working model. Problems only existed to give the satisfaction of discovering a solution. This time, although he knew the solution was an endlessly carefree life with Dorothy, he had no clear idea about how to get there, and his lack of a concrete plan seemed to make him disintegrate a little further every day, pulling him apart molecule by molecule. Whenever he snatched some time with Dorothy he was briefly restored, but the moment they parted the dance of the movies of dangerous silent predator versus lusting thrusting stud began all over again, every time worse and more detailed than the last showing in his uncontrollable mental cinema.

* * *

Charlie had been planning a cosy assembly of six at his house and was irritated that his wishes seemed destined to be thwarted.

"It has to be somewhere neutral and public," Harold said following another evening full of thinly veiled references to "lowering standards" and "fallen women" by Sis and Alma, "otherwise they'll eat her alive. It's not fair and I won't put her through it."

Charlie suspected that while Alma was genuinely morally outraged by Harold's choice of mate, Sis was eliciting enjoyment solely from having hauled herself up on to Dorothy's bowed shoulders to finally attain the moral high ground for herself. Having reached the apex she was now being energetic in her efforts to remain glued to her pinnacle of social respectability, a quest which made her far more strident in her level of condemnation than Alma ever was. However, between the two ladies the full gamut of character assassination had been undertaken and judgement had been passed. Dorothy was wanton and contemptible, and the two females who had initially been an anathema to one another had become uneasy partners in their righteous feeding frenzy and their crusade to protect their vulnerable men folk from the petrifying gaze of Harold's Medusa. For his part, Charlie was thoroughly looking forward to an introduction to such a reviled young woman.

"All right then, let's make it the Lyon's Corner House at Liverpool Street, that's far enough away for her safety, but make it soon, if Sis becomes any more pious I might as well take her to a nunnery instead of the registrar's office."

With a nod Harold slung his jacket over his shoulder and headed out of the door to his afternoon rendezvous with Dorothy.

* * *

Entering a tea shop to meet your lover's father and best friend for the first time is sufficiently nerve wracking under normal circumstances, but these weren't, and in the twenty-four hours since the arrangement had been made

Dorothy's mind had worked overtime on the vast number of clichéd assumptions that would have been ascribed to her person by those around the table long before she ever appeared. There was a concrete understanding that all women belonged to one of two categories, there were "nice girls" and "the other sort" and Dorothy had no doubt that every one of the party in the tea shop would have decided she was irrevocably in the second camp.

Standing on the other side of the street she was behaving like a nervous mare refusing a jump, while Harold attempted to calm her mounting panic and coax her forward.

"It's only Dad and George, you'll charm the pants off them Bill."

"… and their wives?"

"It will be fine. Believe me, they're going to love you."

She had dressed conservatively in a navy suit with low-heeled shoes, minimal make-up and a small hat, yet the clothes could not conceal the feature people noticed first, the flaming head of hair which lead to all the usual quips about fiery tempers and wild dispositions. Although Harold had always made her feel proud of her appearance, as he pushed open the tea shop door for her, Dorothy earnestly wished for a swift metamorphose into a five-foot-two plain brunette of whom nobody could form any disreputable first impressions.

* * *

Only Charlie was enjoying himself, willfully ignoring the doom-laden dames that sat on either side of him and lapping up a great opportunity to ogle the Nippies. They were his sole reason for favouring Lyon's Corner Houses over any other tea shop, their uniforms were always pleasantly tight, and slimness was a prerequisite of getting a job there, ostensibly so the girls could move easily among the closely packed tables, but Charlie reckoned that was just an acceptable public reason for the shrewd lure created by the management to ensure the country's men were just as happy to go for a cup of tea as head to the pub for a pint drawn by a buxom barmaid. The Nippies were everywhere, all eager to ensure patrons had everything they desired, with red smiling lips and the delightful curve of well-shaped bottoms showing through their skirts as they tottered back to the kitchen with the orders. In Charlie's view it would be a national disaster if Lyon's Corner Houses altered their uniforms to bring them in line with the flat shapeless fashions of the era, it was the only place he knew of where he could legally stare at beautiful young women without being accused of voyeurism.

As Harold entered the shop behind a stunningly elegant woman Charlie's flanking granite pillars remained seated while he found it quite impossible not to rise in effusive greeting. A stuttering small talk began which Charlie would have found uncomfortable had he not been concentrating so hard on Dorothy's figure. He hadn't expected this at all. She reminded him of some sublime image of a Greek goddess, all immaculate pale skin, long neck ending in pulled down shoulders, giving just a glimpse of the gorgeous line of her collar bones, every part in sleek proportion to all the others and topped by a great volume of silky hair whose refusal to be tamed only added to the idea of perfection that was already wriggling under Charlie's skin. Even Sis's strategy of sitting ever closer to him so that he was incapable of watching the waitresses properly did not interrupt his reverie. He was enchanted. All Charlie's intention to remain business-like, even slightly stern, seeped straight out of him as he viewed his son's choice and knew that, given half a chance, she would have been his own. He was unable to restrain giving in to the full flow of the genial enthusiasm he felt and with every moment in her company his smile became wider and his gestures more expansive. Harold had caught a magnificent woman, free from the awkward naivety of younger girls, educated and achingly graceful yet clearly with a fairly uninhibited sense of humour judging from the occasional witty comment that would dart out, an unstoppable bubbling intelligence which erupted from her mouth and shone out from the calm grey eyes whenever they peeked from beneath the demurely lowered lashes.

By the time the party left Charlie was affecting a flowery bow and hand kiss to Dorothy, despite still having Sis pasted to his side. Harold and George were grinning broadly and Charlie believed he could even detect a minuscule thaw in Alma although he was careful not to catch her eye in case he should inadvertently wink and send her scurrying back into the ice age. Only Sis seemed to be committed to remaining in the "brazen hussy" camp and Charlie knew full well he could force her to relinquish the role of ethical high priestess when it became necessary.

* * *

Being accepted by Charlie and George marked a turning point for Dorothy, the couple no longer had to find places to meet now that they could spend afternoons at Harold's home, admittedly they still had to brave the lingering disapproval of Sis who would float through the house exuding the air of a powerless Mother Superior trapped in a brothel, but this was a minor inconvenience compared to the difficulties they had already overcome.

Dorothy was careful to be unerringly polite to the potential mother-in-law who was younger than herself, but in private she was buoyed by Harold's disregard for Sis's vexation. His assurances that Charlie would eventually command his almost-bride to climb down from her pulpit, enabled Dorothy to smile at every sarcastic comment which was whispered in her direction. Day by day the time spent with Harold seemed to forge new steel within her. It was no longer the contrived aloofness she had adopted during her years with Jean that lifted her chin and straightened her back, but instead a feeling that, just by Harold's presence, her world was now a safer place to be in. Although they still had to tackle the huge obstacles of escape and secrecy, Harold's constancy offered irrefutable security that her life was destined for a brighter future, and Jean's repeated volleys of slights and insinuations began to bounce off her strengthened armour plating, as she drowned them out with Harold's voice inside her head ridiculing Jean's demeanour and his stream of daily criticisms.

Yet the very emotions which were giving her strength were in danger of becoming her greatest weakness as her new confidence left Jean balanced on the brink of knowledge that in some indefinable way she was unravelling back towards her natural untrained self.

Dorothy recognised she was losing her battle against detectable change but she was powerless to check her slide into the light. Jean began by blaming too much contact with her ill-disciplined sisters as the cause of her unacceptable optimism and banned her from tea dances, insisting it was excessive for her to spend more than one afternoon a week visiting her siblings. Dorothy was wary of compounding her lies by trying to insist Arthur still needed her, and gave the appearance that she accepted the sudden curtailment of her liberty, she would tell Jean either that she had spent her leisure hours reading or running errands for Aunt Sarah, who continued to provide her with an unquestionable alibi. But it was Dorothy's sudden resilience to even Jean's most inventive barbs that left unmistakeable suspicion building in his eyes until one evening he grabbed her wrist as she passed him on the way up to her bedroom, clamping her to him as he stared, unblinking, at her.

"You're hurting me, please stop," she said, still calm, the confidence provided by a vision of years to be spent with Harold only slowly beginning to seep out of her. But his hand tightened further as he shackled her other wrist in the same way, drawing himself up from his chair and forcing her onto her knees as he bent her arms up, pushing her down beneath him, his eyes never leaving her face as his barely contained desire to harm her succeeded in wiping the protective mental haze of Harold away completely, leaving only the reality of the searing pains shooting up to her shoulders and the knowledge that her own deep happiness had spawned a greater threat than she had ever known. Tears of fear sprang into her eyes, "Please Jean ..."

But not until she was sobbing properly did he throw her to one side and walk past her out into the night.

* * *

George knew that altering his wife's opinions did not occur easily, particularly in situations where a conflict existed between what was generally deemed to be unacceptable and what was in front of her eyes, so he was faintly gob smacked when in private one evening, following a celebratory glass of port for George's birthday, she gave voice to the fact that, had she been Harold, she too would have fallen in love with Dorothy. For a moment this seemed like an interesting idea to George, but looking across the worn brown carpet at his wife he mentally conceded that his fleeting fantasy of the two women together was even less probable than the notion of Alma dancing on a table in a public bar dressed only in a Basque top and suspenders. Both thoughts were distracting, so he toasted Alma's final capitulation by pouring himself a second, much larger, glass of port.

* * *

Harold noticed the marks on her wrists, it didn't require huge powers of deduction to tell him he needed a solution immediately. Charlie had been advocating talking to Jean, 'man to man', certain that any husband would agree it was preferable to be 'caught' in a hotel with a prostitute willing to be named in his wife's divorce petition, than to wash Dorothy's dirty linen in public and be cuckolded himself. Harold had initially been sympathetic to his father's idea but the terror any mention of "speaking to Jean" had created in Dorothy stopped him from pursuing it. Her reaction, he remembered, had been similar to that of a street cat he had once found trapped and starving in the cellar. Far from interpreting his purring imitations as comforting, she had employed her last reserves of strength to growl at him from deep within her emaciated chest, puffing her fur out so that her pitiful form appeared intimidating if the sunken eyes and protruding cheek bones were ignored.

The purple and yellow marks on Dorothy's wrists were proof that Harold and his father were perilously innocent of the demons that drove this man, and their earnest desires to 'fix the problem' in a way they considered 'best for everyone' could be quite as blunderingly life-threatening to Dorothy as her reaction had implied. She had spoken of her fear of being forcibly taken to Romania, locked up, unable to ever find him again, and he had half smiled, convinced at the time that she was over dramatising the situation, that her mind was a little unhinged by events, or even more worryingly, that she wasn't one hundred percent sure she wanted to abandon Jean. With the angry welts glaring back at him Harold began to realise that there were areas of people's lives he was woefully ill-equipped to comprehend. Even in the most rebellious stages of his childhood Harold's father had never raised his hand to him, all aspects of the use of physical force to settle disputes were completely alien. He now knew that Charlie's diplomatic solution of chatting to the 'injured' husband was devoid of the sophistication of duress; it was a flaw in the plan that Harold suddenly understood could rape the two of them of their future together.

* * *

Charlie was concerned that Harold was about to panic. His years in business had taught him that dramatic knee jerk reactions, such as Harold's plan of fleeing to America, were often costly and quickly regretted. He would have liked more time to contemplate all possible avenues but he was conscious that Harold was only stalling from putting his luggage on the first boat out of Southampton because his own marriage to Sis was in a fortnight. Charlie had no doubt, however, that by the time the happy couple returned from their honeymoon, Harold and Dorothy would be gone.

Sitting in his living room on a rare afternoon alone when Sis was in town having a final wedding dress fitting and, almost certainly, running up his accounts in a couple of expensive London stores, Charlie examined the idea of losing his only son to the other side of the Atlantic Ocean and found it completely unacceptable. By a process of internal debate he realised he was only prepared to consider foolproof solutions which guaranteed his son remained no further than a pleasant drive away from him. Charlie was orchestrating his nuptials with Sis to perfection and believed he should be able to organise his son with similar panache. Whenever he thought of his surprise gift for Sis a sense of intense satisfaction warmed through his entire being. He felt very clever at having employed her own friend, Mrs Francis, as a go-between in the purchase of a quaint cottage in her home town of Saffron Walden. Charlie had bought the property in what would become Sis's married name. He would give her the deeds on their wedding day and then rent it out for her so she had an income of her own. The extravagant wedding present had given him hours of delight as he imagined how grateful she would be and the promising athletic honeymoon it was likely to ensure.

Charlie liked owning property. Bricks and mortar gave him a solid feeling of personal security that he wanted his young bride to enjoy as well. Maybe some would see it as a gamble, but to Charlie it was important to know Sis was with him because he was the person she desired to spend time with, not merely because he was a wealthy older man. There would be plenty of jealous onlookers who would gossip, saying she was only with him for his money. Let them talk. He would know she was free to go and live in her own house any time she chose, but she chose to live with him. Perhaps he'd put other properties in her name too. He'd fling wide the cage door and luxuriate in the fact that the pretty little bird still returned to his nest. She'd had a hard war, not that she ever spoke about it, as Charlie disliked dwelling on anything likely to diminish the number of pleasurable hours in a day, but she had put down both her maiden name of Long and the name of Fryer on the paperwork they had completed for the registrar's office, and Charlie had been sufficiently intrigued to make discreet enquiries which ended at the French cemetery of St. Venant-Robecq and the grave of Second Lieutenant C.W. Fryer. The occasionally gaudy gaiety, which so obviously annoyed Harold, was greatly preferable, in Charlie's eyes, to a woman who continually re-examined the heartaches of the past which so many had suffered and none could rectify. Although he had not yet mentioned it to Sis, Charlie was already actively looking for a new London home. He felt she had been exceedingly good about moving into his house and he was not insensitive to the fact that it must have been difficult for any woman to run a home which rang with the ghosts of a previous wife and a son who was unenthusiastic about the usurper. Once the wedding was over they would look round some stylish houses in the area, she would like that, he thought, shaking out the paper on the property classified pages of the *Daily Express* with a business-like snap. Buried in the middle of the eye-wincing small print of a left hand page, one ad leapt out at him: Garage and Motor Works for sale, Kelvedon, Essex. Enquiries to Miss Hunwicke's paper shop.

* * *

December 1921
Charlie took the morning train from Liverpool Street and arrived in what seemed, to his London mind, to be a different era. Kelvedon at the end of 1921 was dragging its heels about being pulled into the twentieth century. The perennial scuttle of the capital was wholly absent from the area and Charlie paused to watch the train driver and the fireman cook their breakfast bacon and eggs on the coal shovel before using it to stoke the engine again so the train could continue lazily on its way. Strolling up the hill from the station, he asked for directions to Miss Hunwicke's shop. Horse and carts tramped down the muddy main street. Women called to one another as they drew water from the pumps for the morning chores and boys on bicycles were doing a brisk trade in hot rolls. The yeasty warm aroma coming from the baskets on the boys' bikes made Charlie acutely aware that he had left London soon after dawn and was now exceedingly

hungry, temporarily abandoning Miss Hunwicke, he headed for the Star & Fleece.

Breakfast taught him a great deal about the village. The first major departure from life in town was that in Kelvedon nosiness was so prevalent that it was accepted without comment. A stranger, such as himself, was subjected to an immediate inquisition which left Charlie feeling uncharacteristically on the back foot. The moment he confessed an interest in the garage the entire population of the inn bombarded him with questions about where he would live if he bought it. This naturally led to the revelation that it would be for his son, which precipitated a wave of enquiries about Harold's age, experience and, most uncomfortably, his marital status. The breakfast assault no longer felt like friendly neighbourliness but seemed to mutate into a possible witch hunt before Charlie had even viewed the business, and what had initially seemed like a convenient solution to a tricky social problem became more fraught with traps at every mouthful. Charlie fought a growing battle between politeness and instant flight, employing large gulps of tea as punctuation to his answers, giving him vital time in which to consider his responses.

By the time he approached Miss Hunwicke's shop he was mentally prepared to ensure that he was the only person asking the questions. Setting his hat squarely on his head, drawing himself up to his full height and swinging his shiny black cane in a manner he felt displayed he would brook no tittle-tattle, he strode towards the narrow fronted premises and ducked his head beneath the lintel before emerging to fill the small front room with the newly assumed greatness of his personality.

Piercing green eyes assessed him while hastily wiping inky fingers down the front of her apron before venturing from behind her counter. Feigning complete ignorance of his business in the village, she nodded her head like a woodpecker as Charlie enlightened her of his intentions with brisk efficiency. Wisps of grey hair escaped from the pins holding her precariously balanced bun and Charlie soon became mesmerised by the nodding and steadily unwinding hair-do, wondering if he continued to speak for a further few minutes whether it would tumble down completely leaving Miss Hunwicke in a flurry of indecision as to whether she should continue nodding or attend to her dismantled tresses with the blackened hands she was attempting to hide.

In the end she remained intact and directed Charlie to the garage where, she said, William would be able to help. As he turned to the door, she added "just over the bridge on the right there's a house for sale you might be interested in if your son wants to settle close to the business. It's not been used for a few years since the old gentleman passed on, but it's a nice spot with big windows. My niece used to work there. The greengrocer has the key."

Passing the brewer's dray and the coal cart as he picked his way round potholes and puddles before arriving at the garage, Charlie wondered if his city slick son would be able to adapt to country life. He hoped Harold's abilities at building gadgets could be harnessed into making a home here more like the comfort he enjoyed in London, and that Dorothy would be up to the task of supporting him.

The building of Kelvedon Motor Works looked tired, but William's chattering enthusiasm about every engine currently on the road left Charlie slopping over with paternalism as he experienced regular flashbacks to the better parts of Harold's teenage years. William's eagerness was infectious even to a man who far preferred to drive than have any comprehension of what was beneath the bonnet. Harold would be the perfect mentor for the lad, Charlie thought, and to purchase the business would also save the youngster from the worry that his livelihood was in imminent danger of folding.

With his business instincts satisfied, Charlie turned back towards the village stopping off at the greengrocer to pick up the key for Brookside.

Bending down to open the small wrought iron gate, he looked favourably at the symmetry of the windows, the solid red brick frontage and the neatly tiled roof. Despite the owner's demise the house did not seem particularly neglected, the front door opened with only the slightest stickiness and the hallway, though dusty, seemed welcoming as the sunlight clawed its way through grimy glass. The rooms were pleasantly large with good fireplaces, and the property's proximity to the river hadn't led to a smell of damp pervading the place. From the first floor windows the extent of the back garden could be appreciated in a way that was impossible from the ground floor due to the height of the weeds. Certainly both house and garden required work, but the structure appeared sound and the price was unbelievably reasonable to the mind of a man used to London rates.

He returned to William, spending a pleasant few hours regaling him with tales of the Humber and the array of vehicles he had seen at Olympia. Charlie fired up his new business protégé with stories of tumbling automobile prices making sales boom so that soon Kelvedon Motor Works would enjoy more trade than it could handle and the air pumps on the forecourt would be working from dawn to dusk.

Feeling satisfied with his day's fact finding and aware that he was being observed from behind every twitching piece of lace along the High Street, Charlie adopted an additional swagger as he walked back to Miss Hunwicke's, left an envelope containing a written offer for two-thirds of the asking price of the garage and a further offer at the greengrocers for Brookside, before heading towards the train station just as the lamplighter was stopping his bike beneath each of the silver grey gas lamps, pulling on their chains and lifting his pole to illuminate each in a manner that seemed to light the way, dot by dot, of the flamboyant stranger as he journeyed back out of the village leaving, he hoped, a week's worth of gossip in his wake.

Charlie returned to London gently smiling at the thought of the present he intended to give Harold on his own wedding day.

* * *

Any lingering ambivalence towards his father's marriage was erased when Harold opened the envelope Charlie casually handed to him. The dapper groom arrived at Edmonton registrar's office, resplendent in morning coat and top hat, delivered his gift and continued without breaking stride to march up the steps in search of his bride. Harold followed at a slower pace, eyes scanning the papers as he levered himself up the stone stairway; by the time he was seated among the other witnesses a slightly imbecilic expression had spread itself across his features in perfect imitation of Lewis Carol's cat. The registrar's voice became an ignorable drone, similar to bees in a garden on a summer's day and Harold settled himself into the hard upright chair, luxuriating in it as if it were a lounger kissed by sunlight in the dozy moments after a good lunch in August, here he was able to indulge in an unfettered fantasy of both the business and a home with Dorothy replete with rural bliss.

The end of the droning interrupted Harold's day dreams and he moved forward to congratulate the bride and groom, attempting to convey his earnest thanks by the force of his handshake and a refusal to break eye contact with his father.

CHAPTER TWELVE

January 1922
(Dorothy: 26, Harold: 27, Peggy: 34, Nora: 31, Sybil: 19)
Just after New Year but before twelfth night had robbed pedestrians of the pleasure of seeing decorations in every front room, Dorothy strolled slowly towards Peggy's home, which was only a few doors away from Nora's basement flat. She was wandering as if she were in a park so that purposeful residents marching on their way, washed her aside as she stopped to watch a robin or stare down allies as if unsure of her way. Finally meandering up the front path of 88 Sinclair Road, she let herself in through the front door and walked up the stairs to her sister's flat before tapping lightly as she entered the confined hallway. Peggy was clearing away Wilfred's lunch tray from where he sat muffled in scarves and blankets in front of the fire. A mucus-loaded hack burst from his mouth, proclaiming that the winter dampness was adding to the difficulties he had suffered ever since being gassed in France and the likelihood of him ever becoming sufficiently well to go out to work was lessening rather than improving with the years. As Dorothy looked at the scene her stomach tightened and her feeling of unworthiness increased; how was she to tell her gentle, accepting sister that she felt her own pampered life with Jean to be so intolerable that she had decided to run away with a lover? Whenever she saw Flo or Peggy a surge of contrition left her struggling to form the sentences she wanted to say. Their endless grinding hard work left her humbled, guilt-ridden at her own regular lucky bolts from life's difficulties, while at every turn they appeared more trapped in the service of their dependents.

"Come an' put the kettle on while I wash up," Peggy said when the greetings were over and it was clear Wilfred would be happier to snooze than listen to the women talk, for which Dorothy was deeply grateful.

"Somethin' tells me you 'aven't come here just to be neighbourly," her sister said with her customary unnerving perspicacity as they sat down at the kitchen table.

"Not exactly," Dorothy admitted, already beginning to squirm beneath Peggy's intense stare as she talked of her unhappiness with Jean and began inching towards admitting her intention to elope.

"But there are thousands of women endurin' marriage problems Dorothy," Peggy interrupted. "Even the government says that women's contribution to the Great War 'as only just begun."

"Jean was never *in* the war," Dorothy challenged, "it's not like Wilfred or all the others. I never had the first bit when you're thinking about him all the time and counting the hours till you're together again."

"Then why in 'eaven's name did you marry 'im?" Peggy demanded.

"I don't know," Dorothy wailed, "Uncle Edward really liked him. Not that I'm blaming him. It just sort of happened. But now with Harold I know what it should have been like..."

"What? Dorothy I don't need to know this. You're married. That's it."

"But you *do* need to know. We're going away."

"Dorothy! No!"

Slowly the weeping and recriminations were diluted by the tea, but her sister put up a creditable fight in favour of marriage vows and stoicism even though it was not an argument Dorothy could allow to take root in her brain and the continual pleas lead only to renewed cloud bursts as she sobbed her apologies that Peggy's sound advice had no chance of changing her mind. Eventually her sister ceased talking completely, sighing deeply as she moved towards Dorothy.

"I wish I'd stayed at Maddox Street," Peggy said, rubbing the shoulders that had not quite ceased shuddering, "I'd 'ave made you spend proper time with 'im first, then you probably wouldn't 'ave blundered into a weddin'."

"I was really stupid," Dorothy admitted still punctuating her sentences with the need for extra gulps of air, "and I know your beliefs must make it hard to see ..."

"What I believe ain't important at the moment," Peggy conceded. "Sybil will be 'ome by now, are you going to tell 'er and Nora?"

"Yes, but I'll wait to tell Aunt Sarah until the day before I go in case it puts Uncle Edward in an awkward position."

* * *

"I told you she'd gone daft over 'arold Willand," Sybil shrieked in triumph. "You said you were goin' to talk to 'er."

"I thought it 'ad blown over," Nora said quietly, "when you stopped going to all the tea dances."

"You *know* this man?" Peggy interjected, her voice becoming even shriller than Sybil's.

"Oh yes, 'e's good fun, a toff though."

"Sybil! He's not a toff!*"* Dorothy retorted.

"Maybe not to you, but none of my mates will ever drive a car like that," Sybil countered, feeling quite exuberant at being finally proved correct in her suspicions even if the situation was horribly serious, after all it wasn't her who was in trouble and there had been slight hints from Nora since Sybil had voiced her romantic hunch, that she thought Sybil's imagination was too energetic to give credence to anything that came out of her mouth if it was not backed by published scientific evidence.

"So 'is Dad's settin' you up somewhere?" Nora confirmed.

"Yes, and he'll bring letters from me until things have quietened down, so you won't be lying if Jean asks where I am and you say you don't know."

"That's good," Peggy said, "it wouldn't feel right to be rude to 'im if 'e came round. I know 'e's got 'is funny ways and 'e's often not kind, but it ain't Christian to turn a bloke away without so much as a cup a tea."

"You're too soft, that one's never been keen on any of our family apart from Uncle Edward," Nora said as she began peeling potatoes for the evening meal, "thinks we're beneath 'im."

"Yer, your 'arold may 'ave a bob or two, but at least 'e don't look down 'is nose at people," Sybil offered. "When are you going to tell Flo and Vera?"

Dorothy sank her head onto her hands in a gesture of weariness that almost succeeded in making Sybil feel sorry for her, "not before I go, that's for certain, she's only thirteen, she won't understand, she's so simplistic in the way she sees things, she likes Jean because he gave her pretty cakes and flowers, she doesn't like Mr Whitaker because he's frowny, it's all black or white to Vera, and it's going to upset her which will make Flo more terrifying than an angry wasps nest," Dorothy's voice had begun shaking dangerously again.

"Don't make that 'ankie any soggier," Nora said. "Flo's not goin' to be the easiest but she doesn't need to know straight away. Jean's not likely to go chargin' down to Bexhill. She's made it plain she's never been keen on 'im. So long as we don't upset Vera, she may not be as bad as you think. Leave me a letter for 'er and I'll send it when you've gone, then she can choose 'ow and when to tell Vera."

"That would be wonderful!" Dorothy said, breaking into a wobbly smile which unclenched her jaw muscles from the spasm which Sybil could see was only just keeping her sister's tear ducts dammed. "I'll tell her I'll keep writing to Vera and sending little things and she can send back any letters through you."

"God knows why she can't live a normal life like the rest of us," Sybil thought as Dorothy went to the hall mirror to affect some damage limitation make-up before heading back to Jean. "It's all 'igh drama with 'er, seven days a week!"

* * *

The Kelvedon Motor Works' pickup truck stood outside Charlie's house, Harold's olive green Harley Davidson and his beloved brown leather armchair were already loaded on the back. Inside Harold was busy packing up many of the items Sis had deemed unsuitable for their own new married home. Dorothy shot through the front door having power-walked from the underground station in order to prolong their time together as much as possible. For the past month they had survived on snatched hours with Dorothy being religious in her zeal to avoid attracting Jean's attention.

"Has the truck had a new lick of paint? I love the red lettering," she panted.

"William and I are painting the whole garage, you could hardly read the name everything was peeling so badly," Harold said, kissing her forehead, both her eyelids, her cheeks, her lips, before moving down one side of her neck, across her collar bone and back up the neck ending at her mouth.

"I hope you're going to be all right there Bill, it's horribly countrified. Do you think you'll mind terribly being in a village where there isn't a single flushing lavatory?"

"Harold! I haven't always lived in an ivory cage," she laughed. "I spent my first five years on a farm with no amenities at all."

"Maybe you'll be better at this than me!" he said beginning to wrap a pretty blue vase in newspaper, "I bought a second hand Tortoise stove from Skingles to put in the privy as it's totally freezing without it; and I've arranged a telephone line."

"Isn't that awfully extravagant when we haven't got the business going yet?" Dorothy asked.

"Dad insisted. We'll be Kelvedon 4."

"So who has the three other lines?"

"Not the station that's for sure, I saw them tapping out Morse code. I think the doctor has one, I reckon he needs it, I thought most of the children were suffering from bubonic plague for the first few days, every one of them seemed to be covered in black daubs of gentian violet."

"But do you like it?" she was worried that the upheaval from his natural habitat might create too much of a strain on his affection for her.

"It's very quiet, but we'll have our work cut out for the first few years modernising the house and building up the business, so we may not notice as much," he replied slowly while taking concentrated pulls on his pipe, "I'll tell you the best thing though, the bakers still use coal ovens so the bread's divine!"

"And the worst thing?"

"No contest there, the Band of Hope Temperance Society."

"Oh goodness, you haven't already given them the impression we're godless drunkards have you? We have to be extra careful, we'll be thrown out of the village if there's a whiff of scandal, country places are far more judgemental than cities" she said unable to stop smiling at his guilty expression even though his recklessness made her stomach turn cartwheels and hot acid creep up her throat.

"Honestly Bill, the old spinsters who run it have no sense of humour at all! They're positively asking to be shocked, it livens up their day!"

"Is it better if I don't know what you've said to them?"

"Probably," he replied gently removing the mirror she was wrapping from her hands and lifting her onto his knee. "You will come, won't you?" She looked down into his anxious eyes and laid her inky fingers on his cheeks tracing them down to his lips.

"I'll be on the three o'clock train unless I'm tied down," she replied. "When are you leaving again?" she asked softly.

"Directly you go, I'll drive back up there. Please don't let anything stop you on Tuesday."

"I won't" she promised, silently praying her intuition that Jean somehow knew everything she was about to do was unfounded.

* * *

(Aunt Sarah: 56, Uncle Edward: 72)

Dorothy timed her arrival at Aunt Sarah's to coincide with Uncle Edward being at his barbers. A regularly neatened haircut and beard trim was something that Uncle Edward would not do without, and his weekly routines were more predictable than the movement of the planets. Nora and Sybil had agreed to join Dorothy there half an hour later to give a partial character reference to Harold whom their Aunt would, they believed, perceive as a wrecker of marriages and a male predator of the worst kind.

Although Sarah had doted on her niece since she was a small child, their personal conversations had been stilted and few. Any intimate revelations that had occurred had always taken place when they were doing other chores such as polishing the brasses or washing up, so that they didn't actually have to look at one another whilst the exchange of information was taking place. Aunt Sarah had even made a point of stating openly that it was always best to discuss awkward subjects whilst busily engaged with something else. As Dorothy walked up the front steps she felt a wave of remorse surge through her nervousness as she realised her Aunt's customary avenue of escapism had been sealed shut by the fact that she had absolutely no idea that a delicate conversation was in the offing. Furthermore, having agreed to the imminent arrival of Nora and Sybil and, with Uncle Edward's appointments being conducted with digital precision, Dorothy had no option but to dive straight in. This was completely contrary to the preferred way of doing things; such a blurting of news gave Aunt Sarah inadequate time either to compose herself or to consider an appropriate response, and Dorothy knew the situation was uncomfortably unfair.

To make matters worse, her Aunt was largely insensitive to any vibes people were giving off and so, in contrast to Peggy, she was unlikely to recognise that there was an urgent cause prompting Dorothy's visit and would remain unaware that the call was for anything other than a morning cup of tea and maybe to borrow and knitting pattern or a book until the sorry truth was deposited all over the brightly coloured Indian rug that was spread between the chairs in the living room.

Since confiding in her sisters and seeing Harold every time he returned, the scheme to leave London had become substantive to Dorothy, and although, as her Aunt was likely to face the brunt of Jean's wrath and questioning, she should have felt more apprehensive than she had when telling her sisters, in fact she was brimming with agitated determination and instead of shrinking from this interview she dispensed with the normal niceties of enquiring after everyone's health and fortunes, opting to come directly to the point. "I'm sorry Aunt Sarah, I have some bad news," she declared before she had even sat down.

Her aunt turned slowly to face her, "Oh?" she said, "Nothing wrong with Jean I hope."

"In a way," said Dorothy a definite redness beginning to extend up her slender neck, "although he doesn't actually know about it yet."

Aunt Sarah lowered herself carefully into a tall straight backed chair, "Dorothy please, if you're going to come in here verbose and flustered, could you at least stop talking in riddles."

Dorothy sank down onto a facing chair, fidgeting with her hands and paying close attention to the pattern on the carpet, suddenly losing the courageous momentum that had been churning through her since breakfast. "I'm sorry Aunt, but I've been awfully unhappy with Jean. We have no children; we really have no life together. He's incredibly jealous and suspicious and possessive and has been ever since I married him."

"Yes," said Aunt Sarah dragging the word out as if her thoughts were trying to catch up with the unexpected tirade, "I was aware that it wasn't a particularly happy union, but many aren't," she said as she lent forward in a kindly manner, "What are you *really* saying, Dorothy?"

"Um, well, in the last few months I've met a man who is very different to Jean. He's only two years older than me and, oh Aunt Sarah ... he makes me laugh. It may sound silly, but he's the only man who's ever made me laugh like that and he loves me and I want to be with him more than anything in the world," by this time she was gabbling, her words running away with her like a brakeless train hurtling down a hill. She felt like the engine driver peering out of her eye sockets, observing her mouth as it streaked towards the base, hitting the upturn with terminal velocity. "His father is being incredibly kind, he's bought us a house, and Harold and I are going to go away together to set up as man and wife."

"Dorothy!" by this time Aunt Sarah was out of her chair and on her feet, "you *are* already married!"

"Yes, I know, but Jean won't divorce me I'm sure of it, and if he knows about Harold he'll do something rash. If he can stand up and nearly strike a stranger for looking at me on a bus when I wasn't even being looked at, can you imagine what he'd do to Harold or me if he caught a whiff of this?"

"Dorothy, you cannot *marry* this 'Harold'!"

Dorothy slumped to a halt in front of her outraged relative, "I know that, and I know everyone in the world will think it's terribly wrong and disgraceful and that I'm shaming my whole family, and I can't apologise enough for causing you such disappointment and pain after all you've done for me, but we *have* to be together. We know we can't stay in London, but we are going to remain in England and I'm hopeful that eventually, perhaps ..." by this time her voice had become little more than a whisper, "that my family will still wish to see me and may come to realise what a wonderful man Harold is."

There was a crushing silence. Aunt Sarah had sunk back into her chair. Dorothy was spent. With both women mute the lack of sound seemed to deepen into a refuge from the wild emotions that had been expressed so inappropriately in the formally furnished room. As it lengthened, the quietude was no longer ominous, there were no harsh unspoken words contained within it, nor any atmosphere of resentment or brewing retribution, it was just exhausted, and as the stillness continued, Dorothy began to relax into the realisation that her Aunt was not going to chastise her and more than this, much much more, she was not going to abandon her either, this was not a 'never darken my door again' moment, it was instead an 'oh my goodness, how are we going to get through this' juncture, and the sound of the doorbell suddenly jangling and Sybil and Nora being shown into the room seemed like an indecent interruption to the telepathic tranquillity.

Aunt Sarah looked up, "Ah," she said, "how long have you two known about this?" Nora looked a little sheepish, "And have you met this Harold?" Aunt Sarah asked bluntly.

"Oh yes," said Sybil, "loads of times, but we didn't really know there was anythin' special between 'im and Dorothy. After all, Dorothy was meant to be my chaperon at those tea dances!"

"Ah," said Aunt Sarah again, "it was the tea dances was it, I wondered. So Sybil, seeing as you, unlike us, still seem quite talkative, are you going to describe this young man to me?" she sighed, resting her head on the chair wing, "but softly please, I feel a little fragile at the moment."

"If you'd asked me to describe 'im before I knew any of this," Sybil prattled while attempting to get properly settled by wiggling her bottom into the chair and rearranging the cushions behind her, "I would 'ave told you that 'e was the greatest of fun, a superb dancer, awfully nice to us and drove a huge flashy car," she concluded unpinning her hat and hooking it onto the chair's arm.

"And now?" asked Aunt Sarah, "now that you do know, how would you describe him?"

"Well," said Sybil, hardly pausing for thought, "I'm certainly annoyed that she didn't tell me before, it's made me look such a chump! Also, to be honest, Dorothy 'as already got an 'usband with plenty of money, I'm not sure why she needs two! Oh I don't mean it Dorothy," she said leaning over and squeezing her sister's shoulder as she did so, "you know what I'm like, first thing that pops into my head comes straight out me mouth."

The tension of knowing she must leave in twenty-four hours and the trial of telling her Aunt had left Dorothy so utterly worn out that the most she could do was smile weakly at Sybil's incessant honesty. Aunt Sarah cleared her throat, "So, would you say that Dorothy's assessment of Harold as the 'man who made her laugh most in the world' was an acceptable explanation for what's going on?"

Sybil and Nora looked at each other, "I'd say it was truthful," Nora said quietly, "If I wasn't so worried about what's goin' to 'appen to 'er and 'ow Jean's goin' to take it, if I was just being asked what I thought of 'arold with no problems attached, then I'd say he's a smashin' chap, but now ... now, I truly don't know what to say."

Aunt Sarah rolled her eyes to the ceiling.

"Do you think Uncle Edward will be dreadfully angry," Dorothy murmured looking anxiously at her Aunt.

"I believe he will support you as much as he can. We've both known for a number of years that the marriage with Jean was perhaps not the wisest decision that any of us has ever taken. Although at the moment I cannot imagine how this is ever going to resolve itself, it has been my experience in life that sometimes the most tortuous problems can be finally ironed out if everybody remains calm."

For such a tall and rigid woman, Aunt Sarah could occasionally be shockingly gentle, "I can see you have agonised over this," she said in a low voice while taking Dorothy's hand in her own and stroking the back of it, "so you have my blessing, but please, all of you, leave me to speak to your uncle. We all of us cause a bit of trouble in our lives once in a while but it's not as if you're a young flighty girl any longer, you're nearing thirty now. If you've truly made up your mind nothing anyone says will stop you from acting on it." She stood, voice steady and quite in command as usual, "Go on, the three of you, it's time you left."

To be completely relieved of the task of telling her uncle was a marvellous and unanticipated windfall. Dorothy half skipped, half flew, down the stairs and into the street dragging her sisters behind her as fast as they would go and with each step she increased the distance between herself and the apartment so that by the time Uncle Edward turned his groomed head back towards Maddox Street she was already soaring far away.

* * *

Sarah lent against the hallway wall listening to the footsteps fade. As the street door slammed she lifted her head and whispered fiercely, "Run Dorothy. Run as fast as you can." She had no intention of saying a word to Edward.

CHAPTER THIRTEEN

Sarah moved swiftly, desperate to escape before Edward returned. Her mind felt as if a flash flood was forcing its way down what had once been a trickling stream; decades of debris was whirling around her brain, gurgling downwards to churn up her heart and compel her wobbly legs to move forward so that she was out of the front door and heading down Maddox Street within the space of two minutes. Almost at a trot she crossed Park Lane but on the other side she slowed, allowing the weakness she was feeling to invade her body and halt her frantic pace. As she moved into the park itself, watching the nannies push their perambulators, the horses being exercised, the couples wandering arm in arm, whispers of peace crept into her as their very normality seemed to sooth the vortex, allowing the first vestiges of clarity and comprehension as her emotional sludge settled and the flow of her thoughts began to clear.

Her feet took her to the Serpentine and an unoccupied bench where she sat and watched the ripplets on the water, guilty recriminations oozed into her mind and she felt a weight of ignorance she attributed to not being a natural mother. Her wish to do the very best for her adopted daughter she now saw as possible despotism. Her worry that she and Edward had created a society misfit, and their desire to solve any problem their meticulous care might have caused, had led them to make assumptions about Dorothy's future needs which now seemed hasty and foolish. She had been easily persuaded that Dorothy's outlook was bleak and that the arrangement that had worked so well for herself could be transferred to her niece without the necessity of explaining the ground rules first. So much had changed since the war; women's emancipation had altered society's perception of the female role in a way Sarah could not even have imagined ten years beforehand. It used to be that unmarried women fell into two broad categories, either they went into service or they were of independent means. Dorothy's antecedents entailed she belonged in neither camp. It had been this stumbling block that had led Sarah to make what she now saw as fateful errors.

She watched the fading back view of a boy on a bicycle who had stared hard at her as he rode past, no doubt he saw a staid but robust aging woman. It was an attitude Sarah had practiced earnestly for decades yet inside she felt hardly different from the four year old child whose father had died leaving her mother with three girls of whom Sarah was the eldest. The struggle had started there, she thought, and in truth sometimes it seemed to have never ended. Sarah, and her sisters Annie and Mary, were quickly introduced to their new father, Thomas Trowbridge, who their mother married two short years after their father's death. Her family had moved to Wiltshire where Mr Trowbridge had his business, but the house soon became overcrowded as their mother produced seven more children. By the time Sarah was twelve she was already out at work in domestic service: Avenue One open to unmarried women. When Annie reached the same age two years later, the pair decided to head for London. Little Annie got work in an Islington home and Sarah landed a position in a grand house on 57 Green Street, Mayfair. Their younger sister Mary never followed them to the capital, preferring to return to the West Country and stay with her mother's family finding agricultural work in Bower Chalke and eventually meeting a wheelwright named Henry Foyle whom she married.

* * *

1880
(Sarah: 16, Edward: 30)
Sarah adored life in London, she was one of many maids in the large house and there was a confident bustle throughout the orderly staff, all intent upon providing unsurpassed comfort for their spinster mistress, Miss Millicent Rowe. The differences between her life as the step daughter of a Wiltshire farmer and a maid in the metropolis fascinated Sarah. Wide streets and smart shops, libraries, art galleries and theatres, sumptuous markets and pristine clothing, all these were to be grasped and savoured as the teenage girl vowed inwardly she would never return to the grime and grind of rural life, the air may not always have smelled as fresh in London but the plethora of opportunities and endless new experiences more than made up for that.

The maids at Green Street worked hard, enduring long hours even though they only had the daily care of Miss Rowe. The mistress had spent her life ensuring she was a pivotal part of the developing liberal intelligencia and maintaining her position entailed having to throw frequent extravagant dinners where London's philosophically adept orators could join together to air many of the most avant gaude ideas. Listening closely as she stood against the wall of the dining room ready to clear dishes and pour wine, Sarah was initially shocked by some of the frank exchanges she heard about poverty and prostitution, Home Rule and child labour, initially fearing she could only tentatively toe the servants line of pride in the level of academic discussions taking place under the roof of 57 Green Street. Around the kitchen table Cook would regularly regale the newer members of staff with tales of when she had cooked for Mr Darwin and his wife and the many evenings Miss Rowe had entertained Mr and Mrs Dickens, but by the time Sarah arrived the house's heyday was heading into its sunset and at least two nights a week the only guests would be Dr and Mrs Lane and their son Dr. Edward Lane. The family ran a string of chic hydrotherapy clinics and also had premises in Harley Street, they had gained significant wealth by pampering the rich and used a creditable dollop of their earnings to demonstrate their social conscience by aiding London's most downtrodden.

Mrs. Margaret Lane, nee Drysdale, was Miss Rowe's closest friend and so the Mistress became regularly embroiled in the social experiments that Dr. Lane and Margaret's fleet of brothers, all of whom were also medical practitioners, propounded. When Dr. Lane died the two ladies increased their philanthropic efforts to fill the gap he had left and spent many of their waking hours continuing the work of the family's reformers and holding meetings about contraception's role in poverty alleviation and other subjects that initially made Sarah squirm with embarrassment as she served tea to the ardent do-gooders and overheard their frank conversation. Dr. Edward Lane would always arrive to accompany his mother home at the end of the gatherings and would often be asked intimate questions relating to the discussion in hand by some of the more brawny women present. It was obvious to the young maid that the doctor disliked many of the topics that were minutely picked over and he would attempt to scurry into the library whenever he arrived before the majority of the reforming gaggle had left, saying to Sarah, if she opened the door, "No need to tell them I'm here, I'll come out when the din dies down," before hastily crossing the hallway and ducking into the tranquil safety of the book-bound intellectual world.

Miss Rowe's collection was extensive; ancient tomes rubbed spines with editions gifted to her by Dickens and Darwin, Drysdale, Malthus and Mill. Every Tuesday afternoon Sarah was charged with dusting the shelves and tables before removing the hearth rug for beating and scrubbing the marble floor. Many times when she was working Dr. Lane would quietly enter the room, always greeting her cordially before immersing himself in the papers and magazines that lay piled high upon the central table. Although he was approaching middle age and his full beard hid most of the emotions his mouth and cheeks might show, Sarah perceived him to be a strikingly sensitive man. His high forehead and long thin nose had initially seemed haughty until she dared to look at his eyes. They were unerringly calm with no trace of arrogance or disdain even when talking to a young servant, they were eyes you could trust not to hurt you she thought, so she was able to continue with her tasks in the library without the apprehension she experienced with other visitors that her presence was in some way disturbing to them. Dr. Lane's quietness was comfortable. Many weeks later however he suddenly began to talk, which was very uncomfortable indeed.

"You might enjoy *The Old Curiosity Shop*, there's a first edition on the third shelf," Edward's soft voice shattered the lazy afternoon stillness making Sarah jump as if she'd been stung.

"I'm sorry, Sir, what was it you were saying?" she replied while stooping to pick up the duster she had dropped.

"I thought you appeared to be a young lady who would enjoy reading, and, if you haven't already read it, Mr Dickens' *Curiosity Shop* is quite wonderful, if rather sad in places." As Sarah stood, unable to decide what he wanted her to say, the Doctor seemed to realise he had inadvertently embarrassed her. Suddenly flustered himself, he reddened and asked her to forgive him if he had spoken incorrectly and she had no interest in books. This outrageous suggestion was sufficient to ungag Sarah who assured him that as a child she had loved reading although she had found few opportunities to get her hands on a book. Miss Rowe's library, so stuffed with volumes, had fascinated her, yet the room remained constantly undisturbed which she deemed horribly wasteful; every week when she dusted the books she would notice that not one had moved. For months she had monitored the shelves and each time she felt a pang of regret that none had been taken down and enjoyed.

"Then why don't you start enjoying them?" Edward asked. "Does your work for Miss Rowe leave you no time to read?"

"No not at all Sir, I have Wednesday afternoons off, but I can't be taking the Mistress's books!"

"Why ever not?" replied Edward. "She wouldn't mind a bit, in fact I'm sure it would amuse her greatly."

"Sir, I'm a housemaid! To ask to read books from the library indeed! Can you imagine what Cook would say about me getting above my station!"

The vestige of a smile broke through the woolly contours of Dr. Lane's face, "Ah well, if it's Cook you're worried about, perhaps it's best she doesn't know about it. However, I think it would be unjust to tar Miss Rowe with the same brush of thinking you above your station if you wished to read."

Confused and uncomfortable, Sarah's usual composure faltered, "I'm certain I didn't mean to accuse Miss Rowe of anything," she blurted, her voice rising in pitch along with the panic that was thundering through her heart, "she's the best of mistresses, for certain she is, I've never been so happy as I have here so I'd never say anything against Miss Rowe and I'm exceedingly sorry if I did, as it's not what I meant, indeed it isn't …"

The doctor's smile faded and he began to look concerned, "no indeed, you said nothing of the sort. I was, in fact, agreeing with you that you have a marvellous employer who would be happy to allow you to borrow her books should you wish to do so." Gently raising his hand as she began to prevaricate, he continued, "would you object if I were to ask whether she would allow me to guide your reading from her library?"

Never usually lost for words, Sarah nodded mutely before hastily bundling up the rug and almost running from the room.

* * *

1888
(Sarah: 24, Edward: 38)

Speaking to his mother and Millicent later about the incident, Edward discovered they were both charmed by his unlikely student but they urged him not to terrify his pupil more than he already had. The following Tuesday Edward was installed in a deep buttoned leather chair by the fire when Sarah entered to complete her weekly chore. Edward knew that Millicent had taken the precaution of speaking to Sarah some days beforehand to assure her that he had no unworthy intentions towards her but was merely attempting to aid her education.

The relationship between literary guide and the guided progressed from distant mistrust towards an uneasy friendship and each week Edward's interest in his pupil increased as he realised he had unearthed an individual who had a genuine craving for books, a desire that would, in the natural course of her social position, have been left wholly unfulfilled. First she tackled all the fast paced stories from *Treasure Island* and *Gulliver's Travels* to *Oliver Twist* and *The Adventures of Peregrine Pickle*. Edward would wonder how she had found the time or the light to finish reading a lengthy novel he had given her the week before, but she would bound into the library unable to contain her disgust at the Yahoos or her compassion for Nancy and her outrage at her death. One aspect that surprised Edward was Sarah's dislike of romantic novels. He had assumed she would relish them but she described *Sense and Sensibility* as "foolish" and even the towering heartache of *Wuthering Heights* did not move her as he expected it to. Within months Sarah's natural deference when speaking to him or the Mistress had become palpably diluted when they were discussing books, her opinions on the characters that now populated every moment of her leisure hours were strong and emotionally charged, so that eventually Edward interspersed the novels with pamphlets produced on current social problems and became particularly enthralled with the natural logic of her rural perspective on subjects that had been discussed and written about by innumerable city gentlemen of wealth – a million miles away from the experience of a young woman in service.

Whereas his mother and Millicent gently teased him about his 'star scholar', Edward did not feel as if he were a moulding mentor to Sarah. Certainly he had put the books in her hands, but her understanding and appreciation of what she learned was uncontrovertibly her own, and often, just because her views were not the prefabricated responses handed out to public schoolboys, Edward found talking with her quite spellbinding. Conclusions which appeared on the surface to be naïvely quirky were often revealed as obvious common sense once Edward's probing dug out the altered starting point of someone whose antecedents matched that of many of literature's poorest characters far more closely than the vast majority of the book's readers or authors.

It was this unconventional relationship that proved to be Edward's lifebelt when his adored mother died suddenly of influenza in early 1891. As the pandemic of Asiatic flu swept the nation every drop of his medical knowledge proved insufficient to save her and Edward watched his mother slip away from him within a matter of days. Without her, Edward's port of refuge became Millicent's house. Although he no longer had the need to accompany his mother home, he continued to call at Green Street when he left his office each afternoon, in fact he became so unwilling to stay in the house full of family ghosts that Millicent was able to persuade him to sell up and buy a smart apartment in Maddox Street.

With lonely hours to fill herself after the loss of her friend, Millicent seemed happy for Edward to continue to visit and even to increase the amount of time he spent discussing books with Sarah, and the mistress frequently joined them when the conversation centred on a current pamphlet or social problem. Within their intimate threesome, Sarah's position was subtly changed but Edward noticed that whenever she prepared to leave the library she would take a moment to straighten her cap and apron, and the impassioned shine her eyes had acquired during the debate would be replaced by a slightly downcast deference, so that by the time she reached the door handle her manner had transformed back into the most lowly servant. He suspected this conscious character change kept her safe from Cook's acid tongue.

* * *

1895
(Sarah: 31, Edward: 45)

Sarah was arranging some daffodils on the hall table when there was a sharp rap on the knocker and the housekeeper, Mrs Haracett, opened the front door to find Dr. Lane's uncle, Dr. Charles Drysdale, on the steps. As the Mistress emerged from the drawing room, Dr. Drysdale strode passed Mrs Haracett to address Miss Rowe directly.

"Is Edward here?"

"Yes indeed, we were about to take tea."

"I need to speak with him, and you too, please instruct your housekeeper we are not to be disturbed."

Looking flustered and confused by his rude insistence on giving orders in her own house, the Mistress turned to Sarah and Mrs Haracett to relay the instruction they had already heard, and an unnatural hush seemed to descend upon the rest of the house as it held its breath while the trio closeted themselves away. As Sarah continued with her chores she could discern occasional volleys of raised voices, mostly Dr. Drysdale's but punctuated by Dr. Lane's, none of the sentences were properly audible but the whole aura of anger was so unnatural to the house that the walls themselves seemed to throb with its intrusion.

Forty minutes later, soon after the grandfather clock had chimed five, Sarah heard the drawing room door opening as she sat frozen on the stairs, her duster stilled from working its way between the banister rails. The Mistress walked out into the hallway followed by Dr. Lane who was noticeably pale, Sarah lowered her gaze and pretended to concentrate furiously on polishing the wooden poles while Dr. Drysdale began to take his leave. Thanking his hostess for her time, he then turned to his nephew, and grasped the younger man's shoulders, looking straight into his eyes, "Don't over excite yourself, I only came to try and ensure that those who seek to embarrass and discredit me are unable to pursue their low aims. Nothing more. I'm sure forewarned is forearmed, eh?"

Edward nodded, bid his uncle an abrupt goodbye and turned immediately towards the library, extracting a cigar from his pocket and closing the door behind him before Dr. Drysdale had crossed the hall.

Miss Rowe looked up at Sarah from the black and white diamonds of the marble floor, while the maid continued to feign she was both insensible and deaf.

"Please light the fire in the library for Dr. Lane," the Mistress commanded.

"Yes Madam, I'll get Kate right away," Sarah replied.

"No, I want you to do it yourself," Miss Rowe said sharply as Sarah snapped to attention and scurried off to the kitchen for the fire box.

Attempting to turn the door handle without a squeak, she eased her way into the room, sideling over to the hearth and laying the sticks of kindling and coal so gently that the performance was almost silent as she prayed it would not disturb the hunched form that sat cocooned in a cloud of rich cigar smoke a few feet away from her.

"Have you read Charles Mackay's *Extraordinary Popular Delusions?*"

"No Sir, I don't believe so. Is it in this library?"

"Yes, indeed, I'm sure there must be a copy. Mackay was a great friend of Dickens and in the past I'm sure Miss Rowe had him here to dine."

"What's the book about Sir?" she asked whilst striking a match and attempting to coax her sticks into life.

"It deals with the peculiar contagiousness of the notions of the mob. The chapter on Witch Mania is particularly apt for Britain at the moment."

"I would be very interested to read it Sir, if there is a copy here about Sir," she replied uncertain whether this was merely a new assignment or if he was expecting her to react in some different way, "Are there witches in London, Sir? I've never been a believer in them."

He half smiled, it was the weary reaction of a kindly man but it made her feel ignorant, "Not witches as such, no, but many who demonise their fellow man for their own ends. You don't seem to latch on to the gossip and rumour mongering that can destroy others, maybe it's a privilege of the bored rich to whip up the rest of their clan against an individual as a sport, like hunting with one of your own as the fox."

He fell silent again as she remained kneeling on the floor, ensuring the chimney was drawing strongly before she left.

"Will you walk with me next Wednesday afternoon?"

The request was in such a low voice that although a jolt of fear had shot through her when she heard it she could convince herself her ears had deceived her, until he continued, "Say at two, by the Serpentine."

*　*　*

Part of her hoped Wednesday would be wet and windy so the walk would have to be cancelled, but the gods denied her an excuse to avoid the outing and as she drew back her curtains and saw the first rays of mid-week sun

Sarah felt as if the solid ground she had taken for granted beneath her feet since she arrived in London was about to shift.

Once the morning's work was over Sarah avoided lunch, going to her room to change out of her uniform and into her Sunday dress and hat. She neatened her hair in the glass before slipping down the back stairs and out of the house whilst the other servants were eating in the kitchen below. She chose to be early rather than run the risk of meeting a member of the household when dressed in a fashion certain to invite speculation. There was an unpleasant sensation in her stomach and throat; her heart was racing as if preparing herself for a shock. Curiosity and the need for politeness was driving her to this meeting whilst her physical body emitted every signal that it wanted to flee and return to the status quo, silently protesting that to enter Hyde Park was to somehow be doomed. Had she been given any clue why he wanted to meet her away from the house she would have felt easier, instead she was adrift, unable to compose herself and wandering at the whim of she knew not what.

Perching on a bench overlooking the Serpentine Sarah waited for the doctor, she still thought of him as that even though she knew he had abandoned his medical practice years before and adopted the cleaner profession of stock broking. Anyone watching her as she sat would have noticed that despite the tranquil setting there was no hint of relaxation in her body. Her spine did not touch the back of the bench and the hang of her dress seemed a little too high for her thighs to be more than grazing the seat, her feet were sharply together and her gaze did not gently observe the water or the people but flitted constantly, never resting for more than a fraction of a second in one place. She intended to afford herself some moment of preparation by seeing Edward before he saw her, but in this she was foiled as he approached her from an oblique angle, causing her to start when his deep voice greeted her before the corner of her eye had registered he was there.

"Good afternoon Miss Holloway, thank you so much for coming. Will you walk with me a little?"

She rose, he matched his stride to hers, yet neither of them spoke, the usual pleasantries of the weather and the flowers were ignored in favour of a palpitating silence which grew heavier with every step. They passed Speakers Corner, continuing down to Achilles Statue, here Edward paused momentarily, "Every man has a weak spot somewhere, it's what makes us human I believe."

He spoke so quietly that Sarah was forced to move a little closer. Her eagerness to comprehend the reason for this meeting would not brook her missing a syllable, and it was clear that Dr. Lane was struggling greatly with that which he needed to say and it would cause him anguish to be asked to repeat himself.

"I wish to speak to you of a business proposal," he continued walking slowly onwards. "It involves an unconventional arrangement and I am not confident I know how you will receive it. Over the years we have discussed books and ideas and I have formed opinions about you, as you doubtless have done about me, but now I am unsure if they will prove to be true."

Still completely bewildered about his purpose, there was no reply Sarah could give. Meeting his eyes, she nodded, willing him to explain properly.

"As you know, my uncle came to visit myself and Miss Rowe last week," he stated, "he brought some disquieting news. Mr Wilde's conviction has left London in uproar and whenever the masses are roused from their lairs there is always someone who will attempt to direct them for their own ends. Unfortunately, today's appointed wolf pack leader is my uncle's greatest adversary. He believes the Drysdales and the Lanes to be corrupters of public morals in our drive to educate women so they may limit the size of their families and extricate themselves from the miserable poverty which drives so many of them into prostitution. Every time a Drysdale or a Lane publishes papers or holds meetings to gain support for social reform, this man is tireless in his attacks on us as godless meddlers in the order of nature and defilers of the minds of the populous. With the frenzy following Mr Wilde's disgrace, my uncle has been informed that this viperous fiend is preparing to attack the sole unmarried male in the family, namely myself, smearing our name with rumours of what he terms "unnatural acts" with the aim of discrediting everything that my father and uncles have striven to achieve."

He breathed deeply, fixing his eyes on his feet as each one moved rhythmically forward.

"It is at this point that I make assumptions about you which may prove to be incorrect. If this occurs, forgive me," he said, toying feverishly with his watch chain before continuing. "Since my mother passed away the many hours we have spent discussing literature have been some of the happiest interludes of my daily life, and I hope I do not delude myself in believing the study of literature and the acquisition of knowledge have been more enjoyable for you than scrubbing floors and dusting chandeliers." At this point Sarah would normally have interrupted volubly asserting that her life as Miss Rowe's maid was completely to her liking, but she recognised that protestations could be a distraction from the point Edward was battling to make, which would entail keeping her ignorant of his purpose for even longer, so for once her lips remained resolutely shut, a further slight nod of her head being her only response.

"I also believe, and here I may do you a grave injustice for which I apologise …" he thrust his hand into his waistcoat pocket, pulled out his watch and looked at the face determinedly.

"Yes?" she prompted.

"I also believe," he began again, staring harder than ever at the movement of his feet, "that, like myself, you have great love for your fellow man, your family and your country, but do not experience the searing physical pangs of love so often detailed in romantic novels."

"I have never wished to take a husband if that's what you mean sir," she replied almost in a whisper. "I've seen the toil and heartache of my sisters with babies coming every year and I know I prefer the life I have with Miss Rowe to the one they live."

"That is as I thought. Do you believe, however, that you could entertain the possibility of being able to continue your reading and also accompany me to the theatre, art galleries, dinners, and cease to work for Miss Rowe?" he lifted his hand to stem her interruption. "This is not a proposal of marriage, as I said before, it is a business proposal. I enjoy your company immensely and I need to give the impression to London society of having taken a wife but the flighty young women I am acquainted with do not interest me in the slightest and would, I am certain, within a short space of time cause me much grief with their demands and expectations. As I appear to be forced into the position of taking a female companion, I wish it to be one whom I will not find irksome and the only woman I know who would suit me is you. No wait," he said lifting his hand once more, "let me finish please, then you may speak and take as long as you require to consider your response.

"I offer you your own quarters in my apartment and a generous clothing allowance with complete freedom to spend the entire time I am at my office reading to your heart's content. In return I would like your company when I have to go out to functions, your complete discretion and your compliance in being presented to the world as Mrs Lane, and for you to act as such when we are in public. I make no other demands on your time or your energies."

He stopped abruptly, leaving her unprepared for the simple starkness of the offer.

"And what happens when your uncle's tormenter leaves off? Am I to be let go and have to find a new situation with no proper reference?" she said testily.

"I can see you are confused and surprised but I think that assumption is unworthy of you as well as me. However, Miss Rowe was present at my meeting with my uncle the other day and does know of that which I speak. She believed you could be concerned for your future and to that end she gave me this note for you in which I believe she offers you your current position back if you should ever grow to dislike your place with me." He handed her a folded piece of paper. She took it and carefully broke the seal to reveal what he had said was correct.

"Would you mind if we sat down for a moment?" she asked hesitantly. "I don't mean to be impudent sir, but I could do with it, I skipped lunch and with all this walking and talking I feel a little light headed."

Instant concern spread across the doctor's face and he guided her towards a small tea room beside the lake, ordering refreshments for both of them. He refrained from pressing her to speak but watched her calmly. She felt the drink coursing through her, its warmth straightening the slight slouch in her spine and bringing up her head until she was ready for her eyes to meet his.

"I don't see how you could pass me off as your wife without becoming a laughing stock unless I'm mute. The minute I open my mouth everyone in London would know there was something fishy."

"Said with the compelling logic that makes you so much more interesting than the groomed debutants my uncle was suggesting I wed!" he said, visibly relaxing at the turn the conversation was taking. "I had thought the same myself and if you are interested in the position of mimicking Mrs Lane I suggest we arrange our initial meeting and supposed courtship in Brighton where there lives a certain Miss Solomon, now of advancing years, but who in her youth was a talented dancer and actress. I am sure she could transform you with a handful of elocution and deportment lessons. It is, of course, a gamble that by giving you the voice and physical stature of a high born lady I will alter and destroy the very serenity and prudence that make me believe you to be the perfect companion for an unsociable middle aged man like myself. Do you think that might occur?"

"Oh no sir, I don't think so sir!"

Slowly his face broke into a broad smile, it began with his eyes, spread to his cheeks and as they lifted higher the buried lips emerged from beneath the beard and Sarah recognised the expression of friend and protector she remembered from so long ago when her father was alive and she was so small. He had seemed so big then and so genuinely interested in hearing her recount every detail of her childish day. Now as she relived the security of those fleeting moments she remembered with her father, she felt a deep surety that everything would be just fine because a true friend was there to guide her.

"So how long do you think it will take to make me speak like a gentlewoman sir?"

"Probably less time than it takes for you to stop saying "sir" and get used to calling me "Edward", but I think you will convert into a perfect lady with very little trouble at all," he said lightly taking her elbow to help her up as they made to leave the tea rooms, the deal demonstrably agreed upon.

* * *

1922
(Sarah: 58, Edward:72)

And it was, she thought sitting on the same park bench decades later, an irreproachable non-marriage. Without the encumbrance of physical intimacy and expectations they had retained the joy they experienced in one another's company in exactly the same way that best friends will always delight in spending time together. The "Lanes" were the genuine perfect partnership; they confused their friends with their unbreakable unity. No telling gossip could be extracted from Mrs Lane when the ladies left the gentlemen to their port and cigars. Neither of them ever emitted a twinge of anything other than the deepest respect for one another and whilst their voracious appetites for learning made them formidable individually, together they were unassailable.

Yet now, older and sitting in the cooling afternoon sun on an unforgiving wooden bench, she wondered if the very success of her lifelong relationship had blinded her to the aspects that made it impossible to replicate for her niece. Somehow she had believed the role of companion and wife would be easier for Dorothy, but the lack of need for romance and intimacy in her own life entailed that as part of the ingredients of a marriage, she had almost wholly overlooked them for her niece. Becoming slowly chilled as she sat, Sarah felt vulnerable and foolish. Her shoulders sagged with the weight of her incomprehension as she observed the young couples walk arm in arm, sharing a secret she had somehow missed. She felt the sting at the back of her nose which always came with high emotion, and the pressure behind her eyes of tears she knew she would never allow to fall. People no longer cried over mere disappointments in themselves or others, the war had seen to that. Yet, resisting the physical signs of her anguish did not lessen the shame that was enveloping Sarah, as she confronted the idea that Dorothy's marriage had taken place with complete inevitability; she could have been a figurine on a conveyor belt inexorably travelling towards her mate with whom she would be boxed together to use as wedding cake decorations – cold, unfeeling, plaster castes with painted smiles. With all their literature and learning she and Edward had by-passed lessons in love that Dorothy, unworldly and innocent though she was, had eventually embraced by instinct. The act of allowing Jean, an older man and friend of her beloved uncle, to court Dorothy was pitiless; in so many ways they had encouraged her romantic daydreams when he sent her flowers and chocolates during the austere years of scarcity, whilst on a deeper level they were aware that this man was playing a part, taking trouble to affect a role it was easy to perfect when one's audience was so much younger and less experienced than the Thespian himself. At a time when there were few available young men in London, and even fewer with their own successful business plus the desire to take on the care of a gauche teenager, was it surprising that Dorothy had stepped into the comfortable slippers her uncle and aunt had carefully laid out for her? Yes, she and Edward had studied philosophy and ethics until she had occasionally felt a certain smugness at the ignorance of some of the society ladies she had to mix with, yet all the learning had blinkered both of them to the dangers of paternalism. Certainly there had been no malice in their plans for Dorothy, but their overwhelming love for her had lead them to jump at shadows in her future which, since the end of the war, had ceased to exist. In the seven short years since Dorothy's marriage so much had changed, women could vote, almost nobody wore a corset any more and women of all classes had breathed in new freedoms and fresh determination to live their lives in conjunction with their male partners rather than in subjection to them. How could she have known, she thought as she vaguely fought against blaming herself for the whole sorry mess, with her ankles still safely shrouded from view, Sarah felt as if her comprehension of how life worked had slipped away in a few short years, she may not have agreed with many of society's mechanisms before but at least she understood how each of the engine parts fitted together so that the whole could move forward. Increasingly it seemed as if she was missing a vital bit, or several bits, it wasn't just the changes for women, the whole fabric which had appeared to make up the great British Empire she had grown up with, was being rent into pieces, there were so many radical ideas mushrooming up from the mud of the trenches that even those who had prided themselves previously on progressive thinking were fleeing for the safety of old social norms, and she found herself wanting to hide from the trampling population who moved relentlessly into this new world.

How could she have known it would be like this? Their schemes to rescue Dorothy from the poverty the rest of her family had experienced had led them to believe that imprisonment with the strange jealous creature that Jean was, would be a salvation. Instead their precious flame-haired beauty was showing them a path to emancipation they had never even considered.

CHAPTER FOURTEEN

February 1922, Kelvedon, Essex.
"Where's Harold?" she croaked attempting to pull away as George helped her to her feet.

"Harold? Oh yes, really wanted to come but some wretched woman from the parish council came round and it would have seemed jolly rude if he'd turfed her out, so, to avoid any unnecessary commotion I said I'd pop over and pick you up myself. Crikey, you look as white as a sheet, do you want to sit down?"

"I'm fine George," she said, attempting to move the sides of her mouth upwards, but knowing it must look like a grimace. "Harold does want me here, doesn't he?"

"Dorothy are you sure you don't need to take the weight off your feet for a mo? You know how Harold feels about you, he's hardly going to disappear into darkest Essex if he's having second thoughts! Come on girl, the porter's watching and the entire village knows that Mr Willand's wife is arriving from London, so act the part," George raised his hat to the porter before balancing one suitcase under his armpit and seizing the second by its handle, he used his free hand to take her arm in a surprisingly tender gesture given his tally-ho nature, and began to steer her through the single room of the station building. "Things are rather spartan around here compared to London, but Alma can send anything you need, it will be a bit like camping out for a while."

"I need to see Harold, that's all …"

"Righty ho my cup cake, car's just out front."

The smells of train and station gave way to a soothing cocoon of car leather, it was a scent she associated with Harold and the familiarity enabled her to concentrate on slowing her breathing as she attempted to gain control over the thundering in her chest and force the hard frightened lump in her throat a little lower. She looked down at her hands, observing with mild surprise that they were twitching like an animal twitches in the final unconscious moments before death. There had been times today when she had believed death preferable to a single second more of the razor-like mental torture she had been living. Retaining her habitual expression of bland boredom had become increasingly challenging during the past month and the last forty-eight hours had been continually punctuated by waves of panic threatening to drown her and obliterate her practiced pretence of normality.

Over the past few months she had slithered almost unconsciously into the decision to escape but it was only with Charlie's unexpected gift that the desire to flee had become a concrete resolve and as Harold commuted between London and Essex, and the clandestine relationship itself became common knowledge to Harold's family, and then to her sisters, and finally to Aunt Sarah, that with each nod of acceptance her prospect of freedom seemed more definite, until the idea became her immutable future reality, shining in front of her, blinding as it streaked forward and she caught hold of its comet tail, incapable of letting go but conscious that its light illuminated her so that anything existing in the shadows might easily line her up in its sights and deliver a fatal shot without her even seeing who pulled the trigger.

There had been several occasions when Jean had suddenly treated her roughly since he forced her to her knees, and she knew that all her precautions were insufficient to disguise the change that was waiting to burst from her as she discarded the chrysalis of her London existence and flew off to her virgin country life. She was unsure if he had noted a minute alteration in her attitude towards him, or whether one of his staff or clients had commented on some tiny change, observing that she looked more carefree or her mannerisms had lapsed from their customary stiff formality, leading them to congratulate Mr. Nicolai on his delightful wife, and so causing treacherous suspicion to creep upwards past his heart and into his head where it grew cancerous, spreading into a quest throughout all the waking hours to find the root of his chattel's happiness.

Every day whilst they ate at separate ends of the dining table, she had felt him watching her, his round head, with lateral receding hairline, perched above his slimmer body, lent him the air of a praying mantis as he consumed his sustenance without seeming to need to look down at his plate. Throughout the final morning's breakfast mixtures of resentment, fear and loathing had threatened to force their way up from her chest, funnelling through her neck before exploding across her features, wrecking the mask of serene joylessness she had moulded to fit her face over seven interminable years. She was convinced he was playing with her; certain that he knew exactly what her plans were and had chosen the time when he would obliterate them. The suspicion wreaked havoc with her stomach and bowels. Pursing her lips against the impulse to scream, she pecked at her breakfast whilst Jean sketched petals and ferns on the side of *The Times* with a pencil, still watching her whilst eating and drawing. The images were perfect, flawlessly correct down to the last stroke of shading.

At last he released his pencil, dabbed the corners of his mouth and stood up, looking down at his wife. Wisps of her thick wavy red mane had already worked their way free from the pins which attempted to control the acres of hair. He kept telling her to have it bobbed like everyone else these days, her sisters had truncated their locks as soon as the first cloche hat hit the high street, but her persistence in retaining what he called a "romanticised relic of a hairstyle" was just one in a long list of non-conformities that she knew continually irked him.

She looked up, "I hope you have a good morning," she offered without emotion.

"Yes, see you at lunch," he replied, not breaking eye contact, before quietly leaving the room.

The trains to Kelvedon were either early morning, which would have been impossible, or mid afternoon, so she had no option but to also endure his visual dissection at lunch. She spent the morning moving continuously through the house, paying innumerable visits to the bathroom and feeling as if her abdomen had contracted so forcefully that there was no width occupied by her vital organs, just her spine and skin stretched around it. Lunch was a struggle similar to forcing pieces of cloth down her throat and then desperately trying to swallow in a body that craved to regurgitate everything. Observing her efforts he asked with a slight sneer what was wrong with her and why she wasn't eating like a "normal girl". She blamed cramps.

The end of an interminable lunch arrived and she handed him his hat and opened the front door. "Goodbye, have a pleasant afternoon."

Closing the wall of oak between them she leant against it breathing heavily, unsure whether to wait a while before running upstairs to pack, as she had packed at least twenty times before. For a month she had practiced every day when he left the house, perfecting the art of fitting her most essential belongings into two suitcases, small enough to carry herself without attracting attention. She had known that her packing had to be automatic so she could do it in whatever state of disarray she found herself in when he finally returned to work. She waited, rigid as Lott's wife, frightened to leave the front door; terrified that he might still be on the steps, standing there on the other side waiting for her to emerge and incriminate herself. There he would be, staring at her luggage-laden form, no convincing explanation possible to halt the pyroclastic flow of his triumph at having been proved correct and handed the excuse to slam shut her cell door, flinging the key into a furnace, watching her means of escape become a stream of molten metal. If she failed now she did not doubt she would be in this house until one of them died.

She waited another full minute. A detached part of her mind wondered if she were experiencing a heart attack because the pounding behind her ribs seemed to shake her whole body and everything seemed painful and fuzzy with doubt. Not doubt that she should go, but doubt that she was somehow being duped. She walked upstairs dragging her weighted feet painfully up one step at a time; not with any bounce or like a young woman, deliriously in love, and about to elope with her lover. No, not like that at all. She felt as if she were an animal caught in two nets at once that knows it can escape from one but will never get out of the other, so why try? Why bother?

Reaching the landing she turned into her bedroom, pulled the suitcases from within her wardrobe and packed mechanically; shoes in the bottom, hairbrush, mirror, pins, underwear, a few dresses, almost nothing for seven years of middle-class married life, but then she could carry so little. Quietly closing the wardrobe doors she pulled her hat down low on her forehead and made her way downstairs. She propped a note upon the hall dresser, just two words: "Goodbye", and underneath: "Sorry", nothing so personal as either of their names. Her hand rested on the doorknob for several seconds before she steeled herself to turn it. A tiny out breath of relief escaped her when the steps were empty and in the street it was a normal afternoon with all the normal people around, people who knew her and who called out, "Good afternoon Mrs Nicolai," and, when they saw the suitcases, "Are you off on holiday?" and she'd reply, "Yes, I'm going to visit my sister."

"That's nice, will you still be wanting two loaves on Wednesday morning?"

"Yes please, Mr Nicolai will be here."

"I hope you have a good trip and your sister is in good health."

"Many thanks," and she had hailed a cab, instructing the driver to take her to Liverpool Street Station.

* * *

Leaning her head against the carriage window of the train, watching her own face in the reflection, she had felt frozen and unable to turn around in case she should find him standing there with that knowing smile playing on his lips as if to ask her why she had ever imagined she would manage to elude him. Even now in George's car she envisaged not some local parish grandee chatting to an exasperated Harold in the living room, but Mr Nicolai and Mr Willand gloating over the treacherous woman they had enticed into revealing her vulgar nature. She ached with wishing this day was over, or had never begun.

"This is it," George swung off to the right into a semi-circular close with a wide-fronted house at ninety degrees to a small green which bordered the main road. As he skidded to a gravely halt a blur of a man projected himself from the gate to the car, wrenched open the passenger door and kissed her fully on the lips.

"Bill! Thank goodness you're here," he said pausing for breath, "I'm so sorry I couldn't get rid of that awful woman, but you know what it's like in small villages, we've got to make them all think we've been married for ages or else they'll be gossiping day and night – it's not like London you know, they all know what you're going to do before you've even decided upon it yourself! All I wanted her to do was leave, but she wouldn't take the hint so I had to send George, I'm so terribly sorry. No, no, don't walk, I'm definitely going to carry my 'bride' across the threshold of our new home."

Stopping below the front door lintel to kiss her again he noticed, "You look horribly pale my darling, hey George will you grab the bags, I think we all need a good stiff brandy."

She kept her arms clasped around his neck as if they were welded in place and buried her face in the crook of his collar bone breathing in the comforting residue of his pipe smoke mixed with coal tar soap. Very slowly the muscles around her stomach began to unclench, the nugget in her throat softened and a plague of fatigue flooded through her as slices of pleasure filtered into her brain whispering that maybe, just maybe, they were going to get away with this, and everything would be all right.

Striding through the hall, Harold placed her gently on a patched sofa in the living room, knelt and carefully removed her shoes stroking the length of each foot before tucking her legs alongside her. "Bill, you look all in, it must have been grim. I've been imagining what you've been going through all day, I was so worried that he would come back or that you would get caught or decide not to come at all ..."

"*You* were worried!" she said, but her voice was so low that the exclamation hardly raised the tone. "It was hideous, even when I saw George at the station I thought it was because somehow Jean had found you. I kept imagining what he would do, how he would force me back to London ..."

"We need a drink darling. George! George! Come on in and let's toast the arrival of the most beautiful girl in the world." He handed her a cigarette from the silver case on the coffee table and lit it whilst George clattered around with glasses and decanter.

* * *

The furniture in the house was of good quality but sparse. Bits and pieces had been retrieved from London and a few essentials, including the curtains, had been purchased with the property. To the rear of the house was a scullery and from here a back door led to a large untamed garden. A brick path wound through the flower beds, waist high with weeds, to arrive at the privy on the right hand side. It was here, an hour later, lantern in hand, that Dorothy's throaty laugh rang out at Brookside for the first time as from the other side of the door, Harold refused to bow to her wish for dignity and goaded her with the need to be quick as Mr Whittaker was due to arrive to empty the soil buckets and she could be suddenly left with nothing beneath her, warning her that, if a vacuum were to occur, she should not cry out as Whittaker's horse was known to be skittish and the last time it had bolted the haulage company had taken over a day to clear up the mess. As she sat on the rough wooden seat she realised that she could not remember a single time in her marriage when she and Jean had laughed together, the idea seemed almost indecent.

Back in the house her exhaustion became insupportable and she refused the offer of a meal at The Sun Inn in favour of surrendering herself to sleep. Harold led her up the stairs and along the corridor to a room overlooking the garden where the fire had already been lit in the grate and a high bed was covered by a plump eiderdown which looked irresistibly inviting to anyone so bone weary as Dorothy.

Although her eyelids felt they would close with or without her permission, the sight of the bed reminded the deepest parts of her that she was beginning a new life with her lover and all the horrors of the day were because she had to be with him. He was her addiction, not just occasionally, when convenient, but urgently and with a joint promise of forever. She moved towards him slipping one hand beneath his jacket to feel the muscles rise up his back. Lifting her face to his, he nibbled her lips so lightly that she looked at him fully as he seemed to pull away each time she leant in towards him. He looked down, pleading, "I can't, I'm going to explode, George is downstairs." She drew back taking in the significant interruption to the normal lie of his suit trousers and smiling with self-satisfaction as she buttoned his jacket across it. Lifting his hand to her mouth to kiss the back of it, she never took her eyes from his face, until finally she released him to attend to the needs of George's rumbling stomach.

Yet once Harold had left and she began to unpack and prepare for bed her thoughts became infected once more as the hissing gas lamps threw sinister shadows around the room, where before their glow had seemed cosy and welcoming. The unopened doors she had seen along the corridor threatened to contain hoards of devilish figures sent to spirit her south again and, twitching the drapes she imagined a gently swaying shrub to be Jean emerging from beneath a cover of vegetation, and so when rapid footsteps suddenly hammered up the stairs she moved instinctively towards the wardrobe to hide. The feet halted abruptly outside before a light tap heralded Harold's head which appeared round the door's edge grinning broadly, brown eyes twinkling with even more mischief than usual as the door swung open to reveal him tussling with an eager bundle of white fur.

"Sorry Bill, I forgot I have a present for you and he's just reminded me he doesn't want to wait in the basement until morning."

A small bedraggled face looked up at her, its head inclined while two wildly hairy eyebrows moved up and down alternately. As her surprise was replaced by pleasure an uncertain twitching began at the other end of the unkempt body which crescendoed to the entire rear being swept from side to side as she bent down to put her hand by his nose before moving to stroke him.

"To be honest I didn't know whether you'd like him or not," Harold confessed, irrepressible boyish exuberance bubbling from him, "it's been hanging around the garage ever since we got here and I asked William if it belonged to him, but he said 'no', it just seemed to have turned up a few weeks ago. William gives it some of his sandwich now and then, I think that's why it stayed. Anyway it nearly licked my hand off when I passed the time of day with it this morning so I decided maybe it wanted to come home. His eyebrows only stop moving when he goes to sleep and he's certainly the sorriest specimen of canine mongrelism I've ever seen, but then I'm not exactly pressed and neat most of the time, and you liked me!"

She smiled up at him, scooping the eager bundle into her arms, "He certainly walked into the right place didn't he. No collar? Nothing at all to say where he's from?"

"Nothing. I asked around because I didn't want to take him if he belonged to someone else, but his origins remain a complete mystery."

"So what shall we call him?"

"That's up to you old girl, if you want to keep him that is."

"Of course I want to keep him! I can't abandon something with such piteous devotion in its eyes, look he's licking my hand off too! I think we'll have to call him Lucky."

"Sounds appropriate," he said, watching her greedily as she fondled the dog's ears.

"You should go darling or George will join the nearest Hunger March."

"Yes, I know. I'll try not to disturb you when I come in …"

"… Will you?" she asked, a coquettish grin attempting to replace exhaustion on her face.

He growled at her through gritted teeth, the smile never leaving his eyes, before galloping down the stairs to join George. Relief surged through her, the demonstration of Harold's desire percolated into her sedated brain as the long hours of terror gave way to a feeling that together they would be invincible and the simple honesty of their fusion would overcome even Jean's most ingenious manipulations. She looked down at Lucky, he really was an incredibly scraggly dog, even if he'd been bathed and brushed she doubted his appearance would have been greatly improved. His eyes were his best feature especially when his tufty white eyebrows moved independently of each other but in perfect timing with his tail. She found a spare blanket in the cupboard and put it down by the side of the bed, the dog settled onto it without hesitation. "There," she said, "Lucky's bed."

Unwinding her hair, she took off her dress and slipped between the sheets. Leaving one arm drooped over the side of the bed she fell asleep with Lucky's tongue periodically wrapping itself around her middle finger.

* * *

Jean Nicholas Nicolai took the stairs two at a time, right fist clenched around the note with the offensive pair of words on it. Red faced from the unaccustomed exercise and emotion, he burst through the door of the Lanes' apartment causing them to jump from their dinner seats as he hastened into the room without hat, eyes staring and shaking with indignation. Waving the crumpled paper at Edward he shouted, "Did you know about this?"

Sarah blanched a little and lowered her eyes whilst Edward looked benignly confused. In an instant he assessed the scene and turned his full head of steam onto Sarah. "You know about this, you definitely know about this! She's my wife and she is to come back immediately. I married her under the laws of your country and I have a right to her remaining in my house," in his anger he seemed to be spitting the words at Sarah who flinched as he moved ever closer to her face. He had expected her to stand, using her height to humble him, but she dissolved into meekness which allowed the years of resentment he had felt for her previous haughtiness to build uncontrollably.

As the reason for this violent interruption to his evening meal filtered through to Edward he turned to the chastened woman questioningly, "Has Dorothy left?"

"I believe she may have done," Sarah said quietly, "she came here yesterday and confessed that she was not happy and that she intended to leave, but I have no idea where she has gone. She said that she would contact me after leaving London but she completely refused to tell me or her sisters where she was going because her mind was quite made up that she did not wish to return…"

"… did not wish to return, what unbridled foolishness is this? She has everything she wants. She doesn't work, she has the sort of life that families from my country, and many from yours, could only dream of. What is this spoilt childishness! Of course she must come back I have a right to her being here."

"Please calm down Jean."

A pervading stoical wisdom seemed to swirl around the elder man as he drew back his chair and got laboriously to his feet, but tonight its very reasonableness was teetering on the brink of infuriating Jean.

"We need to talk. Sarah, would you be kind enough to bring a couple of brandies into the study for us, and leave us to ourselves for a bit."

"Certainly Edward," she said almost bobbing a curtsy as Jean strode passed her, all her formidable character erased by his own fury.

* * *

"Please take a seat."

"I'd rather stand."

"As you wish," Edward said allowing his suddenly aching joints to be swaddled by the soft leather of his favourite smoking chair as Sarah scuttled in, setting a small silver tray with two large brandy glasses down on the table between the men, before scampering for the door, eyes never raised from the rug.

"I am deeply sorry that you have been caused such anguish," Edward offered after the first liquid mouthful had sent its glow through both of them. "It is important we discover why she has done this."

"It will be another man. She has the morals of a rabbit."

"I accept you're distressed, but I'm not convinced that's a fair appraisal of your wife," Edward cautioned only a shard away from testiness. "Clearly there are problems and we need to find a mutually acceptable solution."

"There is only one solution, namely that she has to return. By your own country's laws I have a right to her living in my house," Jean sneered, "Surely even you are not suggesting she's above the law!"

"Indeed our legal system may not be faultless, but we also have a law guaranteeing freedom of speech, and I think it's important for both of you to air your opinions and find a satisfactory resolution."

"Once she's back in my house I don't care how much she gabbles," Jean paced in front of the mantelpiece, while Edward noted that his friend's knuckles were outlined by the raised veins on his left hand as Jean seemed intent upon shattering the glass bowl clasped within it. "She has a legal duty to live with me and from now on she'll work as I say, eat as I say, even blink as I say, and any bastard brats she's carrying can be tossed into an orphanage."

"We don't yet know what her story is," Edward said quietly, "and there is nothing any of us can do until Sarah hears from her."

Throwing the remaining brandy roughly down his throat, Jean began walking from the room, "inform me immediately a letter arrives," he ordered, leaving every door wrenched open as he launched himself into the darkness and a chill rush of night air from the street made Edward shiver while the orderly piles of papers on his desk were blasted into disarray.

* * *

Jean did not walk directly home and the light drizzle which left him frosted in water droplets did nothing to quell the fiery rage that was restoked every time he thought of his wife's temerity or her uncle's ridiculous calls for patient reactions. The frenzy inside him dehumanised all the people involved, they were no longer beings who felt pain or pleasure as he did, or who, by their very kinship of species, deserved certain rights or considerations, they were vile defiling insects who should be splattered in the foul gutters that ran below the pavement he marched along. None of them deserved his mercy. The hours of walking and the clamorous voices within his brain solidified his anger into a white phosphorus of fiendish intent to pursue this alien family that was trying to amputate him from their midst, he would dog them until every one of the clan would beseech him for clemency as he trashed their lives, dragging them so low into the mud that the bog would swallow up their genteel pretences, removing them one by one in his righteous crusade.

The flickering street lamps were not sufficient to illuminate the purpose that etched itself into his face as he traipsed onwards in the anonymous company of the thousands of other souls who walked at night. Jean mingled among the widely spaced crocodile of veterans while working feverishly at hatching some nightmares of his own, only dropping into his bed shortly before the foggy sun crept up the sky when he slept from pure exhaustion.

In the morning he casually informed the tradesmen and his staff that his wife had gone to look after a sick relative. Whether they believed him, he cared not a jot.

* * *

The sun did not peep over the window sill on Dorothy's first morning at Brookside, the sky was draped in heavy grey clouds hanging so low they seemed about to engulf the chimney pots. The leaden mounds sat above the one road village encircling it with slight dampness but there was no harsh wind or rain to curtail her exploration of their new home. After Harold had shown her what was behind every door in the house, they meandered round the tangled flower beds to the end of the garden where clusters of trees and ferns slipped gently into the River Blackwater. Harold and George had rigged up a hammock which they presented to her as her "recovery area" and certainly the rustling plants and the slapping of the stream against its muddy banks offered a tranquillity that had been absent from her life for more time than she cared to think about.

"Sit in it Dorothy," George instructed, "it's perfectly safe, we tested it."

Wobbling into a seated position with Lucky on her lap, she was suddenly tossed backwards by Harold who launched himself into the netting sending the little dog's body into gripped-out spasms as the canine calculated whether it was safer to leap off or stay and growl at the tempestuous intruder.

"Hold it right there," George commanded, organising his Brownie Box, "this is an historic moment, you have to have pictures for when you're old and grey," he said before attempting to organise them into a variety of poses he deemed 'moody', 'romantic' or 'arty'.

"Madam," he simpered, mock bowing to Dorothy, "your official nuptials photographs will be delivered on my next visit, but now I must be off or Charlie will think I've stolen his car for good and he'll not manage to deliver your note to your aunt today."

Walking out of their private paradise, back through the house and waving energetically as George roared out of the crescent and onto the main road followed by a balloon of dust and grit, Dorothy finally got her first daylight view of her rural surroundings. The road sign adjacent to the house read, "World's End Lane."

"What a wonderful name, it's like something out of a book," she cried, looping her arm lazily through her 'husband's'. "And those sweets are such lurid colours we might be in a nursery rhyme!" she said pointing to the broad window of the sweet shop across the road where huge jars of red aniseed balls, black liquorish, orange barley sugars and yellow lemon sherbets jostled with other bottles of stripy humbugs and bright pink sticks of rock.

The sweetshop appeared dwarfed by the ancient timber-framed Sun Inn it was joined to. Three triangular rooves pierced the skyline and its black beams strutted across the broad white frontage. Slightly to the left of the inn, a hump-backed bridge spanned the stream truncating the area from the rest of the main street which continued into the heart of the village and was crowded by an impressive succession of small stores and workshops. Kelvedon Motor Works was also on this one street which constituted the main road through the county of Essex. Strolling onto the forecourt, Harold introduced 'Mrs Willand' to William before explaining to her how the air pumps worked, and what the virtues were of each of the six different brands of petrol on offer. The hard standing area already had three vehicles awaiting Harold's magical touch and a further one was mid-surgery in the workshop.

"Come round the back," he said, pulling her away from conversation with William, "I've got something to show you." He pointed to a collection of bits of metal and a bench suspended above three wheels.

"It's our car!" he said as she struggled to look impressed and worried she was failing horribly. "We've only got the tow truck and the Harley Davidson at the moment, although we can both ride on that of course …"

"I've never ridden a motorbike …"

"Nothing to it, just fling a leg over and off you go!"

"Said by someone who's clearly never worn a dress."

"Well, how *is* a lady meant to ride a motorbike then?"

"Side-saddle I imagine, like you ride a horse."

"Bill, if you insist on side-saddle, fair enough, but that's not what I'm talking about," he said with an air of barely repressed exasperation, "I'm building a car. Look, this is a two-stroke engine, this chain will drive the back wheel and I'm going to mount the seats above these two front wheels, and then the one at the back will steady it, and I'll make a nice rounded body from aluminium so it's light … I've even got the number plate for it organised, see WNK 23."

"You only need one vowel and it would be called The Wink!"

"Brilliant!" he said almost hopping from one leg to the other in his excitement, "The Wink it is! I can take you down to the shops and out on Sundays like your very own chauffeur."

"What about when it rains?"

"I can put a hood on it with a strap to pull over if you like," he said drawing thoughtfully on his pipe. "Or you could always put up your umbrella if it's not too windy."

As they continued to wander through the village arm in arm she was conscious that every set of eyes from every window was looking down on them, and she prayed that no one was questioning their masquerade of a married couple. Walking up the tree lined road towards the church of St. Mary the Virgin she looked in past the wooden gate along the winding path that led up to the porch, slanting rays carved their way through the leaves and the scene seemed as far removed from city life as it was possible to be, yet Dorothy felt on loan to this euphoria, as if she were attached to Kensington by a long spring that at any moment could ping shut and whisk her back once more.

* * *

Flo was cutting out pastry leaves and fixing them to the top of the meat pie she had just made. It had not been a good day, first Dorothy's letter had arrived and then her father had turned up without a word of warning and was threatening to stay several days, she wondered if there was a third horror waiting to land on her, everyone always said bad luck went in threes.

"Typical of 'er with all that luxury 'eaped on 'er 'ead to end up no better than a Whitechapel wench," Charles Terrill ranted. Flo was hoping she could drown him out by concentrating on her pie, but it wasn't working and she prayed his tirade would run out of steam.

"Thank goodness your mother's not still alive to witness the shame she's bringin' on the family. All that money and heducation just to run off with a fancy man!"

"Keep your voice down Dad, I don't want Vera to be hearin' you."

"You should make sure Vera forgets all about 'er. It's your job to protect 'er from bad influences."

"She's our sister, Dad," Flo said with a deep sigh.

"Not any more she ain't, not with the disgrace she's brought to our good name. I'll wager Thomas won't own 'aving 'er as a sister no more, 'e's got 'is reputation to consider. 'e'll be 'ead of the family when I'm gone and you should follow 'is lead my girl!"

"Seeing as we don't see 'im from one year's end to the next that could be a bit difficult," she said archly, sweeping the excess flour off the table and smacking her hands together loudly over the stone sink.

* * *

Hanover Mansions
39 Maddox Street
London
My Dear Dorothy,
It did not take long before the storm clouds gathered at our apartment after you left London. In fact, Jean was in such a rush to get through the door he nearly knocked poor Mary over as she was opening it for him.

Your uncle talked to Jean in his study and wonders if you would agree to return here to speak with him as Uncle Edward is concerned that without at least some explanation or attempt at a resolution, Jean may behave in an extreme and rash manner. I recognise that in your new found happiness this will be an unwelcome suggestion and I do not honestly know if I myself am truly suggesting it, or merely passing on a message.

If you do choose to return briefly to London we would try to ensure you were protected and not bullied in any way. Having said that, we would also not condemn you if you decided against this course.

Uncle Edward sends his love as do I,
Your Aunt Sarah

Sitting at the breakfast table, Dorothy passed the letter to Harold, she could imagine Aunt Sarah sitting at her writing desk agonising to ensure the perfect diplomatic turn of phrase so that whatever Dorothy's final decision she would never feel she had disappointed them.

Although Dorothy recognised she had been graciously offered the chance to evade the duty of speaking to the husband she had dumped so abruptly, the second paragraph of her Aunt's letter niggled around the edges of her conscience. Her uncle was enduringly unflappable, not given to dramatics in the way Charlie Willand or even her own father occasionally enjoyed if her sisters were to be believed. If Uncle Edward expressed concern at the notion of Jean's rash behaviour, it was a definite statement of inner dread; she imagined this lion of carefully considered logic being swamped by a tsunami of animosity which threatened to sweep him down to he knew not where. Although the request for intervention was put with feather-like gentleness its effect was to diminish the man, whom Dorothy had revered for decades, into an elderly, helpless shell, still calmly attempting reasoned discourse in a situation that required fieriness capable of vapourising the threats that were emasculating her uncle. Nevertheless, the realisation that she must return to fight her own battle was not swift. The creases in the letter became deeply worn as she re-read and re-folded the sheet dozens of times in repeated attempts to discover new meaning in its few paragraphs so she could avoid both a confrontation and the feeling that she was cutting her uncle and aunt adrift, leaving them to face any consequences of her decision alone.

* * *

Even from the first reading Harold could see that Dorothy was bothered by the letter, but he had sufficient sense to avoid offering any opinion on its contents. Claws of fear mauled him as he waged his own war against taking her in his arms and forcibly preventing her from ever going anywhere near Jean again. Once they had finally got away he had begun to relax and plan, yet one piece of paper threw everything into jeopardy. She had come to him against all odds and he had to trust she would remain. Feeling like a condemned man he stood up from the breakfast table, crammed his hat onto his head at its usual jaunty angle, kissed her on the cheek and strode down the street whistling on his way to the garage, a picture of the blithest spirit in Essex.

* * *

"If your father is being so kind as to offer to pick me up from the station, do you think there's any chance he might agree to wait outside?" she asked with deliberate slowness, aware of the Willand dislike for getting into situations likely to be devoid of any semblance of amusement. "I'd feel much safer knowing he was there and it would be harder for Jean to follow me than if I had to hail a cab."

"I'll come myself," Harold replied eagerly.

"No, I don't want him getting a glimpse of you and I need to know you're still safely waiting here for me, like a lucky charm."

"I'd feel safer if I was with you."

"I know, but I'd be more worried about you getting into trouble with Jean which would make me less attentive to ensuring Aunt Sarah and Uncle Edward are no longer being bothered by him."

"I'd still rather come myself, but I'll ask Dad if you insist. He'll probably bring Sis and George along to jolly things up a bit."

* * *

P.C. Pennings lived above Mr Nicolai's business premises in Gower Street with his wife and twin daughters. A solid six-footer who took the care of his neighbourhood seriously, he only released his playful side from beneath the heavy moustache after his uniform was hanging up, buttons and boots polished for the following day, and his daughters were in their nightgowns begging for a ride to bed on the back of their favourite 'bear'. The policeman was fond of his foreign neighbour whom he considered to be a great artist and also believed to be in possession of a phenomenal memory, not once did Mr Nicolai miss a birthday or an anniversary, on every occasion that marked the passing of years a small box, tied with an expansive ribbon would appear on the steps leading up to his flat and inside would be one of the Romanian's exquisite creations, which left the constable in a state of awe at the transformation of sugar and colouring into a floral scene, literally, too good to eat.

After several years of living in tranquil harmony with the successful business and its four industrious staff, P.C. Pennings was surprised to find Mr. Nicolai pacing up and down in front of the street door anxiously awaiting his return.

"Would it be possible to have a private word?"

"Certainly, please come up."

Startling his wife and daughters with his guest, he ushered his family out of the living room before settling the confectioner into a chair.

"How can I help you?"

"I'll come straight to the point," the smaller man said as the constable mused over possibilities that the landlord wanted to evict everyone from the premises and other such undesirable thoughts. "My wife left a few days ago, no explanation, and even her family claim not to know where she is," he twisted his hat in his hands before running on quickly before P.C. Pennings could interrupt with one of his sympathetic stock responses.

"She's arriving at her Aunt's residence on Wednesday afternoon, and I was thinking that if you were able to come along with me to this meeting it might encourage her to come home," his neighbour said in a tight controlled voice. "I'm aware that although she has violated my conjugal rights, I cannot restore these by the use of force, but Dorothy is a flighty young creature and has probably just run off because she wishes to coerce me into taking her on holiday or some such frippery, and I feel that if she were to see a figure of authority was involved it would sway her not only to be rational about this, but also to stop using her uncle and aunt to harbour a deserting wife, which in itself is something that one can go to the law for and take to court."

P.C. Pennings shifted his weight uneasily as he stood in front of the fireplace, it was always a bad idea, he felt, to get involved in domestic issues.

"Ahh, well, but …" he stammered, "You must realise that there's no way I can put her in handcuffs and bring her home, that has to be her choice."

"But she is breaking the law by breaking our marriage contract…"

"I'm certain this is a most distressing time..." the policeman began, trying a new tack whilst putting on his best condolence face, "but the force is strict about taking a softly, softly approach to domestic issues."

"But I have rights! We have a contract of marriage, and she has no grounds to abandon it."

"Indeed you could bring a private prosecution, but usually these things can be resolved by a chat between the parties concerned, we, in the police, would always want that avenue to be tried first before any official involvement."

"Yes indeed, I do understand," Mr Nicolai said dropping abruptly into a softer tone, "but if she fails to see sense and doesn't come home I will eventually need to undertake a suit of restitution for conjugal rights and, if it came to that then I at least need to have an address of where she is living so that I know where any demands can be sent to. This is all I'm asking for at the moment, just to know where my wife is residing. Perhaps I've been working too hard and haven't paid her as much attention as I should. If she were to come home the whole thing could be resolved and I would take her away for a few days and make a fuss of her. I would happily do all the talking, but as we've been good friends over the years I thought it would be acceptable to ask you to accompany me, no more than that, just to accompany me."

The idea of merely standing there and nodding occasionally began to seem so innocuous to P.C. Pennings that it appeared unnecessarily rude to refuse, and so without him quite knowing how, the arrangement was made that the constable, in full uniform, would go with Jean to the Lane's on the following Wednesday afternoon.

***

Wednesday dawned crisp and bright complete with a light frost dusting the spider's web outside her bedroom window, a robin warbled to a mate on the lawn and the first crocus buds appeared beneath the gnarled apple tree, all of which rather confused Dorothy because she was convinced that on a day when she had such an unpleasant task to undertake it should be grey and damp with gusts of freezing wind guaranteed to leave her looking as dishevelled outside as her brain felt her to be within. She dressed carefully in the plain green suit she had arrived in, her hair smoothed into place, her hat securely attached, and walked to the station with Harold.

"You can still change your mind if you don't want to go Bill," he said.

"You know full well I don't *want* to go, but I think I have a duty to do so."

She bought a second class ticket, Harold had been trying to insist on a first class one but she claimed it was an unnecessary extravagance. Slowly chugging through the villages on such a climatically cheerful morning she could almost pretend she was off on a pleasant jaunt. They stopped at country stations and more people clambered on and off as the day's trade in humans got underway. She watched the people, trying to gauge what each of them was doing, wondering if it was obvious from her appearance that she was on an disagreeable mission, and yet from looking at the other passengers she realised it was impossible to predict anything about their day or their problems or even much about their particular lifestyles other than was obvious from their clothes and the types of things they pulled out of their bags. No, she could be any young woman going up to the city for the day to meet a friend, nothing marked her out as being on an abhorrent assignment.

After almost an hour the train stopped abruptly, there was a signal that was red and it stayed red. Nothing happened for a very long time. It was curious to note how individuals reacted to this; children were still running up and down the corridors, the adults in the first five minutes continued as normal, then became slightly less chatty, then there were some voiced opinions on the state of rail travel and whether they would ever be underway again followed by a smattering of dry jokes. Eventually everything became completely quiet as people seemed to hold their breath as they waited for an explanation. Some forty minutes after the train had come to a standstill a guard entered their carriage and announced that there had been accident on a crossing just before Hatfield Peverel and it wasn't certain when the line would be clear again. A motor lorry had got its wheels stuck on a level crossing and a freight train had struck it, certainly there had been some serious damage and they could be in for a considerable delay, in fact there was even a possibility that the trains would not be able to run to London at all that day. The passengers were asked by the guard to remain seated whilst a decision was taken about whether it was necessary to get them off the train and move them back up the line.

Dorothy asked the conductor if Kelvedon village would now know that there had been a rail accident.

"They'll know all the way up the line very soon, we don't want any more trains coming down at the moment," the guard said stroking his goatee seriously.

"Will they know that it was a freight train that was involved in the accident rather than ours?"

"Can't say for sure, I would have thought so but you know how messages sometimes get jumbled."

There was nothing to do but to sit there and wait. She couldn't contact Charlie who was meeting her at Liverpool Street, she couldn't contact Jean, she couldn't contact Harold. She felt utterly frustrated. The three men involved could be guaranteed to have very different reactions. Harold would be worried silly and running around like an agitated blue bottle; Charlie would be concerned but would find something thoroughly enjoyable to do to pass the time, and Jean would think it was a conspiracy that she'd created to avoid meeting him.

An hour and a half later another guard appeared in their carriage and informed them that the line was clear above them and that they were going to be escorted a mile along the tracks to the nearest road where they would sort out transport. There certainly wouldn't be an afternoon train into Liverpool Street and even tomorrow's trains were looking dubious as the amount of wreckage to be removed from the site was considerable.

Tottering along the stony track in her heels, Dorothy noticed how quickly a crowd of normal people began to look like a herd of refugees. They trudged diligently until a young man appeared running towards them, tie flying behind him, waistcoat rent open, waving violently and Dorothy realised that the dark haired sprinter was none other than Harold.

"Crikey Bill, I was so worried it was your train that had crashed."

"Harold, you shouldn't have come shooting down here!"

"It's all right, I thought before I left, I didn't bring the bike as I knew your suit was far too smart for any side-saddle riding today," he said panting and grinning at the same time. "Anyway, with the tow truck I can take a few more of the walking stranded in the back. Hey Bill, at least it's not your fault you didn't get there ..."

"Harold, you could at least try not to look so ecstatic about the whole thing, there's a serious accident back there!"

They walked the final stretch down the track arm in arm with Dorothy realising that the brightness of the sky and the sound of the birds singing from the reeds edging the railway embankment was in perfect keeping with the day.

***

The maid had been given the afternoon off so it was Sarah herself who opened the door to a uniformed policeman and Jean. She withered at the sight of the officer, half closing the door to try and shield Edward from the sight as he peered into the hallway.

"She's not here. The train never arrived, you can check at Liverpool Street," she said tripping over her words to get the truth out. "We had word just ten minutes ago that there will be no further trains down the Eastern Line today."

As Sarah raised her pleading eyes to meet those of P.C. Pennings' she was surprised to see restrained nervousness transform itself into ill-concealed relief. "Indeed Madam, in that case there's no need for me to trouble you further. I'll leave your good selves and Mr. Nicolai to discuss how to proceed in private. Good afternoon to you," he said touching his hat to both parties as Sarah opened the door fully to usher Jean inside, correctly anticipating that it was only the constable's continuing presence in the building that was containing the jilted husband's verbal eruption and that, when it occurred, it would be much better if the front door was closed and the neighbours were deaf.

* * *

"I don't believe it! Where is she?" he screamed as soon as the street door thudded behind the retreating policeman's back. He began searching the living room and opening every door in the apartment, as Sarah followed, softly closing them, in an attempt to contain the noise of evolving savagery.

"There was a train accident on the line, Jean, there may be no trains for several days."

"But you have an address. You know where she is."

"No Jean, all we know is that she was coming from somewhere in Eastern England."

"This is ridiculous! I have a right to her return immediately," Jean's voice rose to a screech on the final word.

"Today's meeting could only ever have been one of reconciliation and discussion," Edward tried in tones Sarah thought he would have employed if cornered by a snarling dog. "She might not have agreed to return."

"I've done nothing wrong. I have a marriage contract with her, a right to her presence in my home. P.C. Pennings had no qualms about coming to explain her duties to her. She will return, she must, or I'll drag the tale of her filthy conduct through every London court."

"To what purpose Jean?"

"To show the world I've been wronged by your family. That your respectability is a sham and your ward in a faithless slut."

"You have no proof of that."

Sarah could see the vein that ran diagonally across Edward's forehead was beginning to pulsate alarmingly as he spoke, "my family has been consistently supportive of you, even in attempting to arrange today's meeting, but I'm not sure you can honestly argue Dorothy was receiving everything she might expect from a marriage."

"How dare you say that to me! You! With your wife from the slums and your pretence of a family. Should I too adopt an urchin to satisfy English hypocrisy? You forget, I'm a foreigner, I don't care a fig for your trumped up airs, I'll have her back or I'll make such a spectacle out of the righteous Edward Lane and his ward as will keep the gossiping classes riveted to the news stands for weeks."

A slim-fingered hand suddenly grasped Jean's arm, twirling him with surprising force before shoving him in the direction of the door.

"I may not be high class, but I'm not so base that I'd threaten an old man who's never done a bad act to anyone in his life."

Now she was pushing him hard as furious intent to remove him was surging through her slight tidy body. "Get out of here, do whatever you like but don't come near us again."

"Call your witch off, Edward!" he yelled as she wrenched him forward with unnatural strength born from the red haze of rage that hurtled down from the front of her brain, into her arms and legs. She had never experienced such violent emotion before, not over anything, but now she had one aim, to evict the tormenter from their area. Grabbing the door and flinging it wide she expelled him into the hallway slamming shut the heavy wooden slab without caring whether or not all Jean's fingers had escaped the doorframe.

**

An hour after Jean's eviction, Edward took a cab to his lawyers. He returned later to a barrage of apologies that were only muted when he grasped Sarah and placed her firmly in a chair, placing a glass of brandy in her hand – an act so unusual that it silenced her more effectively than any words.

"It would be utterly barbaric to ask Dorothy to return to that man. I want you to arrange for a letter to be sent instructing her not to come to London and not to let any of us have her address. Jean cannot file a petition for restitution of conjugal rights until he has made a written demand to Dorothy to return," Edward explained, "he cannot do that if he doesn't know where she is, and we cannot be put under duress to divulge her address to him or the police if we honestly don't know it."

She looked up at him meekly, still holding her glass exactly as it had been placed in her hand.

"Drink up," he said, smiling down at her, "I also paid a quick visit to Peggy before coming home just to warn her Jean had taken things badly. Number sixty-four's for sale and I think I should buy it."

"What for?" Sarah's face registered total confusion at the sudden change in the conversation.

"If Jean does manage to go to court and drag my name through the mud, the story will be far more titillating if we still live in Mayfair than if we're in Hammersmith. The house looks very pleasant and now Dorothy's not here it will be nice to be close to Peggy and Nora."

"Would you really not mind moving?"

"I think it's time for a change. I'm no longer working much but we can have all the post redirected to my office, no need to announce we're off, just do it quietly," he concluded raising his glass and gently clinking it with hers as she stared at him. He could see she couldn't quite believe she wasn't going to be burnt at the stake or at least put in the stocks. She had deflated since her surprising display of defiance and had the air of a dog anticipating a whipping, whereas now that he had investigated the legal situation and decided upon a defence, he felt positively elated. There would be no further emotional confrontations, no hurled insults, no wrestling of accusers out of the front door, they would simply remove themselves from the arena and hope that it put an end to any further dramas.

CHAPTER FIFTEEN

(Peggy: 34, Nora: 32)
Peggy gazed hungrily at the chubby baby resting contentedly against her sister's breast, Patrick Fry was one day old having arrived at the basement flat of 156a Sinclair Road after Nora had struggled through a seemingly interminable labour while her sisters and aunt downed endless cups of tea as they waited nervously in the kitchen. Now that it was over Peggy watched the two of them in their milky contentment and was relieved when the noise of the front door rescued her from her musing and Uncle Edward, or, in his present guise, the doctor, entered the room.

The move of Edward and Sarah into the same street as the sisters had coincided almost exactly with Nora's announcement that she should be eating for two, which had the immediate effect of reigniting Edward's medical interests. As Peggy helped her aunt and uncle to unpack he directed her to set aside all his tattered medical tomes from the 1870s placing them in pride of place on the polished cherry wood shelves in his new study. He spent days re-reading them before concluding that their information was out-dated and ordering every current paper and thesis on pregnancy and childbirth he could locate. Peggy and Aunt Sarah were sent out to post letters to some of his former colleagues for clarification on modern nutritional recommendations, and he urged the utmost attention to hygiene in all the family homes in case the expanding Nora should visit. Once or twice a day he would arrive at Nora's house and instruct her to put her feet up while he made her a cup of tea before regaling her with his latest nuggets of advice, telling her to take regular warm baths and make ample use of the relaxing properties of lavender water. Although Nora gently ridiculed all the fuss when she spoke to Peggy, her sister could tell she had loved every moment of it.

Their uncle did not restrict himself to digesting the notions propounded by the medical profession and would also devour books of folklore remedies, often arriving at Nora's door with small bottles of oils for her to rub into her stomach, or herbal ointments to massage into her swollen ankles.

Arthur confided to Wilfred and Peggy that the presence of a doctor in the family was a huge comfort, enabling him to abandon the whole baby business, leaving it to the women to fuss and coo, secure in the knowledge that Edward would be consulted about any important queries or problems. It wasn't that Arthur was uninterested in his offspring, he said, but rather he was quietly terrified of the entire production process after his initial input had been made. Peggy and Aunt Sarah were similarly relieved that Uncle Edward had taken control of the practicalities, but now that Patrick had finally arrived they were both so enchanted by him that it bordered on veneration.

***

Patrick smiled and gurgled happily from his first breath. Whether this was due to excess wind or the fact that he was continually doted on, was immaterial, wherever he went he melted hearts so that Peggy was happier if she cleaned her house with Patrick balancing on one bony hip, whilst Wilfred would smile and let the little lad grab his big rough finger as the baby lay down beside him on the sofa for a nap. Sybil would dash through the door after work not even bothering to remove her hat and coat before scooping up Pat and tossing him in the air or bouncing him on her knee making him giggle until Nora told her to stop because the baby was becoming dangerously red in the face. Aunt Sarah and Uncle Edward insisted on daily infant fixes and everyone encouraged Nora and Arthur to go out in the evenings so they could baby-sit.

"Sometimes I wonder if he'll know which of us are his parents," Nora said to her sister as, once again, the couple were being ushered out of their home on a Friday evening by a clucking Peggy who was on the brink of sulking at having not cuddled her nephew for nearly twenty-four hours.

* * *

Every day the Kelvedon postman delivered letters full of the minutia of Patrick's achievements; how much hair he had, how plump the creases around his knees and wrists were, how his gurgles were certain to turn into words far sooner than other babies, and how each of the letter-writers were secretly certain she was his favourite. The reams of enthusiasm streaming out of Hammersmith made Dorothy increasingly homesick. She yearned to see Patrick. The correspondence exchanged through Charlie's butchers' shops fed her craving for physical contact with all her family, but their obvious peaceful contentment made her even more reticent to divulge her whereabouts and possibly jeopardise their utopia by her own need for inclusion within the contented clan. Not that she was unhappy in Essex, far from it, but the wish to be reunited with her own family became stronger daily, seeming to increase tenfold when one of Peggy's letters mentioned that their uncle seemed unusually tired and that the family were joking the birth had taken more out of him than it had out of Nora; this piece of information was followed by a missive from her Aunt which announced her Uncle had been losing weight so she was trying to build him up by tempting him with all kinds of fattening delicacies. Such problematic droplets from the stream of life had probably been resolved by the time the stamp on the envelope had been processed, but Dorothy would read them over and over again wondering if they were the symptoms of something greater and whether her actions may have been in part to blame for any distress her uncle was suffering.

* * *

(Charlie: 53, Sis: 28)
It was a phone call that announced the next change in the family.

"You're going to have a brother or sister," Charlie balled down the line, ensuring the girl on the Kelvedon switchboard was fully acquainted with the proof of his continued virility.

"Oh god," Harold blurted honestly, before swiftly adding, "Congratulations. When's it due?"

"Beginning of July. Didn't tell you before because Sis was all superstitious about tempting fate before she was further along. We're motoring up to view a beach house at West Mersea on Saturday, come and meet us for lunch."

"We'd be delighted," Harold replied, inwardly recognising he was more in a state of disturbance than delight.

"Imagine if he starts having a whole brood of them," he moaned to Dorothy later, "My step-mother's younger than me and now I may have a clutch of siblings who won't be out of nappies until I'm about thirty-five! Why can't he grow old with dignity!"

"He's quite dignified in his own way," Dorothy laughed, "He's just completely unaware that he *is* growing old!"

George and Alma had also added to their family and spent regular weekends up at Kelvedon where Dorothy helped with baby Frank and Antonia who was toddling around putting everything into her mouth. Once the women were happily settled together, Harold was able to take George off to the garage or to play tennis, but on their jaunts although his friend had become noticeably happier he was also more preoccupied with fatherhood which left Harold worried that he was somehow missing out.

* * *

1923
(Dorothy: 28, Harold: 29)

"Dad just telephoned," Harold announced as Dorothy came in from the garden clutching a couple of lettuces. It was a promising spring day and they were intending to travel to the beach house for the Easter break, the lettuces made up part of the hamper they would be taking with them. "He says he has a surprise for you."

"Oh goodness, I hope it's nothing that's going to make me jump, did he give you any idea?"

"None at all, he just sounded extremely smug."

"Maybe you should call him back and get some more information."

"Why are you so worried? I'm sure it's nothing life threatening."

"It's just that I think I should be careful about surprises at the moment," she paused hoping he'd be just a little telepathic.

"Eh? Why?"

"Well, sometimes it's recommended …"

"What is?"

"I think I'm pregnant."

"Oh God, Bill, oh my God," she found herself plonked into a chair, the lettuces were removed from her grasp and Harold's actions resembled a punctured balloon as he darted around the kitchen depositing the green leaves in the sink before pulling an empty chair in front of her, lifting her legs onto it then sitting down, standing up, and finally sitting down again beside her. "You're not to move again, just leave everything to me."

"I think it will be a little tricky to stay here until Christmas," she ventured, "and there have been some children born over the centuries to women who didn't sit on a kitchen chair for the entire nine months."

But Harold wasn't listening, "Goodness Bill, do you think you were in this state when you came off the back of the bike?" he rushed on, referring to the time a month before when he had taken the hump-backed bridge rather enthusiastically, dumping his side-saddle passenger on the roadside while he hurtled onwards still chatting to her until the silence alerted him to his departed pillion rider and he sped back a couple of miles to find Dorothy hobbling home. "I might have damaged it!" he exclaimed, horror running across his features.

"It will probably be a good idea to avoid any further flying lessons for a while, but I don't think you should worry, I feel fine."

"Really darling?" he said, gently lifting her onto his knee and nuzzling her neck, a grin slowly taking over his face, his cheeks physically incapable of lifting any higher, "Whatever surprise Dad has, we definitely have a better one!"

* * *

Charlie left his spherical wife in the front seat of the car whilst he hurried to help Arthur load luggage before installing the family of three on the back seat. He wanted to ensure they arrived at West Mersea before Harold so Nora and Patrick would be playing on the sand when Dorothy walked round the corner of the beach house. He had it all planned down to the last detail. Charlie knew how much Dorothy wanted to see her new nephew and the fact that he had secretly orchestrated a whole weekend together gave him the warm fuzzy feeling he so enjoyed when he knew he was about to receive copious amounts of adoration for his actions. He anticipated that a delighted Dorothy might also engineer a thaw in Harold's rather frosty reception towards his forthcoming sibling, so that father and son could revert to the easy relationship that had been flourishing pleasantly since the purchase of Brookside and the garage.

In Charlie's opinion the beach house was the perfect venue for tranquil reconciliation, so long as the weather held. The timber cabin contained four adequate sleeping areas and a broad covered veranda with rocking chairs looking across the beach to the endless glistening sea. Early risers could sit and watch the sun stretch itself over the horizon, spilling orange over the blue-grey water until the rays crept across the bubbly black seaweed, tiptoed over the sand, inched over the wooden lip, covered one floorboard at a time until it clambered up the legs of the morning spectators, heralding another day of salty fresh air which would leave them all with tight faces and weary limbs when they dropped beneath their blankets and were lulled into slumber by the rhythmic crash of waves on the shingle followed by the long hiss of tiny stones being pulled back into the ocean before the surf sprawled itself across the shore once again.

* * *

"She must come back to London," Charlie said to Edward. He had walked down the street to the Lane's house for an impromptu visit the minute Patrick had been swept into his squabbling aunts' arms and Arthur had started unloading sandy luggage onto the pavement. "They don't even have flushing lavatories and bathrooms there, let alone modern medical care. My wife's having the best available and I want the same for Dorothy."

"I couldn't agree more," Edward replied, appearing jubilant at the news. "Mortality rates for first pregnancies are far higher, I will write to her immediately suggesting she live here for the last two months of her pregnancy so that she is well rested before her confinement. We've had no further trouble from her husband and there are enough of us here to keep her safe and protected."

Judiciously soliciting advice on some of Sis's childbirth queries, Charlie left half an hour later happy that his grandchild would be delivered in a proper metropolis manner. Climbing into the Humber he reflected upon how well Edward Lane had looked, almost as if he'd just returned from a turn of duty in India, which was curious considering how Nora had been fretting that he had not been himself since the New Year.

* * *

Spring 1923
(Aunt Sarah: 59, Uncle Edward:73)

The promise of Dorothy's return to London was a gleaming bright spot on a horizon Edward knew was shrinking. The increasing weakness and nausea he felt had been joined by a pain on the right side of his abdomen and the 'healthy tan' that Charlie noted at Easter became tinged with orange as spring wore on. Edward knew it was time to consult some of his former colleagues but before he tackled the truth of what was happening inside him, he was determined to put his own house in order. Telling Sarah he was going to collect the post from his office, he returned more than two hours later than normal to find her nervously pacing the hallway waiting for his return.

"I was so worried you'd been taken ill," she said, her fearful eyes meeting his as he gripped the hall dresser with one hand and lowered himself onto one knee.

"Oh you are! Let me help you to bed, oh you should have let me go instead! It's far too cold today..." she cried in panic, but he continued to look steadily at her, grasping the hands she offered to help him up and pulling her down in front of him, as he tried to force her hysteria to subside with his calm eyes and the whisper of a smile emerging from his beard.

Putting his right hand into his waistcoat pocket he withdrew a small box and opened it to reveal an opal in an oval setting surrounded by a narrow rope of silver, the three strands of which led down to mould themselves into the shank of a ring.

"You have cared for me for almost thirty years. You have been my housekeeper and, when times were hard, you have undertaken even more domestic duties than you had at Green Street, yet you never complained and you have always been a loyal and exemplary companion and, to be honest, my very best friend," he momentarily dropped his eyes from hers, trying to compose himself and edge away from detonating with the emotion he felt.

"You put on that gold band when you moved into Maddox Street and you have been the perfect partner ever since," he paused again, swallowing deeply to keep his composure. "I have chosen this opal for you because it is said to be the stone of hope, happiness and truth – all the things you have given to me – and I would like you will wear it beside the yellow band and consent to become my wife."

Holding up his hand to stem her interruption he continued, "I have made enquiries and we could go to the registrar's office tomorrow. I want to formalise this Sarah, I am a doctor and I know I am not in the best of health, please agree to marry me, my dear."

On her knees, yet held ramrod straight by her undergarments, Sarah's damp cheeks and heaving chest gave away what her deportment never would. Through the haze of tears they looked at each other, Edward searched the face of his life-long non-wife, for years they had lived their subterfuge where every touch was clouded by the ambiguity of play acting, but now he could see the relief flowing from her that finally the charade was over and beneath it he discovered a love more guileless and true than he had ever dared believe in. She reached out her small hand, unusually small for such a tall woman, the skin no longer smooth or white and the fingers beginning to bulge at the knuckles and joints with the onset of arthritis, but Edward willingly lent in to her touch as she stroked his cheek, both of them unabashed for the first time in three long decades. Holding his eyes with hers in a moment of unparalleled tenderness she said, "Yes."

***

On July the sixth Charlie's daughter, Madeline, slid into the world. Three weeks later Edward Lane was fighting for his life as some of the capital's best surgeons collaborated in a high risk operation to remove the cancerous growth that had engulfed his liver.

As the fog of morphine-induced dreams parted, Edward found Dorothy in a veiled hat, sitting beside his hospital bed lightly holding his hand. He could not be sure she was real, the borders between hallucination and solid matter were not yet definable, but the individual he believed to be next to him appeared subtly different with the roundness of pregnancy glowing through her usually sculpted cheekbones and wearing clothes he had not seen before.

"Dorothy?"

"Please don't speak; you must use all your energy to get well."

A weary twitch at the sides of his lips as his eyelids drooped back down with the exhaustion of sudden effort, was all that showed of the elation that was feeding itself through his veins and arteries, fattening his will to fight back to health and return to Sinclair Road with Dorothy and Sarah, relishing spending whatever time remained to him wrapped in their care and company.

***

While Dorothy visited the hospital and attempted to sooth her aunt's nerves, Harold had visited his new sister for the first time.

"Is she pretty?" Dorothy asked when the couple met up at Nora's house that evening.

"She still looks a bit squashed," he said handing Arthur one of the bottles of beer he had brought round with him to wet the baby's head. "She's the spitting image of her mother, I can't see any of the old man in her yet, not that I said so." He chinked glass with his brother-in-law "It's going to be weird having a sister and a child of my own who are the same age."

The yank back towards London was becoming overwhelming on Dorothy and her talk with Harold was regularly punctuated with lines that began "if I hadn't left …" and wound their way through Uncle Edward not having endured stressful encounters with Jean, not having moved house suddenly at an advanced age, and concluded with "maybe he wouldn't have become ill." Harold sat tight-lipped throughout these episodes feeling as if her guilt was being slightly off-loaded onto his lap. He was grateful whenever Aunt Sarah rebuked her for being "fanciful" and claimed her condition made her in a heightened emotional state, yet irrespective of whether her decisions were hormonally charged, she was intent upon remaining in London to help with Edward's care and there was not much Harold could say against it that did not sound extremely petulant.

Dorothy's decision left everyone content except him. Harold found Brookside too big and the days too long without her, he began to leave William in sole charge of the garage on Saturdays so he could take the last train down to London on Friday evening not returning again until Monday morning. He dedicated his solitary hours to dragging his personal part of the country firmly into the twenty-first century, building a generator and startling his neighbours with the first electric lights in the village. Within weeks the house had lost the flickering glow of gas and the unofficial town criers were put into a frenzy of chattering activity as a lorry unloaded a shiny American Frigidaire, which was carefully manhandled into the pantry, and then the next day Harold was gratified by the reports of the awe struck neighbours who had seen Mr Willand and William enjoying lemonade in the garden from a jug whose sides ran with cool condensation even though the day was unusually warm.

Harold had applied to the post office for a radio license before Dorothy went to London and his set was soon known to work better than anybody else's for miles around. There wasn't a person in the village who didn't acknowledge that where new inventions were concerned, Mr Willand was the man to answer all questions. More items were ordered up from London and the station porter was surprised one morning to be charged with unloading a matching porcelain bath, wash basin, lavatory and water tank to be delivered to Brookside for Harold's most ambitious project that left the outside soil closet and tin bath redundant.

With Dorothy gone and his family in London, there was even time for Harold to finish The Wink. Although it was late November when it enjoyed its first proper test run and frigid air whistled past Harold's goggle-clad eyes, he refused to take the train down to London that weekend preferring instead to show Dorothy at least one of the fruits of his industry in the hope it might hurry her into giving birth so she could be home in time for Christmas. Manoeuvring the swollen belly into a bucket seat was cumbersome but Harold was determined Dorothy should not shirk from the full motoring pleasure however sizeable she was. Edward and Sarah watched from their front window as every resident member of the Terrill clan was given a turn, before the time came, far too soon, for the mercurial man to leave Sinclair Road again so its occupants could slow their heart rates and their living speed as Harold and The Wink trailed northwards behind Charlie's gleaming Humber, a tiny ugly duckling behind a statuesque swan, yet constructed with such obvious quirky attitude that it left smiles in its wake along every mile of the journey home.

* * *

None of Harold's household improvements or innovations succeeded in hurrying up Dorothy's gestational period and it wasn't until the fifteenth of December, almost exactly a year after the arrival of Patrick, that the pains of labour ripped through her. For hour after hour she gripped and bit her pillow until the cover was torn and frayed, the feathers beginning to escape through the many nicks in the fabric. Moaning through waves of agony, vowing never to become pregnant again if God or the doctors or nurses or anyone at all with the power to keep her alive, allowed her to survive, she finally felt the need to push.

Crumpled, with a few residual white slimy patches, a tiny girl wrapped in a maternity home towel was placed into Dorothy's arms. From the moment her eyes locked onto the downy head, miniature mouth and stiffly moving fingers, Dorothy knew she had become capable of murder. A feral instinct to protect her child snapped into place and with terrifying immediacy she recognised that all her rational arguments, such as that it was never acceptable or necessary to use violence against another person, had been wiped out by the first gasping cry of her daughter and there were no lengths from which she would flinch in her compulsion to keep her child safe from even the mildest harm. Prior to that moment she had believed it would be impossible for her to love anyone more than she loved Harold, yet in one silent instant she discovered a love so reckless in its devotion that it trampled qualities of restraint and reason in its stampede of adoration. Assailed by an emotion so brutally base in its reaction to any hindrance, Dorothy realised she could never again hoodwink herself that she was a rational individual; she was an animal, just as wildly driven by instinct as anything that lived in the African savannah, and the intense feelings she had labelled love in her previous childless life were as far removed from her current experience as a child's crude drawing of a rose is from the velvet petals, drowning perfume, godlike symmetry and brutal thorns of the real thing.

* * *

The traditional three week rest in the maternity home entailed Christmas had to come to Dorothy. Although Sarah had planned that each of the family should visit at specific hours, Matron melted from the "two-visitors-at-a-time" rule under the combined charm offensives of Harold and Charlie, allowing the entire Terrill and Willand clans into the ward after church on Christmas morning. Edward sat in the single chair provided by the side of Dorothy's bed while the rest of them milled about, Pat and Madeline crawled and climbed around Sybil, while baby Nancy slept in her cot; Sis and Nora swapped infant tales both lecturing Dorothy on what was to come; Arthur, Wilfred and Harold made clandestine plans to sidle off down to the pub directly they were released from hospital visiting, which Sarah was pretending not to hear. It was all too beautiful for her to scold the men, she thought as she looked on in a benign state of disbelief that she, who had no children of her own, could have become the de facto matriarch of such a robust and noisy crowd. Only one hint of discord threatened the festive mood.

"Hey Granddad," Harold hollered across the room at his father, "any clothes my sister grows out of can be passed in our direction."

"Never! Never! Call me that!" brilliant red coursing up the old man's neck and bursting across his face, his voice shaking with genuine anger. "Your offspring may call me Uncle Charlie."

CHAPTER SIXTEEN

1924
(Dorothy: 29, Aunt Sarah: 60, Uncle Edward:74)
Sarah knew that Edward's medical friends were impotent as the disease ravaged its way through his body for a second time. She arranged for his grandiose carved wooden bed to be carefully manoeuvred downstairs, into the front room so that his ever shrinking body could lie looking out at the June sunshine. Surrounded by pillows that propped him up, Edward was initially able to enjoy short conversations with his cousin George Cochran Kerr, who came over from the Isle of Sheppey twice a week. The artist's soft affection seemed to encircle his dying cousin and draw him gently back towards the family of Lanes and Drysdales who, in the past had skewed themselves elegantly sideways, turning away from the man who shunned high society and had demonstrated his preference for the company of a housemaid and her kinsfolk. Yet now, as the closing acts were being played out, those same cousins, nieces and nephews employed George to convey their sympathy and ensure history's final record would show Edward to be an acknowledged member of their illustrious clan. It was a situation that rent Sarah in two, her philanthropic side was relieved Edward's family were finally forced to acknowledge his many qualities, while the rest of her crawled with resentment that at the end these well shod bigots were trying to assuage their guilt by repossessing her husband.

George lived with his unmarried third daughter, Phillipa, who would usually accompany him to Hammersmith. Sarah liked Phillipa who had herself experienced the slights a proud family would unconsciously heap upon any who seemed not to exactly conform to the ancestral norm. Phillipa was the sole female from Edward's family whom Sarah would class as a genuine friend.

"When it happens, I wish we could just have a quiet ceremony, a private funeral, at the church across the road. It would be much the best don't you think?" Sarah said as they sat drinking tea.

"But St George's was your parish until eighteen months ago, I'm sure Reverent Thicknesse would wish to conduct the ceremony," Phillipa replied gently.

"It's so large and grand," Sarah said with the tinge of a whine, knowing she wanted to squirm away from Mayfair and the unattainable expectations it stood for.

"Yes, but so is your Edward, a man of grand courage and principle," Phillipa argued reaching out gently to take Sarah's brown spotted hand in her own, "he so loved the choir there, and Dr Jolley's Handel recitals."

"Dr. Jolley always makes me jump out of my skin when he suddenly blasts away at that organ," Sarah countered weakly, still trying to avoid the inevitable.

"Wherever it is, it will be a heart wrenching couple of hours, especially for you, but Edward should have the honour of being attended by all his family, his friends and the people from his club. They need to pay their respects, particularly the ones who have guilt niggling at them for past behaviour."

"Leave them to feel contrite, it will do them good!"

Phillipa smiled, "If I were you, I'd feel the same, but what would Edward think?"

"He'd hate the idea of anyone being uncomfortable on his account," she said wearily acknowledging she was losing to the younger woman's logic, "You know that."

"Well then," and the venue was settled.

* * *

Days crawled into weeks and Sarah took to sleeping on the couch in the front room so she could be beside Edward constantly to attend to his needs around the clock. After thirty years of their own private chambers, there was now a fierce impulse in her to not squander the time they could be together. Decades of fully clothed cohabitation, where the only bare flesh showing were hands and face, had died as she washed and clothed him, roundly refusing to let anyone enter the sick room until she had restored the splendour of her weakening lion by a full valetting every morning. As his need to sleep increased and even her voice failed to rouse him, she dared to lie beside him, and take his fading body into her arms where she told him a lifetime's worth of things that the propriety of daily living had kept stoppled.

"I'm frightened, I don't know who I'll be without you ... you've always made me more than I was ... you never seemed to see my uniform, just looked straight through it and found the very best I could be ... dragging it out ... showing it to other people ... forcing me not to be ashamed. I don't know why you were so kind to me ... how you knew, without me ever saying ... my sisters' lives terrified me ... how you knew it would work ... never even acknowledging the possibility that I would let you down." Her face lay on the pillow beside Edward's, her breath so close it warmed his ear, but beneath her cheek the pillow was sodden as her tears rolled across the bridge of her nose, joining the stream from the other eye while her confessional poured out. "I don't know what I will be now. I'm not going to be grand Mrs Lane but I'm not fatherless little Sarah Holloway either ... Who am I? ... I know it's selfish of me, but I so want you to stay ... You've been my rock, my voice of reason ... I don't know if I'll still be able to hear you ... I'll be adrift ... Try to still speak to me, I know you'd think I'm silly, but if it's possible afterwards, please still speak to me."

And in his lucid moments Edward would tell her about his childhood, the things he'd done of which he wasn't proud, the feelings he'd struggled with and others he'd failed to fight against. There were no longer any taboo subjects between them or anything that was not accepted, she now knew all his history as he knew hers, and there was nothing about him she did not love. As they talked, tranquillity wrapped itself around the sick room and she recognised that the final unqualified honesty only made their bond more fused than ever before.

* * *

Humid heat hung in the air and even with the bottom of the wide sash window open there was insufficient breeze to cool her patient. Hours of cold compresses were punctuated by Edward's skeletal remains suddenly shuddering, and then Sarah would hold him to her until the shaking passed. His breathing began to be laboured and at times it was so slow she panicked that she had lost him until a rasping gasp for oxygen prompted her back to changing the frigid cloths on his forehead and gave her a partial respite from the fear that had just gripped her, until the next time.

Nora's head appeared around the door after lunch. "How is he?"

"Not good, the heat seems to be sapping his last ounce of strength."

"You look like a wind-blown scarecrow, let me take over for a while so you can 'ave a wash and tidy and a bite."

Putting her hand to her hair Sarah discovered knotty wisps sticking out in odd places and the side on which she'd lain whilst holding Edward was a mass of damp rubbed nodules. She became suddenly conscious of how sticky her body felt beneath her clothes, realising that Nora's stark evaluation was probably a gross understatement of her dishevelled appearance. She hesitated, squeezing out the next piece of flannel to be applied to Edward's brow. Removing the old cloth, she leant down and tenderly kissed his forehead, sealing the endearment with the fresh flannel.

"I won't be long," she whispered before moving swiftly towards the door, touching Nora's arm in thanks on her way out.

* * *.

Nora plumped the cushions on the couch and folded up the blanket which had remained a regular feature in the sickbay despite the onset of the warm weather; she fetched fresh cold water from the kitchen and drew most of the curtains to keep the afternoon sun from burning into the room, she pulled out a duster and began to clean each of the framed photographs, books and medical paraphernalia that cluttered every surface. Looking round at the bed her legs urged her to walk towards the prone form to check, he seemed so still, and as she stood looking down, she knew she would not find a pulse. He had slipped away so quietly that Nora felt cheated out of telling him how much she would miss him.

* * *

Dorothy stepped out of the car and held her hand out for her aunt. They waited beside the obelisk for Nora, Arthur, Sybil, Peggy and Wilfred to hurry down the street towards them before beginning to climb the three stone steps and pass between the towering Corinthian columns onto the sunlit portico as the church bell tolled ponderously. Groups of mourners spoke together in hushed tones, the men all sporting immaculately pressed black suits, flawless wing-collar shirts and black shoes whose mirror shine was undisturbed by wrinkles of wear; the women's outfits, although suitably austere in colour, displayed the plumage of their class in black mink stoles and understated strings of heavy pearls. Dorothy could not shy away from the stark reality that the sea of affluence was interrupted by one puddle of flotsam; her sisters moved forward hesitantly, resplendent in their Sunday best, yet the wax they had rubbed into their boots was incapable of disguising some of the deeper scuff marks, and their hastily dyed black dresses were demurely covered by dark crocheted shawls. Arthur and Wilfred had both taken trouble to slick back their hair, and Nora had sewn black bands around their hats, Dorothy could see their suits had been freshly brushed to remove any mud but they stood awkwardly with their wives watching the ebb and flow of beautiful people. The people in front of them were all so sure of their next move and their natural right to be there.

The figures of George and Phillipa broke free from one of the clusters and hurried towards them before leading Dorothy and her aunt through the dark wooden doors into the belly of St George's. As the church quietened and the last of the attendees took their seats, the pallbearers shouldered their load, eased their way up the steps and glided passed the waiting family. George took Aunt Sarah's arm without her seeming to notice him but at the softest tug the veiled form, clad in a plain black woollen dress and crepe bonnet, moved slowly down the aisle behind the body of her husband leaving Phillipa and Dorothy to process behind them tailed by an assortment of relatives Dorothy had scant recollection of ever meeting. On either side of the main aisle sat the shiny penguins and their mates, while Nora and the other waifs and strays had slunk to the side of the church before the arrival of the pall bearers so that Dorothy and Aunt Sarah remained the solitary blots beneath the gaze of the great and the good whose clipped vowel sounds spread out above them, and pressed their bowed heads further down.

A solemn tenor slowly built his voice to fill the church, urging "comfort ye my people", until the end of his consummate rendition was demolished by the sharp click of the door latch heralding the arrival of the unfashionably late. All penguins kept their heads locked forward, their ears sufficiently well bred to improvise deafness at any immodest sound, only Dorothy turned her neck ever so slightly to the right, skating her eyes to their furthest corners to catch the merest glimpse of her husband and a policeman moving stealthily towards the back row of pews.

"And now, Lord, what is my hope ..." Reverent Thicknesse's incantation battered her, all she wanted to do was run, yet she was bordered by priest and coffin in front, Aunt Sarah and a pew-full of Edward's family to her left, a further army of gracious penitents to her right, and Jean with his policeman behind her; she was ensnared by a Trojan horse of ululates. Sobs began to surge up her throat. They had nothing to do with the dead man in front of her.

"...We shall not all sleep, but we shall all be changed, in a moment, in the twinkling of an eye, at the last trump ..."

She saw her home blackened by gossip, Harold's business ruined by slurs, and her beautiful baby daughter slapped down by a world obsessed with legitimacy, as the towering malevolence of Jean dismantled and destroyed the castle of happiness she had created.

"Lord, have mercy upon us.
Christ, have mercy upon us.
Lord, have mercy upon us."

Should she go with him, refuse to divulge her address and by her silence protect Harold and Nancy? But how would they be protected? A child without a mother. Harold on his own in rural Essex. Her mind was unstrung, incapable of following the service, she no longer cared how her convulsed body appeared to the penguins, and her aunt seemed insensible, operating in a separate world somewhere inhabited only by her grief and fear at losing Uncle Edward. Encased within her personal bubble of horror Dorothy found herself ushered back down the aisle behind the coffin as it began its final journey towards Brompton Cemetery.

* * *

As Sarah paused at the church door while George spoke to some of the mourners, her hand was suddenly seized and pressed by an ancient crone, before being let go as the crooked elderly lady moved silently on. Sarah watched the bent form hobble painfully down the steps, sluggishly realising it was her former maid from Maddox Street, Katherine Jones. Concerned at not having spoken to Miss Jones, she almost missed the significance of the soft, almost childlike, hand that next grasped hers.

"I saw it in *The Times*," he said before turning to the muted Dorothy, "We'll wait at the far end until you're ready."

"We must follow the hearse," Sarah said, comprehension that these men intended to interrupt Edward's rite of passage struggled up through the blankets of loss which kept her thoughts smothered and unclear.

"It won't take long," he stated, moving sideways.

* * *

Jean Nicolas Nicolai glowed with triumphal exaltation as he entered his workplace, the day's copy of *The Times* firmly anchored beneath his left armpit. Humming as he constructed some of his most exquisite decorations, he even attempted a few light hearted jokes with his incredulous staff. Finally all the months of presents and kindnesses to his upstairs neighbours were about to pay dividends.

Since the incident at Maddox Street, P.C. Pennings had not appeared as enthusiastic about the little packages his neighbour left, but the lack of vocalised appreciation did not lead Jean to cut down on the frequency of his gifts, far from it, with each cake and posy he knew the policeman's neck was settling itself further into his noose. Now the hunt was coming to an end, and he was ready to pull the rope around both his wife and the constable inescapably tight.

Jean accosted his quarry as P.C. Pennings strode for the front door that evening.

"The task we started over a year ago can now be completed," he crowed jabbing at the newspaper obituary as the moustache of his accomplice sank ever lower with his down turned lips.

"Dorothy will definitely be attending, so there will be none of the problems we encountered last time."

"But Sir, you cannot be intending to go there, when the family is grieving and all, it wouldn't be right!" the constable said nervously scanning the report. "Perhaps you could leave a letter with the verger to pass onto your wife …"

"No indeed," the confectioner interjected with a laugh, "she's far too slippery for that, it has to be done in person. I'm sure your superiors would agree it would be unwise to let her slip through the net a second time."

"My superiors?" the constable repeated, his voice rising a little higher and his hands beginning to clasp and unclasp rhythmically behind his broad back.

"Of course, I'm sure the force likes to see all lines of enquiry followed to their conclusion and a result achieved," Jean reasoned

"But it's a funeral … at St George's! Mayfair! We can't go barging in there!"

"The deceased is effectively my father-in-law, I have every right to be there," Jean said tartly before honeying his tone in response to the waves of horror that were crossing his victim's face, "there will be nothing unseemly, we will just ask Dorothy for her current address so that our business together can be resolved. Nothing dramatic. As before, you will only be present to explain her situation to her, as a man of authority, a representative of the law whom she will respect."

"I may have other duties that day," P.C. Pennings offered lamely.

"I'm sure if I came down to the station and explained how …"

But the policeman held up his hand, interrupting Jean's tendrils of bindweed, "That won't be necessary, I'll speak to my colleagues," he said abruptly before stomping up his stairs and slamming the upstairs door.

* * *

Forty minutes before the funeral P.C. Pennings was still skulking behind a stack of files on his table, hoping his unpleasant conundrum would evaporate if he did nothing, but not having quite sufficient confidence that Mr. Nicolai wouldn't arrive and speak to his boss to risk leaving the police station.

A familiar East European accent at the front desk filtered through to the office and sent a violent electrical charge through his body, jolting him upright, striking his hat onto his head, whipping him out into the lobby where he spattered the clerk with information that he had this case "under control" and marched forth with his adversary, a condemned man whichever direction he chose.

* * *

As the gathering began to thin, Dorothy stood by the doors flicking her eyes at Jean, as he lounged against one of the great pillars and watched the tide of mourners.

"Do you want us to stay?" Nora whispered as she came up behind her.

"No, more of us will only further incense him."

Nora squeezed her arm before moving towards Peggy and Sybil, drawing her shawl tightly around her as if suddenly chilled, looking back briefly as they turned towards the bus stop.

Aunt Sarah was talking to Reverend Thicknesse while the remaining family who were invited to the interment stood in clusters around the cars. Dorothy moved forward slowly unable to look at either of the men, her blinded gaze was fixed upon the stone paving slabs as she arrived silently before them.

"We require your correct address," Jean said, stiffly as it became obvious she was not going to speak. "I have a legal right to know where my wife resides."

"It's just for paperwork," the constable prompted in a tone she recognised as one adults used to pacify small children.

"Paperwork!" she thought, "that would never satisfy Jean."

"You have a marriage contract with me," a bullying tone was creeping into Jean's voice. She knew her drooping form and muteness would be frustrating him and that this would make him even more dangerous and unpredictable but her voice seemed to be floating a couple of feet above her head and she was unable to reach it, her lips and tongue were paralysed, incapable of helping her in any way.

"Why would you refuse your address unless of course you have committed worse crimes than desertion," he stopped, studying her posture, "like bigamy."

She sensed the policeman stiffen, waking up to fresh criminal ideas.

"The constable must ensure you have not committed bigamy to disguise the birth of your illegitimate child," she couldn't stop it, she must have twitched, he knew instantly that he had hit the bull's eye.

"Whore!" he shrieked, "So where is your bastard child who will grow up as low and vile as its mother?"

A primordial sound dragged itself from her guts, echoing round the columns and striking at the hearts of the congregants who still stood there, "Noooooo". Every eye was magnetised towards them, she was aware that the whole portico seemed to be waiting, transfixed by the ghastly sight of her ineffectual writhing body pinned through its abdomen onto the great stone floor.

But Jean seemed unaware of the stares, he shook off the policeman's restraining hand continuing to scream as she cringed before him, the violence of victory feeding his fury so the observing crowd was obsolete in the face of his divine anger.

* * *

Shrouded in black, her chest slowly swelled, more and more, lungs filled to the brim, until a controlled stream of air was vented in a long tedious sigh which brought her veiled head upright, her eyes focusing for the first time in days as inescapable obligation forced her limbs to sweep across the portico, until she stopped in front of the roaring conqueror. Inclining her head towards P.C. Pennings, her low voice contrasting with Jean's shrillness, she asked him with if he would be kind enough to take Dorothy to the other side of the porch so she could speak privately to Mr. Nicolai. The constable gathered up his charge with evident concern, asking if Dorothy would allow him to get her a glass of water or a chair as the pair left Sarah looking through her netting into two exultant blazing eyes.

"Only a man of the cruellest nature would defile a friend's funeral in this way," she began as Jean lapsed into Romanian insults still radiating power and confidence. "But your unpleasant plans to ruin Dorothy fail to take certain changes into account."

"Oh really!" he mocked. "Don't even attempt foiling me Mrs. Lane, you haven't the wit."

"Doubtless I have not because, as you remarked at our last meeting, I am merely 'from the slums', but that is exactly the point Mr. Nicolai, whilst Edward was alive I would have done anything to protect him and the name he held so dear, now I have nothing left to protect except Dorothy, and her needs are very different from my husband's."

"I have a right to know my wife's address," he said labouring every syllable, "once I have that I believe it is my duty to ensure the local population knows what a harlot they have in their midst."

"If you were to attempt to do any such thing, I would be compelled to advise my niece to cite you for divorce immediately for non-consummation of marriage due to your homosexuality."

"Slander!"

"Prove it! No children for seven years of marriage. Only deciding to take a wife when your position in England left you in grave danger; a peculiar courtship where you were more interested in spending time with my husband than your fiancée …"

"You wouldn't dare!"

"I have nothing to lose. You, on the other hand, have everything. Do you honestly believe your business would survive such a scandal?"

"You cannot threaten me!" he said, flecks of spume forming at the corners of his lips as his face passed from deep pink to magenta.

"But you are threatening my niece," she replied quietly. "Why were you such a fool? I truly believed you would imitate Edward and be kind to Dorothy. I thought you respected him, aspired to be like him, I thought there was a common understanding of how these pairings operated. Now I can hardly comprehend why he had so much time for you."

"That *I* should disappoint *you!* What a joke from the domestic servant!"

"That's just it, Edward never made me feel like a servant and so I always treated him as a lord. If you had shown any understanding or care of Dorothy you would have taken in Sybil or let her adopt Vera after her mother died ..."

"So you think I should have paid for the upkeep of another one of your slatternly breed do you?" he jeered.

"I am saying, if you had been kind you would never have been cuckolded," she replied evenly, "Dorothy has always had a deep sense of fairness which she received from her upbringing with Edward. He showed his love of humanity in every decision he ever took and that left people loving him back. You show bitterness and suspicion which leads you to worship manipulation and force, but it also leaves others confined to employing those same tools back on you. Many times you believe you have won, but whenever you face a person who no longer cares about your threats, you will always lose. Today I lost the need to pretend I was a grand wife of a grand man, I am free to do anything, anything at all, if I decide it may help those whom I love."

Jean's eyes seemed to mushroom out of his circular head, red and shaking he appeared about to lunge at the devilish black pyramid that stood immovable in front of him. Flouncing past her he strode up to Dorothy thrusting his face into hers as she shrank back.

"You'll never get away with this," he screamed, gripping her face and distorting it with the pressure of his kneading fingers, "I'll ruin you and every one of your bastard brats," he promised, throwing her face away and running down the steps leaving P.C. Pennings scrabbling to apologise for his presence there and make sympathetic noises as he attempted to align himself with the weeping woman and her aunt. But it was the Reverend who came to the rescue of every remaining sheep in his flock by moving forward, his arms thrown wide to include Dorothy on one side and Sarah on the other as he herded them towards the statuesque family beside the hearse, all of whom suddenly became reanimated, allowing the constable to inch away almost unnoticed.

Holding the door open the priest helped Sarah into the car where she stared forward at the wreath-covered coffin, her teeth clenched together as she willed the cortege to begin moving. The show would go on.

Steph Mason

PART THREE

Steph Mason

CHAPTER SEVENTEEN

1927
(Dorothy: 32, Harold: 33, Nancy: 4)
Dorothy was beginning to waddle, at seven months the bulge in front of her had begun to spring random lumps of elbows and feet as they strained against the taut skin. Whenever they were lying in bed Harold would watch the angular display while expressing his horrified fascination as the alien within attempted to punch its way out of the confined living space. Throughout the day the expectant mother tried to keep up her normal pace of caring for a four-year-old, tending house and garden plus any contribution she was expected to make to village life, but the games of tennis, the motorbike jaunts and even getting into the Wink were becoming increasingly difficult as she became more incommodious. Legs sturdily spread as she stood to scrape carrots in the kitchen, she felt a fleeting twinge of resentment towards her mother-in-law who was due to arrive in an hour and who would, she knew, be dressed in the latest London fashions which would model themselves perfectly to her svelte body. Having children, lots of children, was undoubtedly a blessing but the process was barbarously uncomfortable and seemed to last an eternity.

Placing a hand on her swollen belly she massaged in her hope that this time she would have a boy. She could imagine Harold spending endless hours teaching his son about engines and electricity, plumbing and wirelesses, trailing a miniature clone behind him with whom he could share his gadget mania. However hard she and Nancy tried to show interested enthusiasm for Harold's passions there was a glassy film that passed over their eyes and ears after a very few moments so that they were unable to ask the pertinent questions that naturally sprang from young Patrick's lips when he was enjoying the same earnest education.

"If it's a boy," she thought "I'll make him a set of blue overalls identical to his father's as soon as he can walk." The carrot scrapings crept up the sides of the bowl as she pictured two male posteriors, of hugely differing sizes, bent over the latest car to come into Kelvedon Motor Works. Charlie had been correct in his predictions of an explosion in automobiles, even in the wilds of Essex the days of the horse as the main mode of transport had finally gone and Willand's garage had more trade than could be easily handled. Yes, it would make a huge difference if they had a son, there would be a latent promise of future help and they would each have a prodigy to enjoy.

"Should I lay the table in the dining room with the Royal Doulton, Mrs Willand?" Mary stood in the doorway, a grimy cloth and tin of bees wax poking out from her flowery apron pocket, as she waited for instructions.

"Yes, thank you Mary, and after that please take the afternoon off and go and see your mother." Altruism towards the maid was a sure fire way of improving their standing in the town as Mary's mother and elder sister were freewheeling chatterers incapable of suppressing even the most minutely boring details of the entire family's daily life and although Dorothy and Harold had been cautiously embraced as 'locals' after the birth of their first child and were even more firmly accepted now that there was to be another, she still felt the need to make regular deposits into the bank of village approval.

A cacophony of horn blowing made the two women jump and Dorothy whipped off her apron and barrelled towards the hallway as Harold tumbled out of the front door and halted with an awe-struck "Oh my!"

A magnificent curvaceous creature was drawing men towards it like a siren, the long shining beast had glided into the close, magical shock absorbers giving it the grace of a panther. Its tamer emerged, acknowledged the expanding crowd before reclining onto his monster, leaning an elbow on the sleek stretched bonnet, openly exalted by his flagrant extravagance.

"Morning son," Charlie hollered at the gobsmacked Harold, "What do you think?"

"A Chrysler Six!" the statement emerged as a strangled squeak, "high-compression engine ... hydraulic brakes ... aluminium pistons, oh my!" Harold moved towards it with lascivious greed and was mirrored by the small hoard of spectators who gave a mini surge to close in upon the masterpiece. "When did you get it?"

"Ordered it at Olympia. Thought I'd give you a surprise. Look at these they go back and forth to clear away the rain, all electrics, amazing eh!" the two narrow wipers suspended from the roof dutifully moved as he flicked the switch, mesmerizing the gathered ogglers.

Madeline and Nancy raced passed Dorothy indoors to play, supremely unconcerned by the car's accomplishments, while Sis, attired to attract as many admiring female glances as the Chrysler did male ones, sauntered into the house.

"I'll just go and slow down lunch," Dorothy said taking Sis's fur-trimmed tailored black coat, "I think they may be some time."

* * *

"You must employ a nurse," Charlie thundered from the end of the table. "You'll have no life with two children in the house and no nurse."

"I can cope quite well with just Mary," Dorothy replied, slightly peeved that the old man was being so strident in the arrangement of her domestic affairs, "I *enjoy* being with children."

"That's not what a man wants to hear," he bawled, laughing loudly whilst wiping gravy from his chin. "Children are all very well but a man needs his wife's attention when he gets home or he's liable to wander."

The statement sounded uncomfortably like a threat and Dorothy felt her colour start to rise as Sis tittered, placing her manicured hand over Charlie's and squeezing it playfully. Harold began to make soothing noises about "Considering it" and "Sorting it out between ourselves," but Charlie refused to be politely deflected.

"You said yourself that a motoring holiday would be capital. We'll never get away next summer unless you get yourselves a nurse, George and Alma have agreed, so you need to get on with it, make sure you've got someone by the time Dorothy pops and then she'll be more than happy to leave when the warm weather starts."

* * *

Hearing the courteous farewells followed by fading footsteps down the path, Harold folded his newspaper and looked expectantly towards the lounge door, Dorothy walked through it an expression of unhappy resignation on her face as she sat down heavily on the sofa before swivelling round and swinging her feet up onto his lap.

"Well?" he said, pipe still clenched between his left molars.

"I don't like any of them," she replied a perceptible wail creeping into her voice. "They're all so stern, they're either banging on about how much discipline a child needs, or the importance of sleep and exercise, or how babies should be left to cry or whatever, it seems as if they all think I need to be taught something. I feel as if *I'm* being interviewed by *them* rather than the other way around. I'm not comfortable with any of them. I really don't want them living here, I'd feel as if I was being watched and found wanting the whole time."

"Poor Darling," he said, massaging her ankle, "William mentioned a girl he knew who might be good, but when I pressed him he seemed to back track and claimed she'd probably be unsuitable or too young."

"I don't mind someone young, if they're sensible. At least I could teach a young person what I like rather than feel they wanted to boss me around. Please talk to William and get him to send her along."

* * *

Alice Butler had endured a lengthy walk by the time she knocked softly at the door of Brookside. Her fresh face with large pale-rimmed glasses would not have looked out of place on a librarian, although the ragged nails and tanned hands pointed to lowlier work being the norm. As Dorothy opened the door the girl began to gabble at an alarming rate.

"My name's Alice Butler Ma'm, William told me to come 'bout the position." She half turned back towards the gate as if deciding to leave immediately. Dorothy took in the freckled cheeks and big front teeth, the girl before her certainly did look young, not more than seventeen or eighteen if her appearance was anything to go by. Her eyes flickered down the youngster stopping for only a fraction of a second on the protuberance which undoubtedly matched her own.

"Come in please," she said opening the door to its fullest extent to show the applicant that she was welcome to step across the threshold. "Would you like a cup of tea, I've just put the kettle on."

"That's very kind of you Ma'm," the girl mumbled as Dorothy encouraged her into the warm kitchen and pulled out chairs for both of them. "That's a change," Dorothy thought to herself, "I took all the others into the dining room and asked Mary to fetch tea, and we seemed stuck in dining-room-mode for ever, this one I'm happy to have in my kitchen." Slowly Dorothy thawed her way through the girl's shyness. Alice revealed she had lived in Kelvedon all her life and was one of eleven children, seven of whom still lived at home in a rented cottage at the end of Swan Street. She'd left school at fifteen, later than many girls because she was good at her lessons and the teacher wanted to keep her on to help with the younger children, but since numbers at the school had dwindled Alice had spent the last year doing odd jobs in shops and picking peas, strawberries and plums as the harvests came due. Smiles of encouragement from Dorothy and reviving quantities of tea slowly relaxed the youngster transforming her from a terrified tight-lipped teenager into something resembling a female Mad Hatter. The round glasses gave her a quizzical look which was brightened into enthusiastic curiosity by the buck teeth which emerged from her wide smile. Dorothy postponed the question she needed to ask for as long as possible, in case it transformed the façade back to the one she'd encountered on the doorstep. Unable to tackle it head on she dodged around the subject by asking when Alice thought she would be able to start full time work.

"William said you wanted someone after January."

"And do you believe you will be ready to work then?" Dorothy asked gently.

"Oh yes Ma'm, definitely Ma'm."

"It's a live-in post you know. Would that leave your mother in difficulties with any, er, younger children in the house?"

"No Ma'm, only at picking time when everyone's out but we've a good neighbour who might help out."

"Or, any younger children, or perhaps babies, could come here during picking time, if you felt you could manage more little ones in the nursery."

A smile the size of a slice of watermelon lifted the freckles up underneath the big rims to be magnified by the spectacles, while the green-brown eyes shone above them.

"That would be wonderful Ma'm."

* * *

The appearance of the Misses Docwa on her doorstep sent Dorothy into a flurry of apprehension that she had forgotten to return a book to their excellent library, or, less worryingly, that they were collecting funds for one of their many charitable causes. The tightly-bunned grey spinsters were the founders of Kelvedon's Band of Hope temperance society whom Harold had fallen foul of before Dorothy even arrived, consequently she was always nervous of further inflaming the local tongues of righteousness by an inadvertent lapse of her own.

"May we come in?" the older Miss Docwa asked in a tone which appeared to dispense with the question mark.

"Certainly," Dorothy replied politely, guiding them into the lounge and onto seats where they perched like hungry vultures, openly staring at the silver tray on the sideboard with its content of six glittering decanters each amply supplied with colourful liquids, their expressions displaying undisguised disgust.

"How can I help you?" Dorothy enquired as the carrion eaters appeared in no rush to get to the point of their visit.

Spreading her short thighs so that each sensibly clad foot was moored either side of her stout cane, the younger Miss Docwa leant forward on the handle with the air of a judge questioning the accused.

"There has been talk that you intend to employ Alice Butler as a nurse, and it's important for your reputation that a stop be put to such ridiculous tittle tattle."

"I see." Dorothy could only say the words very slowly so that the majority of her concentration remained fixed on keeping the angry bear that had suddenly taken up residence in her stomach from jumping out of her mouth.

"You haven't said if it's true," the second judge prodded, "Are you intending to employ her?"

"Yes," all attention consolidated onto temper control.

"You may not be aware but she is both unmarried and with child," the first ancient virgo intacta intoned, her lips curling as she pronounced the words as if to draw themselves away from the unpalatable subjects that were being vented.

"Her mother will care for the child whilst Miss Butler is working."

"You seem to have missed the point," putrid contempt was pouring from the duo onto Dorothy, "you have joined a god fearing community Mrs Willand, with a respect for Christian values and clean living. In addition you have a young daughter, yet you propose to expose her to the evil influence of an unwedded mother. What kind of example does that give her, or the other young impressionable girls of the town?"

The battle for control of her voice box left Dorothy speechless.

"Furthermore," the other old trout trumpeted, "you overlooked both Miss Whiting and Miss Johnson in favour of this young trollop, both highly qualified for a nurse's position and with excellent reputations."

"I wish to employ someone to *help me* take care of my children, not someone to *take over* the care of my children," Dorothy enunciated, trembling with the rush of emotions, her face flushed, the lump in her throat only just allowing her to keep her tone rational rather than dissolving into the shame and fury she felt. How dare they brand her an unfit mother, a bad influence on her daughter, a trollop.

"When Miss Butler helped with children at the school I believe everyone thought her to be most suitable, nothing you have said has led me to alter that widely held opinion. I would appreciate it if you would leave immediately," she said already on her feet so that the two antagonists would be forced to pass beneath her scornful stare as they took their potent disapproval out into the windy afternoon to be spread around the village.

* * *

From her front window in World's End Lane, Mrs Pickford was one of the first to see the Docwa sisters emerge, scarlet and visibly quivering with indignation.

"What's Mrs Willand's Christian name?" she called back to her husband as she let the edge of the net curtain fall.

"No idea," came the reply.

"I'll have to ask if we have another girl, I fancy giving a daughter of mine the same name as someone who can stand up to those two!"

* * *

"He's got your red hair but he's a boy too, it couldn't be more perfect," Harold said allowing the chubby finger to grasp one of his own, stroking the plump dimples on the back of the hand with his gigantum thumb.

The treatment of this baby was rather different to that of its predecessor, once home Alice was regularly deprived of her charge as Harold would march upstairs to the nursery, seize the baby basket and bring it back to the kitchen where he would set it down on two chairs whilst he fixed radios, small generators and household gadgets at the table, providing his offspring with a running commentary of why solder should be used in one repair, or why one particular wire must not touch another. Dicky would lie dutifully quiet, placid eyes studying the ceiling, gurgling occasionally as if in response to the instructive monologue, while Lucky sat beside the chairs, head on one side, eyebrows twitching attending to his master's voice, remaining with the constant sound in case it should herald a titbit magically dropping from above.

"It looks as if Lucky's learning more than Dicky," Dorothy laughed as she came in from the garden.

"You don't understand Bill, he's probably absorbing everything I say and his first word will be 'car' instead of 'mama'"

As soon as he could toddle the locals would see Dicky walking hand in hand with his father, a miniature overalled mechanic employed every Saturday morning to watch and learn. Seeing the duo return from their labours Charlie was heard to remark that he should have given Harold the same treatment so now he'd have a useful butcher in the family, but the battle for Dicky was not always won by Harold, Nancy adored having a playmate, even one younger than herself and, frankly, the wrong sex. Once her brother began to object to being dressed up as a doll and wheeled around in her pram, she would haul him off to Blackburn and Davis general store where Mrs Blackburn would let him ride one of her Great Danes and Nancy would parade the huge dog with its jockey round and round on a lead pretending to be a circus entertainer as she put on a lavish display of twirls before guiding the Dane over a series of improvised jumps as Dicky hung on to the enormous collar.

Holidays at Mersea saw Harold rolling up his trousers to paddle with his youngsters, finding hermit crabs to crawl towards their small toes and make them squeal, teaching them how to pop the big black pods on the seaweed and using razor shells to poke washed-up blobs of jelly with their long stinging tentacles. In previous years Harold had swum with George or sat in his deckchair chatting to the other adults while the kids amused themselves, but suddenly conversation bored him as he relived the wonders of the English seaside through the eyes of his son.

"For goodness sake Harold, leave them to play by themselves," Charlie cried as his son flopped onto the sand and began building elaborate moated castles while Dicky dashed back and forth to the sea with his bucket, never managing to stop the water from draining away, and Dorothy, pregnant again, sat watching them and smiling.

* * *

May 1930.
(Dorothy: 35, Harold: 36, Nancy: 7, Dicky: 2)
Great Aunt Sarah grasped Patrick's hand as they walked up to the main road from Kelvedon station. At the grand age of eight he felt he was far too adult for such treatment but the doughty vigour of his elderly relative remained insensitive to his squirming, and kept him forcibly attached until Nancy rescued him by racing down the front path and out of the gate to greet them. Dicky trailed the older children round to the back garden where their vocal interpretations of awesome aeroplanes startled the thrushes and chased the starlings off the lawn.

"I'm Amy Johnson flying all the way from Australia," Nancy cried, arms out wide as she banked around the continent of a hammock.

"I'm Charles Lindburgh," Patrick countered "and I know far more than any girl about aircraft, even Miss Johnson."

Dicky soared and guttered among the flying aces until the Great Aunt called them in for tea when the early May sunshine gave way to long shadows and weary limbs.

As Patrick sank into the comfortable dip in the middle of his bed that night he sent up a silent prayer that Aunt Dorothy wouldn't have her baby too quickly so that he could stay in Kelvedon for weeks. Although Great Aunt Sarah was determined to keep everything running smoothly while Dorothy was confined, Patrick was certain Uncle Harold could help them evade her evil eye, leaving Alice to bear the brunt of the Great Aunt's ministrations, while the kids ran wild through the countryside and Patrick was freed from at least some of his many aunts.

* * *

"You have a beautiful healthy son," the comfortingly rounded midwife announced to Harold as he ceased his hours of corridor pacing at her appearance.

"Is my wife all right?"

"A little tired, of course, but nothing a few hours' sleep won't put right. You should get some rest yourself and come back later."

"Perhaps I could pop in before I leave?" he ventured as the nurse's broad smile became set and she seemed to gird herself, ready for a matronly battle, "just for a second..."

"I don't like my mothers to be disturbed," she countered.

"If you could just ask her if I could ..." he pleaded, "... if she's sleeping I'll go."

Tossing the starched white veil of her cap over her shoulders she glared at him while Harold pretended to be duly cowed until she had completed her flounce through the door.

Twenty minutes later a flustered face momentarily reappeared.

"Don't leave, there's another one," she said, causing Harold to sink onto a chair, his face turning chalky as his brain absorbed the fact that he was suddenly head of a family of six.

* * *

It was Saturday afternoon and Arthur Fry was directing a small army of friends and family to move all of Sarah's remaining furniture and boxes from 64 Sinclair Road to number 88. Wilfred had died, seated in his chair whilst the women were at church one Sunday morning and after this it seemed prudent for the two widows to move in together.

Watching four men struggle up the front steps with Edward's black upright piano, Sarah wondered why she hadn't sold it with the medical books and his bed. She herself didn't play and although Peggy had occasionally asked Dorothy to teach her tunes when they all lived at Maddox Street, as she couldn't read music it seemed unlikely any future use of the instrument would justify the effort necessary to get it up to the first floor. Her vague protestations that it could be left in the hallway and she would arrange for the furniture shop to collect it resulted in the men becoming considerably more animated than before and an air of masculine pride and determination took over the procedure making her wary of saying anything more in case she upset the very people who were giving up their afternoon to help her.

Half an hour later, amid much backslapping and expansive stretching, the piano stood in Peggy's living room its carved front panels proclaiming "Music exalts each joy, allays each grief" and below, in smaller copperplate, "There's music in all things if Men had ears."

"I'm goin' to learn to play it," Peggy announced running her fingers up and down the yellowing ivories, "by the time Nancy comes down again I'll be thumpin' out *Tipperary* and *Beautiful Doll* and she'll be singin' and dancin' all round the place."

Sarah grimaced slightly and hoped the windows and doors fitted tight enough to give some sound proofing.

* * *

Sis was reading a magazine in the lounge when she heard Charlie boom down the phone, "You'll have to have a big bash with two to do."

"Hey Sis," he yelled after replacing the receiver in its cradle, "Harold's had twin boys, reckon country life doesn't leave them with enough to do in the evenings!"

"I guess so," she replied, closing her magazine and quietly going upstairs where she ran a deep bath and lay in it with her eyes closed until the water had turned cold.

* * *

Seven gleaming vehicles swept into the close in front of Brookside disgorging themselves of numerous well-shod shapely calves and dapper men in double-breasted suits. Sis watched little Dicky running between the cars, climbing onto the running boards and dragging open the heavy doors with their rich leather interiors to test each horn in turn as proud owners looked on while their women cooed over the tiny creatures in their long white christening gowns. The twins were being passed around the elegant crowd their almost bald heads being gently supported by a succession of glamorous doting women each of whom, Sis reckoned, would be praying her carefully chosen outfit would not be anointed with baby sick.

She sat for a moment in the passenger seat not wanting to become swallowed up by the throng, but Madeline was already stepping out onto the dusty road and so, resplendent in a fashionable suit, three strings of pearls and a full fox fur, feet and tail in situ, which was draped around her shoulders despite the warmth of the June day, she grabbed her daughter's hand, steered her round the baby bevy and headed directly into the house to find Nancy.

Painting on a smile she persuaded the two girls it would be pleasant to walk to the church and that they could feed the ducks on the way if they left quickly, but as she exited the front door she was besieged by the maternal crowd and an infant was placed in her arms as cameras clicked and the chic London party made appreciative noises about being in the countryside, if only for a day. Depositing little Peter in Alma's willing embrace, which had only just released baby John to an eager auntie, Sis wiped her hands down the side of her skirt before almost running to rejoin the girls.

As the walking trio rounded the final bend before St. Mary's a procession of cars roared past them, Charlie's Chrysler leading with a triumphant Dicky perched upon his grandfather's knee, his round face beaming as he steered the dazzling leviathan for the first time.

CHAPTER EIGHTEEN

April 5 1933, Kelvedon
"Come quickly Mrs. Willand!" Mary's shout drove through the open front door and down the hallway with such urgency that Dorothy dropped the knife she was using running into the street still holding the potato. Her fast walk became a trot as she saw the maid running across the grassy island towards a car stopped on the other side surrounded by a growing crowd. As she saw the flash of red hair on the ground, almost beneath the front wheel, her legs began to sprint.

On her knees in the dirt and grit, the heat from the engine searing the side of her face, she cradled Dicky onto her lap, bending over to kiss his soft cheek, using her left hand to brush away stray locks from his forehead and to pull the arm, which wore a black armband the width of a tyre, up towards his rounded tummy, stopping it from flopping down, trying to warm the ten small fingers in hers while meaningless chatter went on above her as the driver repeated over and over to the gawping onlookers that he had swerved to avoid him but the child had abruptly turned and run straight back in the direction from which he had come. Mary's voice, shrill and crying that it was all her fault, pierced into Dorothy's mind on occasions until, almost by absorption into her body rather than through an interruption of her concentration on her child, she knew Mary had seen the car coming as Dicky ran across the street to the sweetshop and had called to him to be careful, causing him to hesitate and run back towards her straight into the path of unforgiving steel.

A head bent down to her, "They've gone for Dr. MacKenzie and your husband."

She nodded, "Can you get a blanket from the house, he feels cold," she said and the head left, returning minutes later with a green woollen blanket which anonymous hands helped tuck around him while she tried to use the warmth from her own body to compel heat into his. As she poured out the love that erupted from her onto her son she felt an irrational certainty that its power was so great that it must wash away all the physical hurt leaving him clean and well.

A chafed brown leather bag appeared at Dicky's feet which were lolling down from the arm his mother had beneath his knees. The doctor gently requested permission to see him as Dorothy kept her child clasped to her while the acrid scent of the ointment Dr. MacKenzie put on a white cloth clawed at her nostrils as he used it to wipe away the slow trickle of blood that stretched from Dicky's right ear to the curve of his jawbone. It was only a little blood, really very little, far less than when he had cut his knee tripping over the front step and had made such a mess of the hall. He'd been fine then and was even quite proud of the small white scar the accident had left. Surely this would be the same, they'd all be smiling at the scare he had given them next week. And then Harold was there, the mass having parted as he ran towards them, skidding down to the ground beside his wife and child as the doctor looked up at him with a dull expression, his lips sagging down, she felt quite irritated with him, where was his jovial bedside reassurance when you needed it? He was frightening her.

She would not give him up, not even to Harold. The two men took her elbows and helped her from the gravel still hugging her boy.

"We need your car, Sir," she heard Dr. MacKenzie say to the driver who was sitting on the damp grass, his head in his hands which kept flexing over the top of his thinning hair.

"Of course," he replied, face snapping up.

The doctor guided Dorothy into the back seat with her burden, getting in beside her to continue monitoring his patient. Harold leapt for the offside door, "I'm driving," he stated, coldly relegating the owner to the status of a passenger. She knew she would usually have softened the atmosphere by making a joke about Harold always wanting to drive other men's cars, but she couldn't, even to make the stranger feel better, not while her stomach felt so sick and the doctor still wasn't smiling.

"Call the hospital and tell them we're coming," Harold shouted to Mary as he crashed the engine into gear.

Sitting beside the doctor a surge of intense hope relaxed her forehead as the small green eyes flickered open. Leaning over Dicky she expected his head to turn and focus on her, and with that her will for him to be well would somehow enter him as their eyes locked, the power of her love flooding through him and healing whatever injuries there were inside her beautiful boy. But the doctor did not show any response to the miraculous awakening and the small copper-framed head did not turn, so she was forced to curl herself above him, deluging him in her love, but his eyes gazed past her with no recognition that an obstacle blocked their view and her outpouring turned into an entreaty to any higher power there might be as she realised that although her chest felt as if it were drowning, there was some barricade to her adoration and she was unable to reach her child and draw him back to her.

As they sat beside the hospital bed, Dorothy held the cool clammy hand between her two as if sandwiching her son into a prayer. Harold mirrored her on the other side but his head was down as if he was attempting to avoid acknowledging that Dr. MacKenzie had remained with them. Known as the Flying Scotsman, the doctor was notorious for the speed with which he dispensed with his patients. To see him sitting almost still beside Dicky, gently swabbing the chubby arm and picking out the tiny stones that had been ground into its white flesh by the welt of the wheel, consulting his pocket watch and taking the flickering pulse every few minutes, with no sign of preparing to leave, was more sinister for Dorothy than the sight of her son lying on the bed. This lack of hurry swathed the room in ominous resignation and seemed to place a brick wall of fate in front of her which she hurled herself against with her tortured silent supplications.

* * *

"You need to wait outside now so that the specialist can work on him," Dr. MacKenzie said gently taking Dorothy's arm, persuading her to relinquish her vigil, "I'll stay. We will do whatever we can."

Like ghastly somnambulants she and Harold grabbed at each other to steady their walk from the room, sitting outside encased in their separate orbs of agony; silent, with complete concentration given to the begging pleas that flowed from her throbbing temples into a universe that did not appear to be listening.

* * *

A china doll lay on the bed, the face pale and set. She could not look at the face. Climbing onto the bed and cuddling the pliable little body to her, the unearthly expression was hidden against her ribcage. Harold was kneeling on the other side, his face pressed into the rough blanket, the fingers of his right hand twisting among the soft red curls. A voice above them attempted to engage them in practicalities, trying to interrupt raw grief with the necessities of procedure.

"There will be an inquest, would you like a post mortem to be conducted?"

"Don't touch him."

* * *

She battled hard against her senses, but eventually it became impossible to ignore the tightening of the skin and the rigidity of the flesh, it was as if her vulnerable boy had been swapped for a stone replica from Pompeii which she was left foolishly attempting to resurrect by her embrace. Her arms began to loosen and her torso drew back, she looked down in horror willing herself to wake up.

The men moved forward helping her off the bed as Dr. MacKenzie said, "There's a car outside to take us home."

Home. Where her daughter would be waiting with questions in her eyes, and the twins would rush forward with their habitual leg-hugs, clamouring dual voices each demanding attention, ignorant and uncomprehending that she had nothing to give.

But when they arrived it was a wreath affixed to the front door that greeted them, and a note from Mrs Pickford said she had taken Nancy and the twins to stay with her family for the night. A dull hint of relief flowed over Dorothy that she would not have to try to look sane for her children quite yet.

Dorothy and Harold crept fully clothed beneath the bedcovers in their empty house. Unable to reach out to each other, the bed's width too distant for them to traverse as they curled themselves within their own private hells where the physical pains in their chests and throats choked through their tears.

* * *

The house was alive with people, and cars were double parked in the close, Peggy and Aunt Sarah were queens of refreshments and household orderliness, Sis and Charlie formed the welcoming committee, each of the voices, though hushed, drifted up the stairs and filtered into the sarcophagal sphere of the bedroom. Dorothy had dressed by automation and now she sat on the side of the bed, her legs dangling, her eyes unfocused on her hands which were twiddling the rings on her fingers. Harold stood at the window staring out at the garden. The church bell began to toll, each 'dong' pausing at the bottom of the note before the next sighed into the space its predecessor had left hanging over the town. She stood up as Harold turned and the two of them headed down to the triangular chink of sunlight that lay across the hall floor and out into the road.

The small white coffin balanced on a hand bier was cornered by four men in black suits, frock coats and top hats; men who every day before had been the chaps at the timber yard who would raise their flat caps with a cheery "Morning, Mrs. Willand" but who had today mutated into soulless scrubbed clones of the townsfolk she had known for the past ten years. Falling in behind the bier, vision blinkered onto the compact white box, the procession coerced her up the High Street. She was dimly conscious of neighbours coming out from their houses and their compassionate eyes boring into her as they joined the crocodile that followed the bier like a ghastly dark bridal train, curving round to the right and in through the wooden church gate.

The solemnity that Reverend Croft's initial incantations created was booted out as the organist struck up the introductory bars of the first hymn. Although the usual *Abide with me* and *Oh God my help in ages past* had been suggested by the priest, Dorothy and Harold had shaken their heads, uncertain what the service should contain, but knowing it should not be ponderous songs whose doom laden notes would frighten their precious baby. Eventually it had been Nancy who had said any service for Dicky should have his favourite music, and provided her own carefully written list.

All things bright and beautiful ...

By the second syllable of the final word all Dorothy's resolve to remain steadfast throughout the next hour had been swept away as she crumpled chin onto chest, chest concaving inwards as her body was convulsed by sobs that came from so deep within her there seemed no space inside for anything else.

And then they were standing above the neat brown hole, incongruous spring flowers merrily bobbing their colourful heads in the regularly tended beds around the church perimeter, and Reverent Croft was messing up the pristine white box with handfuls of dirt, as from the pit of her stomach her whole being shrieked "No, no, don't take him."

An arm was round her shoulders trying to ease her away as if she needed to be peeled off this spot and stuck somewhere else, somewhere more appropriate, but the glue wouldn't yield. How could she put her child in the cold earth and then turn and walk away? A voice attached to the arm mentioned the other children, making frustration rise within her that the voice misunderstood that it was her child here who was hurt and needed her. It was *this* child she should be with, the others weren't owed her as this one was, and that it would all be put right, she knew it could be made right, if she could just sink into the ground and rest a while beside him, together in the clean white lining.

* * *

She was alone, quite alone, so it was almost inconceivable that it should matter to anybody whether she was there or not. She was alone. Harold was alone. Even Nancy was alone although she seemed to be trying to pretend it wasn't so.

Mary had not returned to Brookside since Dicky's accident and Dorothy made no attempt either to persuade her back or to find a replacement. She immersed herself in mechanical household chores, beating rugs and scrubbing clothes, frenetically polishing furniture and striding down to the shops to hand in daily orders all of which at least made her body physically tired even if her sleep was plagued by dreams where she would hear his voice, or know for sure that he was hiding just around the next corner where she could never quite find him. She regularly woke with her cheeks and pillow damp but instead of remaining with the visions that had tortured her, she would leap from the bed as if stung, wash in cold water and begin her rigorous automation of active work. To stay with the dreams would be to give in to the loneliness and some innate core of self-preservation told her that to lie and think would suck her down into a depressive sludge from which she would never escape.

As spring turned into summer and the heat became oppressive, she was still determined nothing would overpower her resolve to keep pushing on. Striding into the kitchen from the garden, her brow streaked with muddy sweat, she pulled the remaining pins from her straggly bun, seized a pair of material scissors that were poking out of her sewing box and hacked off the acres of hair at her neckline. Tossing the tresses into the compost bucket, she marched back outside to continue weeding.

* * *

Despite all her strident attempts, her strenuous work ethic and abrupt manner, nothing she did could deflect others' sympathy and although her briskness had succeeded in silencing family and friends from making even the slightest enquiry about her well-being, there were many in the town who failed to pick up on the vibes she knew were crackling out from every pore.

"Why the hell do they look at me with their lined foreheads and piteous eyes asking 'How *are* you' all the time?" she ranted at Harold one afternoon when she returned from the shops.

"People don't know what to say," he offered quietly.

"Then they should just shut up!" she said, slamming the broom cupboard door as she stamped up the stairs to clean all the bedrooms, apart from the one that she left forever untouched which had housed a cherubic five-year-old with a glossy red halo.

* * *

Harold lost interest in the garage now that he no longer had his mini scholar to show and explain new things to, it all seemed so pointless and attempting to continue being enthusiastic was a sham he was not prepared to enact. As the weeks wore on he found his steps turning more and more frequently towards the tennis courts, often he would find a fellow shirker there eager to give him a game but when the rest of the world was working he would content himself with bashing a ball against the practice wall for hour after hour until perspiration soaked his clothes and every one of his muscles was pleading for him to quit.

It was after a particularly long session of beating up a tennis ball, that Harold ventured into the Post Office to buy a standard will form. His head had been needling him to put something in writing ever since the fact that all life was fragile had been rudely thrust in front of him. His own mortality was a subject he avoided thinking about, not because he was particularly superstitious of unpleasant retribution for past misdemeanours but because he recognised that Dorothy, with no marriage certificate, would be left in a nightmarish situation should he die early. Consequently, it became part of his character to be unshakeable in his belief that he would always be there for her, forever her rock and protector, immortal during the time she needed him. Yet the mound of slowly levelling earth in the churchyard had shaken his certainty so that he forced himself to sit at the kitchen table, filling in the form with all his details and the stipulation that he left everything "to my life's partner, Dorothy," before signing it and putting it away beneath a number of other papers in a rarely opened drawer.

* * *

Alice kept the twins with her almost constantly, with just two young charges now she redoubled her efforts at making them happy and active. She built wigwams for them at the bottom of the garden, playing cowboys and Indians until they curled up in front of their unlit camp fire and fell asleep. She taught them to swim in the river, to ride their tricycles and to sail paper boats, but for all her efforts she could not erase the empty place that assaulted everybody when the family sat down together three times a day to eat. However much they shuffled around the table to try to disguise the absence it stared back at her during every interminable meal. When the weather was fine Alice would suggest picnics, which her employers readily agreed to. Sitting on a rug outside partially hid the loss of a child and the twins' additional animation at eating in the fresh air disguised the silences. On rainy days she began inviting Nancy's class mates to come and share almost every meal as she saw the little girl trying daily to push away the sorrow-filled chalice she had been handed and haul herself towards a sunnier future.

Vowing she would not abandon the family she had grown to love, Alice strove to keep normality intact for the Willand children while trying to lug their parents back towards some kind of peace.

* * *

It was late summer by the time the ground had settled sufficiently to allow the rectangle of white stone to be placed around the grave, topped by a cross and below it the words:

"Dicky"
Richard Willand
Died 5th April 1933
Aged 5 years
"safe with Jesus"

Dorothy had brought a bowl of chrysanthemums which were in full bloom. Looking down at the stark freshly cut slabs she felt no pressure to linger and a shard of fear stabbed through her when she could not feel her child there. Leaving the flowers she began to wander through the churchyard looking at the inscriptions on the other stones. The gardener had only mowed the paths but she walked straight towards any memorial she was curious about, the long grass quickly soaking her shoes, stockings and the hem of her dress. There were other children buried here, many of them, and she wondered whether their parents were also harbouring some shameful secrets and whether in fact all of them were being put through her daily agony because of some failure in themselves.

If she had shown greater respect for Jean and not left she would never have experienced this dragging hunger for her child, yet she couldn't wish for that, not even now that every moment burned with the need to see her boy again and her blistered brain constantly sought a way to believe in a God just so she could comfort herself with thoughts of an afterlife shared with her son. She could never wish for a world where Dicky's life had not existed.

No one could miss the irony of his death, she felt it was as if a great celestial hand was pointing at her and Harold, singling them out for personalised punishment. Children died of measles and scarlet fever, drowning and falling out of trees, but not from being hit by motor cars. The local newspaper had said it was going to become a growing problem, that in ten or twenty years time there would have to be laws passed to protect the public, but now, the only grave in the large churchyard housing a road accident victim happened to be that of the son of the local garage owner, himself fanatical about cars. Undoubtedly the Misses Docwa would find a chain reaction of divine retribution and nod sagely in their judgement upon her sure that their God had smote the wicked in their midst, and yet they only knew of her minor misdemeanours, how much more sure would they be of their God's all seeing eye if they knew the truth?

Was this all part of Aunt Sarah's adage that "What goes around comes around"? Was there something crucial she was meant to learn from this, and if, by some confusion, she missed the point, might it happen again? Was she guilty of causing this? Could she become guilty a second time by not seeing the connections? By not changing as she was meant to change? She knew she would not survive a second time, already she spent each day swaying on a narrow crumbling ledge above a towering drop where mad people fell. Just the gentlest puff of additional pain would launch her over to where she would spend her days screaming and gibbering, tearing at her hair and scratching herself with long curved yellow fingernails in a frenzied desire to draw endless parallel dripping red lines on every part of her exposed skin. It was her horror of falling into this final demonic degradation that left her oscillating in her emotions towards the twins, first drawing them to her in fierce cuddles, assuring herself they were real and healthy and should be protected and loved with all her strength, while at other times she would view them quite dispassionately, distancing herself from their rough and tumble and the tears of one when the other was victorious, conscious only that they were somehow less perfect than their brother who would always be angelically frozen in time.

* * *

1934.
(Dorothy: 39, Harold: 40, Sis: 39, Nancy: 11, Twins: 4)
By the following year the Sunday routine of lunch with Charlie and George, and Sis and Alma had been re-established although on fine days the party would split into two as the men headed for the tennis court as soon as the beef and gravy had been semi-digested, leaving the women with the brood of children. It was a warm day in June when the women settled themselves into deckchairs in the garden after the racquets and balls had been seized and the washing up done. Alma relaxed to the shouts coming from the river bank, the noise let her know all the youngsters remained in fine voice and so by definition, safe. The sun caressed her as she sat between the two Mrs Willands and she closed her eyes and turned her face directly towards the rays without even the slightest zephyr to chill her and disturb her rural bliss.

"I had twin boys," Sis said, her eyes still shut but her voice clear and firm.

Alma felt Dorothy stiffen and opening her eyes a crack she saw the muscle linking her friend's jaw to her ear clench tight. Alma sat in the middle, her eyes now fully open, looking from side to side at the unseeing faces, almost too tense to breathe, praying that the loaded silence would act as a massive 'Stop' sign to Sis and the three of them would be allowed to slowly relax into the softness of the afternoon. If only some minutes could pass in silence, each one of them could perhaps pretend the sentence had never been slapped into the middle of a summer's day.

"I'd only been married five months when they were born. My husband had been sent to France the month before."

"Even now," Alma thought, "you could stop talking and we could float away from the words into the balmy sky, looking down at the little birds on the lawn and the colourful flowerbeds, don't take us any further away from this beauty. Please, please stop, I'm begging you, Stop!"

"John died the day after he was born, but Robert lived for three weeks."

The statement crashed into the deckchairs scattering them around the garden. Sis opened her eyes and turned towards Dorothy who was staring fixedly ahead as Alma span distractedly from one to the other incapable of rescuing them from themselves, Christ, one of them even had the same name! Why did she have to say it? Why couldn't she leave it alone? Things were getting back to normal weren't they? What was she trying to do?

"I know I'm probably not doing very well," Sis continued, beginning to falter, "but I'm trying to say that although you'll never get over it, and you'll never forget it, you will eventually get passed it. You think time should stop, but it doesn't and slowly it becomes your past and you realise you're still alive and have a future."

Alma raised her eyes fearfully as Dorothy sprang to her feet, her face flushed and her grey eyes unnaturally bright as she looked down at Sis. Alma had never seen anyone look so incensed, Dorothy's expression was one of someone who despised all those in front of her.

"So, how, *exactly,* is your survival of two dead sons meant to make me feel better? Should I rejoice I haven't lost another one yet?" she screamed, spinning on her heel and running for the door as her voice began to shake.

Alma stretched out her left hand and grasped Sis's, squeezing it as she kept the fingers on the right crossed in the hope that losing children wasn't contagious.

* * *

That evening the two of them sat in the living room listening to a musical programme on the wireless. Harold looked his wife over the top of his newspaper, she seemed withered, drained of the steely will power she had cloaked herself in since the accident. George had murmured something about a "scene with Sis", after having an urgent furtive conversation with Alma when they returned from their game and the visitors gathered up their respective offspring, leaving hastily with muttered excuses about having things to do at home.

Getting up from his chair he gently pulled her into his arms as the radio began to play *Up a Lazy River*. Their limbs fitted together as perfectly as before and their bodies expertly avoided the furniture as they swayed and revolved. For a moment she rested her head on his chest, but it was only for one weary minute, by the end of the song she was out of reach again and Harold still felt quite alone, the vacuum of loss separating them as effectively as solid prison walls.

Steph Mason

CHAPTER NINETEEN

May 12, 1937
(Dorothy: 42, Harold: 43)
It was the day after the twins' seventh birthday, Dorothy had spent all day setting up trestle tables and making sandwiches for the Coronation party, she supposed the new King would be all right, after all kings never appeared to have to do anything too taxing, she'd liked the real king though, but she'd avoided most of the endless abdication debates that had raged at every shop and street corner for the past six months. It seemed excessive that he should have to lose his throne over who he wanted to marry, and running away to France was what Harold had initially proposed for them, now she'd seen what the king had to do to be with the person he loved she was hugely grateful she wasn't royal. She wondered what would happen if Mrs. Simpson had children, that would stir everyone up again.

She sat down on a bench to enjoy a brief rest before the town's children arrived, it had been a hard year for her and Harold but their problems probably hadn't done them any lasting harm, they might even have helped them she thought, in a moment of brutal honesty.

A month or so before the king's departure, Harold had been forced to abdicate from his position as Kelvedon's ever-ready tennis partner after his desertion of the garage had resulted in a careless employee flicking a cigarette butt into an open petrol tank which was awaiting delivery of several hundred gallons of fuel. The resulting inferno had torched all the pumps, workshops and six cars that were being serviced on the forecourt, but the first Harold knew of his loss was when the sky above the tennis court darkened so alarmingly that even he was compelled to abandon play. Oily black smoke covered the entire town as the members of the local fire brigade took turns at working their arms until every muscle must have screamed for mercy at the town's manual fire pump which drew tonnes of water from the river as they struggled to contain the blaze. Dorothy had stood watching, a hand on each twin's shoulder, feeling wretchedly impotent as the family's livelihood burnt to the ground. The murk had been so thick that even after the garage was merely a smouldering collection of timber stumps and melted metal, one fireman had attempted to roll up the white line from the middle of the road, mistaking it for a hose.

The destruction of their business had become an opportunity to rebuild, repaint and restructure, it provided Dorothy and Harold with a joint goal at just the time the twins began school and the house became unnaturally quiet, Alice had been able to wield their enthusiastic reference at potential employers who snatched her away from Brookside within weeks of the boys picking up their pencils, and the family had settled into a new routine with a young general home help called Betty who was only a couple of years older than Nancy.

The imminent arrival of a crowd of children, freed from giving thanks for their new monarch at the church, was heralded by the increased volume of excited shrieks floating down the road. Dorothy got to her feet and moved towards the long tables to help the other ladies position the jugs of milk and plates of food. Peter and John wheeled around the corner and skidded into place opposite the largest mound of iced cup cakes, Peter's hand was hovering above one when Dorothy grabbed it, "Sit on them until everyone's here, then you can start," she ordered in mock severity, but it was on John's face her gaze lingered. "It's passed," she thought as her chest rose in a deep sigh, "his face isn't Dicky's any more, it's just John," and she didn't quite know if she was relieved or sad to her bones that John's appearance had inched passed the place where Dicky had stepped out of her life and he was no longer a ghostly shadow of the brother he'd hardly known. Looking at him she realised that for some time now they had all been operating smoothly as a quintet but every alteration had been so minuscule she had never seen it happen. Rebuilding the business and the constantly changing lives of the children had nibbled away at her chrysalis of grief without her noticing, but as she took in the bunting and the rows of smiling faces she acknowledged, almost guiltily, that she could feel the sun shining on her back and hear the brass band playing and that she was looking forward to strolling down to the hall tonight and dancing until she dropped with Harold.

* * *

November 1937
(Sarah:73, Peggy: 49)

The doorbell interrupted Peggy's piano practice, Sarah reached for her stick placing it squarely in front of her armchair where it quivered at the pulse of pressure exerted upon it as she attempted to lever herself out of her chair, the damp autumn weather played havoc with her arthritis making her frustrated by her own body's growing inadequacies.

"I'll get it," Peggy sang out, allowing her Aunt to relax gratefully back onto her cushions. She could hear the door open and a man's voice say, "I believe Mrs Lane lives here."

"Yes, she does, is everythin' all right?" Peggy replied as Sarah went to work once again with her stick and began an urgent hobble onto the landing. She looked down the stairwell into the eyes of a friend.

"Constable Penning! How nice to see you, please come up I'll put the kettle on."

Smiling at such a warm reception the policeman made his way up the stairs two at a time as Peggy stared at her aunt in confusion before closing the door.

Sarah warmed the pot before adding three generous spoonfuls of tea and setting out the strainer, plus the good milk jug, sugar bowl and cups on the pretty inlaid tea tray she usually only brought out at Christmas and Easter. He was undoubtedly greyer than when he had come to her house thirteen years ago. It had been strange how afterwards she had continued to believe that some day she would see him again, that they were somehow kindred spirits, two people who naturally understood and liked one another irrespective of age difference or unfortunate antecedents, but friends often needed a reason to meet, and they had had none. He had come to Edward's house a week after the funeral, dressed in his Sunday suit, all the officialdom of his uniform stripped away as he stood on the doorstep unable to quite make eye contact while apologising unreservedly for the scene that had occurred at St Georges. He said he had been compelled to ask the verger for her address, and although reappearing in front of her ran the risk of igniting anger against himself, with possible career repercussions, his inner moral barometer had not allowed him to shrink from the task. Heaping all the blame for any distress solely onto his own plate, he berated himself for failing to adequately explain to Mr Nicolai the tangible difference in England between the letter and the spirit of the law, and asked her to pardon him. She saw only an honest and considerate soul, out of his depth when confronted by Jean, the expert manipulator, hell bent on convincing an inexperienced copper that his duty lay firmly behind this personal marital quest.

She had insisted he come in even though he had clearly intended to say his piece and leave, but she had known he could not reject a request to join a recently widowed woman for a cup of tea, so he had been forced to enter the living room and allow himself to be plied with refreshments as she had gently teased information out of him about his children and his wife, his childhood and his hobbies until by the end he was chatting to her as if she were his own aunt and he was paying an enjoyable social visit rather than having arrived bowed under a crushing weight of remorse and embarrassment. He confided his passion of philately to her, describing how he would relax by sorting out his albums, adding a new acquisition here and rearranging a sequence there, and she had told him that her husband had taken up the same hobby before the war spending endless evenings clasping tweezers and giving warnings to the household not to open doors and windows in case the precious pieces of printed paper should fly around the room and become muddled or damaged.

Now he was here again in full uniform, and although she was curious to hear the cause of his visit, his face had looked friendly and relaxed so she felt no apprehension at seeing him there. Handing him the teacup she finally asked, "To what do we owe the pleasure of seeing you?"

"There is a group of women who are in a difficult situation and whom you, or rather your niece, may be able to help."

"Oh?"

"I'm sorry to tell you that Mr Nicolai died suddenly a week ago."

"My goodness! What happened?"

"It seems he cut his thumb opening a can of corned beef and the wound became septic, he was dead within three days of going into hospital.

"Mr Nicolai's business has become quite successful over the years, he even patented his methods and in the past few years devoted all his efforts into edible art floristry. His products have become so popular he now has five women who work full time in the business. Obviously their futures are now in jeopardy and all of them have families to keep and bills to pay."

"I see."

"My home is above Mr Nicolai's business in Woburn Buildings, so it was natural for the ladies to ask me if I could find out what would become of the firm. The housekeeper at his rooms allowed me to search for instructions but I was unable to find any kind of will or uncover any addresses of friends who might have known what his wishes were. It appears he lived for his work, the only package of letters I found from Romania dated from before the war so there seems no likelihood of any surviving family suddenly making contact."

She remained silent, nodding at him to continue, "I realise your niece probably will not enjoy being asked to get involved given the delicate situation she is in, but if she remains married to Mr Nicolai, if there has been no divorce, she would automatically be granted control of his estate and could perhaps keep the business running until a suitable buyer could be found and the ladies' jobs made secure," he ended in a rush.

"You're a kind man, Constable," Sarah said thoughtfully, causing the silver streaked moustache to lift upwards in a shy smile. "Indeed, my niece has never divorced Mr Nicolai but she has three children and so the matter will need to be handled very discreetly to have any hope of her agreement. However, from what you have told me she's now a widow and so would be free to marry the father of her children which is something I know they both greatly wish to do."

"Would you permit me to tell the ladies that I have found some family members and their situation may end up being resolved?"

"Of course," she replied, "this isn't the sort of thing to say on the telephone, one nosy operator would put an end to Dorothy's privacy, no, I will take the afternoon train up there and try to persuade her and Harold to come down to London in a few days time, where should I send them?"

"The business and my home are at 2 Woburn Buildings and Mr Nicolai's rooms are at 24 Tavistock Place," he said handing her a note he had written out for her. "Thank you so much," he said as he rose to take his leave, "please don't get up," but Sarah was already hauling herself out of her chair.

"Wait a moment Constable, I have something for you," she said, her joints laboriously grinding across the room towards a dark wood book case. She pulled a tall volume from the top shelf. "For many years this has been gathering dust and I've been wondering why I kept it, now I know it was so I could give it to you," she said handing it over with a flourish, her face flushed from the sudden exertion. He opened the hard outer cover of old brittle leather, "you do still enjoy stamps?" she asked.

"Yes indeed, my word you have a good memory," he said "to think you remember my hobby from all those years back!"

"I don't imagine there's anything to get particularly excited about in it, but there may be some attractive Canadian ones, it's nice for it to finally have a home with someone who will appreciate it far more than I do!"

"I'm certain I'll have many wonderful evenings looking through it," he said, delighted and bashful all at once.

"I'll be in touch once I've spoken to Dorothy," she gave him her hand. "Would you mind if Peggy saw you out? It takes me about twenty minutes to get down the stairs and up again."

* * *

It was as she had feared, Dorothy wanted to run as far away as possible from openly admitting she was Jean's legal wife, and the reasoned discussions Sarah had envisaged were not going to plan.

"It would be crazy to get involved," Dorothy cried her pitch going up an octave whilst remaining pianissimo even though the children were in bed and Betty was out for the evening. "If we sit tight it will all go away and we can carry on as usual."

"We could get married once you're officially a widow," Harold pointed out, in a soothing deep voice while his chocolate eyes seemed to soften into hers, joining Sarah in willing her obstinacy to melt.

"It still won't help the children, there's nothing we can ever do to make that right, we would be taking a risk for nothing," she countered, her hands shaking as she lifted a cigarette to her mouth taking a long pull and inhaling deeply. Harold chewed quietly on his pipe stem, and as Sarah studied him she guessed he had been through this type of scene before and was waiting for calmness to filter into Dorothy's mind, knowing it was prudent to keep silent rather than stir up the confused emotions once again by putting his point of view too soon.

"Of course I'd love to marry you darling," she said, suddenly becoming conscious of how dismissive she'd sounded, "I didn't mean it to come out as it did, and I know it sounds stupid, but I'm still scared of him. Even though I'm being told he's dead there's a part of me that thinks it's another trap, a ruse to expose us and harm the children, that there will be a document somewhere that will be published when I make a move or something. I don't know, I really don't, it's just we seemed to be getting back on our feet and I'm frightened that nothing good can possibly come out of this."

Harold scraped his chair back, moving to stand behind her, gently massaging her shoulders as he watched Sarah over the top of his lover's head.

"I understand why you want to stay out of it but I'm not sure it will go away if we do nothing," he said working his thumbs round her shoulder blades "we already know there's a policeman who remembers he has a wife and there may be staff who also knew you."

"Exactly! There probably are!" she said swivelling round, her eyes begging him to panic with her, "Jean inspired great loyalty, he was a perfectionist but he had patience by the bucket load when he was teaching others. I was always useless at it, but there were ladies in the shop who were very artistic and they worshipped him. If they're still there I'll get no favours or discretion from them!"

"In which case, I suggest Dad and I go up to town and pose as interested buyers, claiming there's some long lost cousin whose been discovered and is eager to sell. Once we've seen the business we'll have a better idea of what to do," he said looking at both the women while Sarah nodded encouragingly. "At the same time we'll use Dad's lawyers to make an application for Letters of Administration in your name, we'll keep it all low key and in London so there'll be no risk of it rebounding back here."

Sitting down beside her again he took her hand, "It's gone too far to do nothing. If we're ostriches about it we'll never rest easy in our beds, but if we sort it out we can get married Bill."

She smiled at him, her forehead still wrinkled but a glimmer of acceptance flickering into her eyes. "I'll take you on honeymoon to see the Loch Ness Monster and if you're cross with me over how any of this has been handled, you can feed me to it!"

"Nessie, here we come," she murmured as Sarah's face relaxed into a smile, convinced Harold would guide Dorothy through this leaving the constable and his downstairs neighbours content while tying up the loose ends of their own relationship, just as Edward and she had done.

* * *

The exaggerated cascading grille of Charlie's latest Chrysler nosed its way into the waiting area outside Liverpool Street Station; an enormous grey hulk of metal with fender skirts and double 'V' shaped windscreens, which were advertised as 'streamlining' for the colossus. Charlie adored his Airflow and would have been content to wait hours for his son to arrive just so he could continue to be surrounded by the throng of passengers who washed passed his sleek bodywork, screwing their heads around for a second glance which, each time Charlie spotted them in his neat rear view mirror, made his chest swell a little further.

"Thanks for picking me up Dad," Harold said as he clambered into the passenger side of the front bench seat and Charlie caressed the wooden gear stick into first making the two dials on the futuristic dashboard take excited jumps into life, as they glided out of the station.

"How do you feel about this?"

"I'm quite intrigued to find out more about him, he's been a bogeyman for so long."

"And Dorothy?"

"Pretty jittery, I don't imagine she'll be able to keep still until I'm home with a full report."

Charlie's lawyers had been pleasingly efficient and by using Nora's address at Sinclair Road they had procured the Letters of Administration for Dorothy in a mere two weeks. P.C. Pennings had alerted the five ladies of J.N. Nicolai's Art Florist to the presence of an absentee 'cousin', and had obtained a key for the rooms at Tavistock Place which he forwarded to Dorothy.

Parking the Airflow boldly outside the shop window, Charlie strode into the tranquil work space trailed by Harold, and kicked off by regaling the shell-shocked females with full details of his success in retailing and his belief that their "little business" would fit in well with his portfolio as he would have no trouble convincing many of the bakeries, which operated close to his seventeen butchers' shops, that they wished to place orders for their wondrous edible decorations.

"I'm not sure how many more orders we can manage, Sir, without training more staff," the elected forewoman offered timidly, "the book's full already but we're running very low on supplies."

Charlie was just preparing to launch into a second monologue when Harold elbowed him to one side and started talking to the women in a very touchy-feely way, which was not nearly assertive enough, in Charlie's view.

"What do you need to keep going?"

"We don't have problems with producing the natural flowers, but we've hardly any gum solution left. That's the stuff Mr. Nicolai used to fix the powder tints onto the rice paper flowers," Harold took out a notebook as the wide middle-aged lady began to explain in detail, which lead Charlie to sigh deeply and begin pacing behind his son.

"Mr Nicolai spent years developing our tinting techniques so the rice paper wouldn't become soggy or smell of tragacanth and then he patented it, but he was always worried someone might steal his recipes so he only ever mixed them up himself. There's his recipe book in the locked cupboard at the back but you'd need to be a chemist to understand it," she said pointing towards the darkest recesses of the shop.

"Do you think it would be possible for me to take a look at it? I have a friend who is a chemist and may be able to make up what you need," Harold offered, but his method seemed no better than Charlie's own as the women began behaving like cornered sheep, shuffling towards the back of the shop where they spoke nervously among themselves while darting glances towards father and son.

"Do they want help or don't they?" growled Charlie. "If they weren't so good at what they do I'd leave now."

"Take it easy, Dad," Harold said over his shoulder as he walked towards the gaggle. "Perhaps you would prefer to give a list of your most urgent requirements to P.C. Pennings and he can hand it to us if we buy the business," he said before cordially bidding them "Good day" and ushering his father from the shop.

Charlie was feeling thoroughly peeved that his son had taken over the proceedings when he knew himself to be so much more experienced at handling shop staff, still, he reasoned, Harold probably had instructions from Dorothy to show them who was boss.

"No point in selling that, son," Charlie pronounced once they were purring back in the direction of the station again, "a full order book and practically running itself, you've landed on your feet there."

* * *

It felt like trespassing in a private guarded place where any intruder was almost guaranteed to be caught, Dorothy's stomach had been queasy for days before the scheduled house clearance but now she had actually entered the hallowed sanctuary she could feel the acid of fear rising up her throat as with trembling hands she moved towards his wardrobe.

She had decided to begin at the far end of his group of rooms, moving steadily backwards towards the door so that when she reached it the entire expanse in front of her would be depersonalised and she could leave the contents of his life boxed on the landing for Charlie's man to dispose of however he saw fit. She pulled the first box towards her and with a sharp 'click' turned the wardrobe handle. Pristine white shirts hung on a rack of identical varnished clothes hangers, starched collars were arranged on one shelf with military precision, perfectly folded under garments on another, evenly rolled ties filled one drawer so that all their colours could be appreciated without disturbing the arrangement of the whole, suits were shrouded in bleached cotton covers as spotless as virgin snow, and the row of shoes were not only polished to a deep shine on their uppers but all small stones and every trace of dirt had been removed from their soles. Despite the demise of the owner a month before, even dust had not dared to defile the sanitised regimental order of the place. Dorothy's discomfort at her intrusion doubled at the sight of the wardrobe's correctness. However carefully she packed each immaculate garment it would be desecrated by her fumbling fingers or her unworthy rough wooden boxes.

She was, she thought, probably the worst person to do this job. One of the ladies from the shop who had passed the test of the pedantic proprietor would have been far more suitable. If an action of the living could cause one of the dead to turn in their grave, this had to be it, in fact, if she survived without nightly visitations from a malevolent spirit it would almost constitute empirical proof against the existence of ghosts. She bent down to pick up the first pair of Italian leather brogues, placing them almost reverently in the nearest box with a mumbled prayer that her husband wasn't watching.

Moving on to the tallboy, it's glossy top patterned with mother-of-pearl, she noticed that his tortoise shell comb, brushes and mirror were laid out in the exact manner she remembered from when they had shared a home. A flashback to feelings of inadequacy tweaked at her gut, recalling how she had constantly tried to put all the household objects back in the identical position they had been before she assaulted each surface with her duster and yet, time after time, he would enter a room she had cleaned and spend the first few minutes deliberating over every moveable item in turn before easing it half an inch in one direction or another, until perfect symmetry was restored after the destructive hurricane of the cleaning cloth had so disrupted his domestic space.

Progressing through the tallboy drawers she arrived at the bottom and removed the perfumed paper liner with a flick of achievement marking the end of the bedroom and the time for her to move into the main living area. A grainy photograph fluttered to the floor and with a lurch of menace she recognised herself, still with the plumpness of adolescent puppy fat on her cheeks sitting in a deckchair with him beside her, outside the country hotel at which they had spent their honeymoon weekend. Her obvious long limbs accentuated the difference there was in their heights when they stood, and a look bordering on contented triumph was on her face. She had forgotten she had ever believed her marriage to be a great catch, yet here it was demonstrated as definitively as if someone had added a cartoon bubble reading: "I'm a grown woman, with my own home and a husband who sends me daily gifts."

Seated behind her on a poof decorated with an Aztec design, was Jean. Both of them looked directly at the camera but his expression was unclear. If she focused on the eyes and the thin lips with her mind unclouded by the events that followed this moment in their history, she could only say he seemed to be pleading.

Confused by its contents but with tangible veneration, she placed the photo into her handbag, snapping it shut before she dragged the half-filled boxes into the living room where Harold was sprawled over the sole armchair, his carefree presence seeming debauched among such sensitive furniture arrangement.

Removing four small paintings of bright geometric shapes from the wall, she then began work on her late husband's roll-top writing desk. Fastidiously kept account books stood next to some suppliers' invoices, neatly pinned together, all of which she passed to Harold to take care of before starting on the cubby holes and drawers. The desk screamed out to her that it had been touched, rifled through by the thorough P.C. Pennings who no doubt believed he had left the bureau in the same orderly state as he had found it in, but odd paper corners were not completely in line and the pens were no longer at accurate right angles with the back panel, all of which left Dorothy strangely relieved that she was not the first to encroach on this final piece of privacy.

A bundle of letters tied with a deep fuchsia ribbon was the only thing in the left hand section, the envelopes had all been opened with a sharpened letter knife leaving no slovenly rips along the top edges. Each one was addressed in the same elaborate hand, a rectangular stamp in the corner showing a man with a long curved nose, groomed moustache and forward pointing beard below the word 'Romania'. Untying the stack she realised how little she knew about him, how hidden he had been from her and how even the letters from his mother were indecipherable to her when the only word she could understand was 'Mama'. They had been kept in date order, the last one showed an eight, the word 'februarie' and 1916, they would have been married just under a year when it arrived. Had he told his mother about her? What had he said? Would the woman who wrote these letters have liked her?

Working backwards she discovered the first one was dated 1897 and addressed to a place in Paris, by 1899 the address had changed to Brussels before altering to Frankfurt and finally London in 1912. She had never realised he had travelled so extensively, but that fact did not bother her nearly as much as the dates. What was Jean doing in France, separated from his mother in 1897 when he would have been just eleven years old? Was life so cruel in his country that children younger than her Nancy were sent abroad to work? And then another move to a fresh country at just thirteen, was it these harsh antecedents that had made him seem so remote and worldly compared to her? Gathering the letters together again, conscious that she was not recreating the perfect bow she had undone, she placed the bundle to one side, unwilling to commit it to the rubbish bin with the other things that had no value now their owner was dead. To knowingly categorise them as 'waste' seemed deeply sacrilegious.

The final desk drawer held official records: their marriage certificate, his patent papers and a foolscap sheet marked "Primaria municipicelui Galati". The date 1873 caught her attention as one of the few items on the document she could understand.

"Harold," she said slowly, never taking her eyes from the sheet, "how good is your Latin?"

"Fairly awful, why?"

"Do you remember if 'Nascuti' means 'birth'?"

"Sounds possible," he said putting down the account books and coming over to look at the yellowing paper with its array of official stamps, "'Naissance' means 'born' in French."

"I think this is Jean's birth certificate" she said, her hand running down the foreign phrases stopping at names and words which vaguely matched remembered parts of schoolroom language learning. "But how can it be dated 1873?" she cried, her hand beginning to shake as she felt the slender control she had over her panic begin to slip away. "He always said he was nine years older than me and that's what I've put on his death certificate."

She steadied herself on the side of the desk, "is it a crime to put something incorrect on a death certificate? I can't do it again, people would get suspicious, it might all come out ..."

"It's not your fault if your husband lied about his age!" Harold said, studying the text over her shoulder, "My God, Bill, this man was as old as I am now when he married you, it's almost like someone our age trying to marry Nancy, I'd chase him out of town!"

"Uncle Edward would never have agreed," she said quietly. "It would never have happened."

Hastily stowing the documents in her handbag she brushed all the rest of the papers impatiently into the nearest box, leaving the rooms hygienically cleansed of all obvious memories of Jean. Not lingering a minute longer she moved briskly down the stairs, leaving Harold to close the heavy front door as she darted across the ornate art deco mosaic steps which announced the property's number in garish golds. Neither of them looked back. With every yard, freedom began to flood through her until by the end of the street she had grabbed Harold's hand and they were running pell mell, grinning like children on the first day of the summer holidays.

* * *

1938.
(Dorothy: 43, Harold: 44, Pat Fry: 16, Nancy: 15, Twins: 8)

Betty was peeved with Mrs Willand; she kept tripping off to London, often staying several days at a time and whatever their mother might think, the twins were not the innocent cherubs they imitated when processing up the aisle behind Reverend Croft dressed in their choirboy robes and effortlessly hitting the top notes of the Te Deum. In Betty's opinion the duo had more in common with Old Nick than any heavenly elements. They'd already caused her grief twice that week with neither Mr nor Mrs Willand around to shoulder the disciplinary responsibility. On Tuesday she'd opened the door to an irate P.C. Johnson, suspending a twin by its ear from each of his large hairy hands.

"They've been caught scrumping apples out of Mrs. Foster's garden, she saw 'em with her own eyes filling their pockets and then taking aim at perfectly good fruit with their catapults, you tell Mr and Mrs Willand to teach these two a lesson before they run riot through the whole neighbourhood," he commanded, releasing the boys with a shove towards the red-faced Betty who was having difficulty controlling her internal volcano. She wanted to shout out that she *would* tell Mr and Mrs Willand if she firstly had any idea where they were and secondly if she believed the couple would display anything scarier than their usual complete indulgence towards the terrible twosome.

Then, today, Mrs Miller had called her into her sweetshop to ask how much the twins were given for the collection on Sunday.

"A penny each."

"It seems one of the pennies is not getting to the Good Lord, as they've passed by here the last three Sundays asking for a penny's worth of aniseed balls and for me to change the other one into two ha'pence."

"Thieving little devils," Betty raged as she left the shop with flaming cheeks. "If they were mine I'd tan their hides off." But they weren't, and even eliciting Nancy's aid at dishing out stern discipline was ineffective when the big sister's face dissolved into a giggling fit directly Peter began to explain the finer points of their latest illegal antic. To a solid Christian girl like Betty their disregard for law and order teetered at the edge of heinous recklessness.

The back door banged open and the handsome young face of Pat Fry grinned round the frame. Betty didn't feel like smiling at him; he was another one of them who seemed incapable of living by the rules.

"Look what the cat dragged in," she said as he stepped into the kitchen, his muddy boots leaving marks on the flagstones.

"You're too gorgeous to be cross," he said leaning down from his towering height over her short dumpy form to elegantly take her hand and raise it to his lips.

"Stop your nonsense Pat Fry, don't you forget I'm a year older than you and head of this household right now," she said drawing herself up to her full five-foot-two, "What are you doing up here anyway?"

"Hitched a lift in the guard's van to come and see you and cousin Nancy, and as I didn't have to pay I've got enough to treat you and her at the dance tonight, so stop being grumpy and get your glad rags on," he said leaving her feebly attempting to repress a smile as he went in search of his cousins who collectively believed him to be closely related to Superman, which was one of the reasons Betty felt it her duty to regularly take him down a peg.

* * *

The evening of Jean's house clearance saw Dorothy and Harold with George and Alma in Charlie's living room for a pre-dinner drink. Taking a velvet ring box from his jacket pocket and sinking onto the carpet Harold flipped the lid to reveal a large emerald surrounded by six small diamonds.

"Although you're a grand lady of wealth and business, would you, Bill, do this humble man the honour of marrying as soon as the registrar can fit us in?"

"It'll be a come down," she said laughing and pulling him to his feet to kiss him firmly on the lips, "but I like a bit of rough!"

"Let's not have dinner here, we should go to the Palais to celebrate for old times' sake," Harold cried cajoling Charlie out of his armchair and irritating Sis into calling a halt to eating at home.

As they entered the dance hall Dorothy was still admiring the big shiny rock. She had been flashing her left hand out in front of her at regular intervals on the walk there, but a roar of voices from the dance hall dragged her away from her reverie as the six of them naturally fell into line yelling out *"doin' the Lambeth Walk, eh!"* as they swayed from side to side straight onto the dance floor.

The fashions had changed and the band played less ballroom music, but the décor and ambiance of the Palais seemed barely altered in the fifteen years since she had left, yet as Harold swung her round to the tune of *"When you're smilin', when you're smilin', the whole world smiles with you,"* and happiness glued her cheekbones high, Dorothy realised how they had changed, finally they had joined the ranks of the carefree couples she had so envied when they had gone to the Tango Tea so many years ago. Throughout their courtship, however much they had tried to play the part of untroubled lovers, there was an aura that someone who might shatter their dreams was watching, someone who could destroy the promise of a life together. Now she danced with abandon born from attaining the deliverance she had coveted for so long; no longer troubled by the shyness of youth or the awkwardness of new love, they matched each other step for step whether moving like whirling dervishes or Coco the clown.

* * *

The blue Caledonian sleeper train clacked rhythmically along the tracks heading from London towards Loch Ness on a clear starlit night which left the full moon flashing through a crack in the curtain whenever the carriage swayed. Harold slithered down the ladder from the top bunk and squeezed in next to his wife.

"It's bad luck to spend your wedding night apart," he said. She greeted him with a crescent of white teeth as she flattened herself against the thin wall. "Did you think we'd ever get this far, Mrs Willand?"

"No, I honestly didn't," she said slipping an uncomfortable arm beneath his waist, "especially after the last few years."

He kissed her softly, acknowledging the truth of what she had said as he looked at her bobbed hair on the pillow, more white than colour now among the strands, 'pepper and salt' she called it but the salt was definitely winning. Her eyes had lines at the corners and her breasts had suffered from a succession of eager mouths, but she was still the only woman he wanted to wake up with every morning.

"We had a beautiful boy," he eventually replied, their bodies forced together by the narrowness of the mattress, their faces stacked cheek to cheek, both of them finally allowing slow tears to fall, mingling together for the first time, his words lancing an exquisitely painful carbuncle, freeing the hurt from their souls.

"We did," she said, and as she lifted her head he could see the moonlight glistening off her moist eyes, "we really did."

Steph Mason

CHAPTER TWENTY

Betty's diary, Tuesday 27th September 1938: Everyone is so worried of the war scare and we were all delivered gas masks.

* * *

3rd September 1939
Harold got up from his chair and turned the wireless power knob to 'OFF', he pinched the bridge of his nose not turning round to look at his silent family. "It had to happen, Chamberlain gave them every chance."

"Nora will be worried," Dorothy murmured, "Pat's the same age James was when the last war happened."

"There will have to be some changes around here," Harold announced slowly revolving to face them, his stubborn calmness was pervading the sitting room so that even the nine-year-old twins resisted the temptation to break into war cries.

"I should write immediately to British & Colonial to let them know my current address. I may never get to play my part on the battlefield like Arthur and Wilfred did but I won't shirk my duty. You children will have to help your mother if I'm needed elsewhere," he seemed to be almost speaking to himself now, oblivious to the rapt audience, making a job list in his mind. "If it lasts a while and there's rationing we may have to close the garage, and maybe the London business too. We'll be all right, pull in our belts a few notches, just need to get organised, that's all."

* * *

Coats, scarves and hats bulged off the row of pegs making the passageway from the front door to Nora's kitchen so narrow it was like walking through C.S. Lewis's wardrobe into Narnia, the five sisters and Arthur sat around the kitchen table thawing their frozen hands around large mugs of tea, Nora was wiggling her toes inside damp, clammy stockings in an effort to avoid chilblains.

Flo and Vera, eldest and youngest of the clan, looked nervously at each other as if they were colluding before Flo launched into the midst of the chatter with, "I don't know if this is a bad time to mention it, but as Pat's room is goin' to be free for at least a couple of years we were thinkin' it might be a good idea to move Dad up 'ere."

An uncomfortable hush blotted out the contrived light-heartedness the six of them had been working hard at ever since they met up on the station platform to wave Pat off on his odyssey across the Atlantic. Sybil and Peggy, with an arm each around Nora had squeezed and cajoled her into drying her tears by pointing out that the seventeen-year-old was better off with an ocean between him and Hitler rather than just a thin channel, and in all likelihood the war would be over by the time the U.S. Navy had finished training him. While she had rallied in front of them Nora still could not imagine her tiny home without Pat's big presence; he filled every room he was in, not just physically but with his good humour, his endless stories and his energy. Arthur said he had ants in his pants, yet it wasn't random leaping about, he was just incapable of containing his enthusiasm for life and it infected her whenever she was with him. Nora had secretly planned to keep Pat's room unchanged in the hope she could take refuge there and inhale some of his optimism when she was feeling at a low ebb, it was to be her little tonic, her way of keeping in touch with him when the wrap-around bear hugs were temporarily unavailable. The image of her father in that room made her draw air sharply between her lips as if she had just bitten into a lemon. She would have to pack everything of Pat's away, all the model aircraft would have to come down from the ceiling and there was no way she would leave the intricate patchwork quilt she had made for her son so that her father could drop his cigarette ash all over it and probably leave a few burn marks in as well.

"It's just not safe for 'im in Bexhill," Flo ploughed on. "At our WVA meetings we're instructed in everythin' we must do when the invasion comes 'cos we'll be the front line," both Sybil and Vera were nodding as backup.

"We were told to encourage all vulnerable people to leave the south coast," Sybil explained, "and there's no doubt 'e's vulnerable, 'e can 'ardly see a foot in front of 'imself, most of the time I reckon 'e gets about from memory rather than sight, although 'e's too obstinate to admit it."

"I've not disagreed with you," Nora said, shooting a pleading look at Arthur, "but wouldn't Thomas's house be safer, it's further north."

"'e won't agree to go there, says Elizabeth's too stuck up and so are 'er family," Flo replied.

"I don't think she'd be kind to 'im the way you and Peggy would be," Vera said in a soft earnest voice. "'E's got nicer recently, 'e even said to me 'e wanted to meet Dorothy's children."

"You must 'ave been dreamin', or 'e's completely lost the plot!" Nora replied half laughing in spite of the railing misery she felt. "When I mentioned they'd married 'e gave me a right earful about 'ow it didn't change nothin', 'e was as full of fire and brimstone as ever!"

"'E didn't say 'e wanted to see Dorothy, just the boys," Vera said simply, "Our WVS leader said the government would protect the capital more than anywhere else, so it must be the safest place for 'im to be."

"'itler seems able to march into wherever 'e wants, but if you think London will be safer then bring 'im up," Nora said mentally reciting the bold print on the bottom of the War Office leaflet that had fluttered onto her doormat and was entitled *If The Invader Comes*: 'THINK ALWAYS OF YOUR COUNTRY BEFORE YOU THINK OF YOURSELF', she'd have to content herself with letters rather than a 'Pat Sanctuary' and pray her son got his wings quickly and the fighting was over even sooner.

* * *

5th September 1940
(Dorothy: 45, Harold: 46, Nancy: 17, Twins: 10, Aunt Sarah: 76)

The sound of the twins sawing through planks of half rotten wood they had found at the back of the shed filled the early September afternoon. John had won a pullet at the school rummage fair that had been held to raise Spitfire funds the previous Saturday, and Dorothy was determined the hen would be properly housed outside before she dropped the boys with Nora on Friday. For only the second time since Harold had left, she had obtained a travel pass to Bristol. They were becoming increasingly difficult to get hold of and she had been delighted when it arrived, promising her a whole weekend away, it didn't matter that they would be sleeping like sardines in a tin at his spartan lodgings eating bread and spam, rather than enjoying a mini-break in an hotel room and dinner with wine.

Nancy and Betty were pleased to be left for two days of undisturbed house sitting, which was to be punctuated by a dance down at the Institute. She could hear the gramophone now, the record was stopped every few bars as Nancy tutored Betty into mastering the latest moves. By the time the hen house was completed Dorothy had no doubt the two of them would have perfected the steps and she would be asked to watch the finished performance before the living room furniture was retrieved from around the walls and put back in place in time for the BBC News bulletin.

"If it gets cold this winter we should have her back in the scullery," John said looking solemnly at his mother. "An egg a day is too valuable to lose."

"Then you need to make the house easy to move as I don't want her in the box again, she just climbs out of it and makes an awful mess on the floor."

John pondered the problem with Peter, "If we make it in sections it will be easier to carry, but it's got to be secure against foxes."

Dorothy smiled thinking how pleasant it was to see John taking control of the operation. The twins were so very different from each other; Peter, the eldest by twenty minutes, was bigger with thick curly hair, always midway through an urgent scheme he was working on, the details of which he often hadn't thought out properly. John was quieter with searching brown eyes. He would listen to his more exuberant twin until the flow of enthusiasm slowed, at which time he would gently point out the fatal flaw in the proposed plan together with his idea of how to rectify it. They were like two halves of a motion picture: John was the camera, taking in all the images, putting them in sequence to make order out of them, while Peter was the projector, showing their joint creations to the world, causing the 'oohs' and 'ahhs' in the audience, the two of them together forming a perfect whole, but in the case of the hen house John was firmly in charge. When he'd gone up to Mr Hutchings amid the clapping and cheers to receive his feathered prize, the school master had been attentive, answering all the lad's questions about how to care for the family's first 'pet' since Lucky.

"She should begin laying in about a month," John said, as Peter narrowly missed smashing his thumb with the hammer, merely bending the nail head over in a hair breadth miss. "If she eats lots of green leaves her yokes will be bright orange but if we feed her acorns they'll go green," he announced with lurid satisfaction.

"We should lock her inside the hen house with a huge pile of acorns and see how green we can get them," Peter chipped in.

"I think I'd prefer normal eggs if it's OK with you two," their mother laughed, walking towards the house to sort out the arrangements before they left.

Since the evacuation from Dunkirk in May the garage had only been open one day a week and it looked likely that it would close completely before Christmas. Every gallon of petrol needed saving and every piece of available metal, right down to pots and pans, was being melted and reformed to produce tanks, aeroplane parts and armoured cars to replace the convoys of equipment that had been left on the beaches of France. She could feel that William was itching to be relieved of any responsibility for the garage so he could dedicate himself to war work and to be honest she wouldn't be sad to see it close, at least then all the remaining petrol would be removed and she wouldn't fret about it falling into enemy hands when the invasion came.

People talked about a German invasion in terms of 'when' not 'if' now and although the general idea was the further north and central you were the safer you would be, she was battling a sensation of being marooned in Kelvedon without Harold or her sisters, or even Charlie and George. Thousands of others were far worse off than she was of course, but she had begun to feel a tight desperation in her chest for the chance to talk to Nora and see the photographs Pat had sent of himself on a Californian beach with palm trees standing tall and exotic behind him, looking a million miles away from grey, war torn Britain. Just an hour of chat with her sister and a couple of days to rekindle the family bonds with her husband was so much more than many women had and the prospect of her weekend pass loomed in front of her, a delicious orgy of familiarity in the middle of such strange times.

The demand for train places and the need to move all goods around the country by rail meant she wouldn't be allowed to take a suitcase, so spare underwear and anything else she needed had to be stuffed into her pockets and handbag. She'd sewn an extra large pocket, more like a calico bag, on the inside of her winter coat in an effort to get around the problem and enable her to take some supplies from the garden and the local farmers down to London to show her appreciation for her sister's care of the twins while she was away.

Harold's letters had been full of his training with the Home Guard. The production of aircraft engines was more mechanical than in the previous war, with fewer demands for Harold's engineering trouble shooting, but the Home Guard had finally given him a uniform to feel proud of and a mandate to 'do his bit'. Weekend courses on guerrilla tactics, first aid and field operations were reported in detail with instructions that Dorothy should read the relevant paragraphs out to the twins. One night in eight he would be on duty throughout the blacked-out time when the rest of the city attempted to sleep, afterwards he returned to his digs at six in the morning for an hour's rest before getting up for work.

For all the pride Dorothy felt in Harold's Home Guard zeal, she was keeping all her extremities crossed that he could avoid doing his duty this weekend.

* * *

Aunt Nora stood with a hand firmly placed on each twin's shoulder, the pressure was nudging John forwards towards the old man seated in an upright armchair in the corner of the basement's tiny lounge. A wormy odour mixed with tobacco smoke emanated from the figure as he took his hands from the chair's flat wooden arms, reaching them straight out as they felt the air for explanations.

"These are Dorothy's boys, Dad," Aunt Nora said giving Peter and John a minuscule shove. The musty smell became stronger as they took the enforced step forward, Peter seized the right hand that was meandering towards his body, shaking it heartily, stopping it from wandering further.

"Pleased to meet you, Sir," he said, wriggling free of his Aunt's clutches as he called over his shoulder, "Uncle Arthur, can you show me those card tricks you promised?" before dropping the gnarled brown limb and hastening for the kitchen.

"I'll make some tea," Nora sighed, moving away, leaving John alone before his grandfather. The eyes that faced him were opaque, the arms that stretched into space, searching for matter, were so covered in liver spots and tufts of course black hair that it was impossible to guess what they would have looked like when young and muscular, wrinkled skin hung off the parts that showed beneath the rolled up shirt sleeves. John had read about blind people, about how their other senses were heightened, their need to touch and feel what the eyes could no longer register, so he moved into the softly flailing fingers, allowing his face to be explored, his height recorded, the breadth of his shoulders measured.

"Which one are you?" rank breath filled the space between them.

"John, Sir."

"You're tall."

"Peter's taller, Sir."

"But 'e's gone to learn tricks, eh," phlegmy coughs seemed to crumple the ancient bony chest.

"Reckon 'e's like my James was. 'e'll be canny with the ladies that one," half a smile cracked across the face, splintering into a thousand deep crevices.

"So, young John, what do you want to do with your life?"

"I'm not sure yet Sir, I'm hoping to get more ideas when I go to Grammar school."

"Grammar school eh! What a posh family I'm getting so late in the day."

"I think I'd like to do something with my hands, rather than sit in an office all day," he ventured.

"If you're good with your 'ands, take this," Charles Terrill reached down to the side of the chair pulling out a pipe and tobacco pouch from beneath the cushion and handing them to his grandson. "Fill me a good pipe, pack it tight mind."

Once the smoke had been enjoyed in silence and the tar from his lungs regurgitated into his stained handkerchief, the sparsely covered scalp lolled against the wing of the chair as he snoozed, John kept sneaking a look at the old man, he knew it was rude to stare but did it count if the recipient couldn't see you? At six o'clock the old man was still sleeping so they left him to go and play whist with Auntie Peggy and the Great Aunt at number eighty-eight.

* * *

Arthur had won one game and Aunt Sarah the other two when the evening was pierced by wailing sirens.

"There's Moanin' Mini," Nora said, "Do you think we should pack up? I've got such a good 'and and last night they gave the all clear after forty minutes."

"Stop messin' about and get the pillows and blankets while I put on the tent. You boys help your Great Aunt to get underneath," Peggy instructed as she produced an elaborate construction of sheets and pegs she draped over the table to deflect any flying glass or plaster from landing on her Aunt while Nora busily stuffed the pillows and blankets beneath the solid slab of oak.

"You lot get going," Aunt Sarah commanded from the floor, "stop fussing around here and get yourselves and Charles under the stairs."

* * *

Dashing down the unlit road, they slid into the cupboard slamming the door shut just as the first whine informed them that this time the warning was for real. There were six of them in the cupboard. Turning his head to the right John could smell his grandfather, to the left was the perfume of Great Aunt Sarah's lily of the valley soap which he assumed must be on his Auntie Peggy's hands, he knew Peter was directly in front of him sitting with his back against the opposite side of the cupboard wall because when he had put his hand out he had felt the fabric of his brother's trousers, but more than that he could not tell as the blackness was total, completely impenetrable even though he kept his eyes open and with each beat of landing bombs his eye lids shuttered further back. The drone of engines was so thick it became background noise, interrupted by the 'pom pom' of anti-aircraft fire, John had heard of air attacks but in his most elaborate fantasies it had never been like this, his imagination had usually placed one or two bombs uncomfortably close, but not this hour after hour of relentless pounding with no let up, crouched in the dark like rats in a hole.

The house juddered around them as a cacophony of explosions seemed to go off almost alongside their cramped refuge.

"I wish I hadn't left Aunt Sarah," Auntie Peggy's voice drifted into the centre of the cupboard during a brief lull in the invisible destruction that was happening around them.

"It would have taken us an hour to get her down all the stairs to here and she couldn't have stretched out," Auntie Nora's answer came back.

"It's not right for her to be all alone."

Cavernous blackness enveloped Auntie Peggy's statement as John pictured the Great Aunt laid out beneath her table, looking as if she had been prepared for sacrifice, stoically accepting she was possibly destined to become a statistic of war.

As the Luftwaffe's next gift detonated no more than fifty yards away, something landed softly on John's head. He raised his hand to his hair brushing nervously, certain a large spider was making its way towards the collar of his shirt, but his fingers encountered pieces of dust and plaster instead of eight-legged creatures, leaving him wondering how long it would take rescuers to find them if the floors above pancaked down entombing them in the rubble. His bottom had become numb over an hour ago, maybe it was two or three hours, he had no real sense of time and it was impossible to tell if all the crashes and bangs were concertinaed into terrified minutes or if, in fact, they had been there so long that dawn was about to break outside in their ruined world. His eyes no longer widened with each explosion and he seemed cocooned in his own small area of inkiness, knees drawn up, forehead on them, his hands linked together spanning the base of his skull. Every so often their burrow would seem to be hit from the inside as his grandfather dissolved into a fresh set of graveyard coughs, but otherwise they remained silent, feeling the dust and flakes of paint trickle down, nobody saying anything that could lessen John's vision of the carnage they would find when they emerged, if they ever did get out again, nor could he erase the picture of the lonely peril of his Great Aunt who had always seemed so majestically invincible.

John could not say when the whines, bangs and droning were replaced by crackling and the groans of buildings, but at some point he registered the noises had changed and he began waiting for the 'All Clear'.

When it came and each one of them painfully unwound themselves from their cramped positions, they were reborn into a world of fire. Ringed by flames, the night sky was so bright they could have read a newspaper even though it was three in the morning. Uncle Arthur began to run down the street towards a group who were working beside a collapsed house, while Auntie Nora and Auntie Peggy sprinted like youthful athletes for number eighty-eight which stood tall, surrounded by burning debris.

As John wandered down the street with his twin, the air drawn into his lungs felt thick and warm as if he needed to chew through dust to breathe. A ruptured gas main in the next road was spitting long tongues of orange while dirt smeared men were keeping residents back, telling them to wait elsewhere until this single incident, among a thousand others, could be rectified. The brothers returned to Sinclair Road, turning towards the heap of bricks and rubble where their uncle was levering up beams and debris with a long crow bar, calling out, then stopping to listen for a living reply.

It came, ever so faintly.

"All right Mrs Higgins, it's Mr Fry here, I'm sending for more help, just hold on and we'll have you out as quick as we can." Turning to his nephews he barked, "Run to the end and turn right, tell the police or any of the official crews you meet that sixty-four Sinclair Road took a direct hit and there's a woman alive inside."

* * *

Nora had no doubt about what needed to be done, the sight of Sarah and Edward's old house in a pile, neatly flanked by numbers sixty-two and sixty-six, which appeared completely unaffected apart from occasional pieces of jagged brickwork that remained clinging to them, left her with no other option

"We 'ave to send 'er to Wiltshire today."

"She'll kick up about it," Peggy replied, "but you're right, she's in too much danger 'ere."

"When we go to the station to give the twins back to Dorothy we'll take 'er too. I'll send a message to Bower Chalke as soon as the Post Office opens, and I'll tell Dorothy if she goes to see 'arold, we'll go up to Kelvedon rather than risk having the boys down 'ere again."

By five o'clock that afternoon Aunt Sarah, armed with a few belongings and her gas mask, was being jostled through crowds at the station with the thousands of others trying to get out of the capital. Nora watched her Aunt's dazed and sorrowful expression, it was the same as so many of the other evacuees, the face of being expelled from everything they had known. Doubts crept through her tired body, what if her aunt didn't survive the war anyway and was being forced to pass her last days among strangers? What repayment was this for her years of care? Did she even understand why her nieces were being so insistent that she go? Leaving her seated beside a window in a second class carriage, Nora watched the train pull away. Her aunt's expression would haunt her for years.

* * *

Harold had been moved north to the Rolls-Royce factory in Cheshire where he was building Merlin aero engines. He and Dorothy had managed to grab a Sunday together, meeting half way and spending most of the day at the station where they ate the sandwiches she'd brought, filled with the jam she and Nancy had made when sugar was still plentiful, but without butter as by the end of the week there was none of their ration left.

She told him about Pat being due home soon and Nancy's wish to join ENSA as a singer and dancer, about the eggs from John's hen and Peter becoming a soloist in the church choir. He had told her about the factory, the PV-12 and how to spot Lancasters, Hurricanes, Spitfires and Mosquitos all of which might be flying with engines he had actually built. He also mentioned Miss Philips and Miss Wright who worked in the office, and how they ribbed Miss Wright by enquiring if she had any inventive uncles. He seemed rather impressed by Miss Wright, Dorothy thought, so under the guise of general chat, smothering the shape of her mouth with a sandwich, Dorothy had asked lightly what the secretary was like.

"Shorter than you, blonde hair, rather pretty really, not much over twenty-five I'd say but devilish efficient at her job."

Dorothy churned the description around in her head and her stomach over every clattering mile of track back to Kelvedon. She lay in their unfilled marital bed staring at the ceiling, picturing various secretaries, all of whom were twenty-five and walked with the surety that they were attractive which gave them the freedom to flirt with the world, and she felt like tearing each one of them into ugly little pieces.

* * *

A tuppence hapenny letter card dropped onto the mat at Brookside.
C/O Mrs Dixon
226 Ruskin Road
Crewe
3/1/41
Darling,
Many thanks for sending letters, and take it that you got home safely, and generally had quite a nice time. I feel inclined to ignore your "nosiness", and am certainly not going to enter into elaborate correspondence except to say that this is not the first time that you have "jumped to conclusions" without knowing the true explanations. So forget it until I see you at the end of the month. Conditions up here are pretty bad, especially accommodation, it is intensely cold, and last night we had two air-raid warnings which lasted all night. I shall probably be changing my digs this weekend to C/O Mrs Yoxall, 230 Ruskin Road, Crewe, where I shall have a

bedroom that is heated and inside sanitation which I have not at present. I hope you got my previous letter O.K. and everything is all right at home. Well cheerio for the time being with my love from
Harold
P.S. Have you packed the electric trains away yet? Don't forget you are the only one.

* * *

1943.
(Dorothy: 47, Nancy: 21, Twins: 13)

Dorothy was practising formal scales and arpeggios on the piano in the living room. Her fingers moved mechanically while her head fretted about producing honky tonk and swing, jive and jazz. The whole area seemed to be sinking under the weight of millions of American airmen and troops. There were airfields everywhere and Saturday night had become party-night in full Stateside fashion. Harry Doughton had convinced her it was her war duty to play in the Kelvedon Quartet at St. Mary's Hall where the town would make a weekly effort to entertain their visitors who were always so generous with their Lucky Strikes, nylons and gum, but Dorothy had strong reservations about the abilities of the Quartet to entertain. Mr Welsh, the trumpet player, was a long way removed from Louis Armstrong, his only regular experience seemed to have been playing the Last Post on the bugle in the previous war, but she knew of no other local who might replace him and was hoping that a few proficient Yanks might step up and relieve them from their hours of embarrassment.

Following a clatter of the letter flap, the twins barged into her scales, elbowing each other through the door with Peter holding an envelope aloft in his hand an inch too high for John to grab it off him.

"There's a letter from Pat addressed to us, can I open it?"

"Yes, but do it nicely, together, or you'll rip it."

Two heads bowed over the small paper that was extracted.

"Oh my! Look how close that must be to the fuel tank!" John exclaimed.

"What is it?" their mother asked, leaning over to see the photo of her nephew standing proudly beside a Bristol Beaufighter, the sides of which wore streaks of perfectly round bullet holes like a polka dot paint job. "I don't know how he stays alive! Nora must be so worried."

"He's written on the back," Peter said flipping the picture over, "'Don't show my mum this photo, it's not good for her nerves!'"

"I'll say!" said Dorothy.

"'There's talk I may get a DFC this time. Hope to drop in on you soon. Cheerio. Pat'."

"I'd better keep back some rations in case," Dorothy mused as she made her way towards the larder to take stock of its contents. "I wish he'd said when."

In the kitchen Nancy was bent over a saucer with a small blob of Vaseline in the middle, adorning it will single drops of beetroot juice whilst mixing with the same intensity of concentration as a bio chemist. Betty stood up from the oven door, an almost perfectly charred stick held lightly in her hand.

"I reckon it's perfect to draw seams if we keep a steady hand. Have you got the colour right yet?"

"I don't know, try some on and let me see."

Betty dabbed her little finger in the middle of the potion before smearing it over her lips.

"We need much more, it hardly changes the colour at all," Nancy commented, chopping a corner off the bleeding vegetable and swirling it around the gunk. "Mother, have you got a cork? It says in the magazine we can make mascara by burning the end."

Dorothy was just considering the cork situation when she landed in a squat position, hands clasped over her head as the most tremendous roar set the windows rattling, the others also dropped by instinct but as they were beginning to unfold themselves the front door banged open and Dorothy realised the twins had dashed out onto the street.

"Get back! It's coming down!" Dorothy screamed, running towards the open door in time to see the plane bank sharply right, lining itself up as if the High Street was to be its landing strip. "He can't land there!"

By now all the neighbours were outside trying to wave the pilot of the dying machine in the direction of fields, but the aircraft was relentless and the townsfolk scattered, cascading down side streets in their final attempt to save their lives, while dogs flattened themselves to the pavements growling at the sky. As the wings skimmed inches above the triple Tudor-beamed rooves of The Sun Inn, almost beheading their tall chimney pots, Peter leapt up pointing,

"It's Pat!"

Unfrozen from their horrified gawp at the impending destruction of their town, Nancy grabbed the twins and in her harshest big sister voice hissed at the teenagers who were already taller than her, "Shut up you idiot, he'll get court marshalled if they find out!"

"No need to keep any rations back," Dorothy whispered as snorting nervous laughter erupted out of all of them the minute the heavy door was safely closed, "he couldn't stop for tea!"

* * *

Summer 1944.
(Dorothy: 49, Harold: 50, Charlie: 74, Nancy: 21, Twins: 14)
The town was quiet, unnaturally quiet, the streets were clear of the choke of uniforms and different accents, the vehicles had gone, the cigarettes and candy almost wiped from the landscape, the band was only needed for local girls to dance together. Dorothy felt flat. The cocky young military men might not have been much older than her sons, but they'd made a fuss of her, winking at her while they danced as she played, presenting her with flowers and chocolate, giving her that heady feeling that she wasn't just some middle aged mother stuck in an Essex backwater thumping a piano, but an important part of the struggle, that she was worthy of being fought for. She couldn't deny that there were aspects of the war that were seriously enjoyable.

Suddenly everything had stopped and the whole country seemed to be holding a collective breath, waiting for their boys, or the Americans, to come marching home and tell them it was over, they were safe. But it hadn't happened yet and although the big push meant aero engine production had scaled down and so Harold had been sent home, Dorothy couldn't relax into family normality as Nancy was already being vaccinated against yellow fever, typhoid and cholera in preparation for donning her grease paint for the benefit of troops in India and Burma. The ENSA troop was to travel via North Africa and Baghdad before crossing the Indian Ocean to Bombay and Nancy was bursting with excitement, practising her routines every minute she wasn't laid too low by the cocktail of vaccinations. Dorothy attempted to share her daughter's enthusiasm instead of thinking of the possible consequences of voyaging across half the world to play a part in this very foreign war.

* * *

"That hen hasn't laid for over a month," Betty announced firmly to Dorothy. "You should have it on Sunday before Nancy leaves, it would be criminal to waste it, you'll already have to braise it for hours to get it tender."

Dorothy was attempting not to hear. "You can't go soft," Betty badgered "not with teenage lads to feed."

"It's John's"

"Rubbish! It's just an old hen, like any other you'd see plucked and hanging in the butchers," she said briskly in the tone Aunt Sarah would have used in her heyday and which always left Dorothy feeling bullied.

"I'll sort it out," Betty said, before giving the final order to her employer, "You go and pull some onions and pick a few sage leaves."

* * *

"I come all the way up here, you put on a splendid lunch and then the whole bunch of you sits round the table looking as if you're at a wake and not eating a morsel!" Charlie boomed at the solemn faces that periodically seemed to be suffering from colds, necessitating frequent handkerchief action, in an affliction that had also robbed them of their appetites. "For goodness sake, much as I'd like to, I can't eat all of this wondrous fowl myself!" he laughed, hoping indifference to their sensibilities would somehow eradicate them.

Charlie had arrived the previous evening, ostensibly to bid farewell to his only grand-daughter but actually to gain comfort from his son after some unpleasant scenes with Sis and Madeline whom he had managed to exile to a pretty cottage in Ugley Green for the past couple of years, by arguing it was safer for them to remain in the country while the constraints of his business glued him to London. Somehow his wife had wised up to the complete lack of butchering business Charlie was actually engaging in, together with the sizeable amount of time he could expend with a certain curvaceous female by the name of Amy, whose stated residence was only a couple of doors down from Sis's previous marital home.

It was awkward, but at seventy-five and during the second global conflict of his life, Charlie felt he should not pass up any opportunity for enjoyment. He had left his wife and daughter well-housed and with generous funds, he was even prepared to visit them regularly if they were amusing company, so he was at a loss to know why they would complain. The cottage was in the same village as Sis's favourite brother lived, an excellent fellow who always informed Charlie if his sister was short of anything that might be available on the London black market so that Charlie could surprise her with it. So why, he wondered, would she scream and shout at him like a mentally challenged fishwife, bandying about wild accusations of infidelity and lack of interest in her and Madeline, which, while admittedly they might be true, were not based on any solid evidence he had given her, and so were clearly irrational. Now she was threatening to return to London, disregarding his tales of Doodlebugs and V2s coming over like swarms of locusts. She had become implacable in a way that could seriously dent his joie de vivre. She was really being completely unreasonable.

"Why don't you stay here Dad?" Harold offered as they sat together once the uneaten hen had been cleared away, "we get fewer bombs."

His son was being gratifyingly sympathetic about Charlie's uncontrollable spouse, but had completely missed the point that he needed to return to London in order to wallow in Amy's charms. This could have been because he had omitted to mention anything about her to his son. The revelation, he felt, could have diluted the level of compassion being draped around him, which was so warming and pleasant.

"Maybe for a few days, but London's my home," he replied, "I haven't been hit yet, so I'll take my chance and hope my luck holds."

"I hate to think of you down there alone."

"Don't you start," Charlie growled, visions of his son interrupting his love nest now beginning to worry him, "I've George and Alma plus a lifetime's worth of friends. I'm happy in my home if everyone just lets me be."

* * *

The crowd of dancers in St Mary's Hall spilled out onto the streets as the blackout blinds were ripped down and sweet fresh night air filled the room that had been stuffy and dim for more than five years. As Dorothy's fingers waltzed over the keys she had now become so at ease with, her face was lit with relief, the wide smile never letting her cheeks fall for a moment as she gave thanks her sons had never become old enough to be called up. Surely now there was victory in Europe the full allied might would be turned onto Japan and they would soon triumph there too and Nancy would return, safe, glowing and enriched by her adventure rather than harmed in any way.

She thought of how Nora would finally be able to sleep at night rather than worry that every plane she heard might contain her son and that this mission could be his last. Nora could rest tonight wrapped up in a blanket of pride in Pat's two Distinguished Flying Crosses and the Croix de Guerre he had received. For years pride had been squashed out of all of them by nervousness that it was tempting fate to luxuriate in courage today when it could be replaced by a deep well of grief tomorrow. Tonight fear had lost, and pride could be basked in she thought.

At eighty years old Aunt Sarah could finally return to her unharmed home, in fact all of them could begin again, get back to normal, whatever 'normal' was going to be. There was one blot on the landscape, but even this seemed to pale into a niggle as Dorothy watched her friends and neighbours whirl around in front of her, serenity on every face.

Six weeks before the final Doodlebug dropped, Charlie had suffered a stroke and then succumbed to pneumonia leaving a four-page will, the contents of which were likely to dog Harold with migraines for years. In his haze of rediscovered youth, Charlie had made more generous provision for his mistress than his daughter which had resulted in Sis becoming as mad as a swarm of hornets and as she was unable to vent her anger on a corpse, she dropped it solidly upon the hapless Harold. The woman scorned remained at her cottage in Ugley Green, close to her own family and, uncomfortably, within the same county as Kelvedon.

Harold had said volubly when he first read the awful final testament that he felt very sorry for his step-mother, but the aura of sympathy evaporated with every fresh volley of lawyers' letters. Having had absolutely no knowledge of what the old man had put in his will, Harold became understandably irritated at being held responsible for its contents and being forced into building legal defences against his father's widow and his own half-sister. Yet tonight, as Harold danced while Dorothy played, the two of them exchanging winks and smiles throughout the evening, she hoped that Sis and Madeline would be celebrating too, and that the deliverance of peace would put their own private war into context allowing a cease fire throughout the family so they could dedicate themselves to enjoying calm prosperity in a nation no longer wondering if the next bomb would spell the end for them.

CHAPTER TWENTY-ONE

1st September 1945.
(Dorothy: 50, Harold: 51, Nancy: 22, Twins: 15)

"Come on John," Peter yelled sprinting out of the door through the gate and cutting down to the river, catching up with the other lads from the Worlds End Lane gang as they slid along the bank, saving themselves by grabbing overhanging branches, flying to overtake the invaders who were already visible skimming along fifty yards ahead. The Coggershall Road gang had been spotted quietly gliding under the bridge and heading en masse towards the boat stack, leaving the World Enders charging for defensive positions as they fought to prevent Coggershall from robbing them a second time in one month.

The canoe battles were intense and the theft of a craft left the pilfered side vulnerable to being surrounded and suffering a crushing defeat of their armada. Capsize and sinking were constant problems even when not fending off the marauding hoards from the other side of the bridge. The canoes were constructed from auxiliary aircraft fuel tanks which the Americans jettisoned once they were empty. Whenever the cylinders were spotted falling from the sky, boys from both gangs would race for the fields, hauling away the bootie before the Yanks could retrieve them. A spot of precision engineering with a hacksaw made a hole for the owner to sit in with ballast placed along the bottom in an attempt to create stability. There had been a few unfortunate moments when the boat builders had failed to cut a big enough hole making escape from capsize impossible. It had happened to Ben Spence and although they had dragged him to the edge and pumped on him until he threw up gallons of water, he had never been quite the same since. Health and safety meant being able to swim in the first place, plus bending back the hole's jagged edges so that they didn't slice neatly through the teenage captain when the canoe was rammed during naval manoeuvres.

Once the war cry went up it was certain that the twins would be fully engaged in defending and counter attack until dusk reminded them that they were hungry and drove them home, Victory in Japan might have arrived a fortnight before, but as far as Peter and the other Kelvedon lads were concerned there were still plenty of missions to be undertaken especially as their source of canoes had dried up, so the existing fleet had to be protected down to the last man.

* * *

Harold sat in the living room not absorbing the newspaper yet surrounded by the peace which settles on a house only after the resident teenagers have left the premises. He should have been feeling relaxed, instead he was restless, it was as if a small boring insect was attempting to enter his brain by way of his temples. To do nothing was to allow the insect to win but he was not at all sure what he should do to prevent it, only that it had to be something decisive.

"Are you going to the garage later?" Dorothy asked as she entered the room armed with her duster and a jar of polish.

He looked at her over the top of his reading glasses, puckering his lips as he thought, "I *really* don't want to, I know I *should*, it's my business and it is stocked with pleasant people and fine engines, but it feels as if all the life will be sucked out of me if I go there, so I'm making all sorts of excuses in my mind to get out of it. You may even persuade me I absolutely have to dig out the compost heap!" Dorothy raised an eyebrow, "Yes, I know I've been putting it off since Easter and to be honest it will probably lose out again to a game of tennis!"

"So it's pretty clear what you *don't* want to do," she said sitting down beside him, "have you any idea what you *do* want?"

"I think I'd like to move, there doesn't seem to be a good reason why we're living here any longer."

She looked startled as if she had expected him to say "go for a walk" and instead he had presented her with a monumental problem, it didn't seem like a good start.

"I don't want to run a garage any more, and we have sufficient to live on from Dad's properties," he argued, "I'd like to sell up, it's a good time, everyone feels the country will get back on its feet now." She moved towards the sideboard, turning her back on him as she rearranged the decanters on the drinks tray, before deciding they all needed cleaning and beginning some earnest investigation into each cut glass gully. Her silence made him nervous, once the idea had been deposited in the middle of the living room it seemed to take on an existence of its own, blossoming into pleasant pictures of a different type of life, closer to the big theatres, cinemas and dance halls of London, with the promise of impromptu days with George and Alma rather than ones that always had to be arranged in advance, a life without employees and accounts, wages and irate customers; to back track on this dream suddenly appeared impossible, vocalising the notion of selling the garage and moving back to London made the yearning inside him grow into a necessity which threatened to choke him if she rejected it in favour of the status quo. He stood up and went to stand close behind her, his breath on her neck, his arms finding their way along the tie of her apron around her waist to gently still her restless hands and draw all of her to him.

"What are you thinking?" he asked, his heart hammering against his rib cage in case she refused outright.

Still she paused before revolving slowly to face him. "I think you should sell the garage if you want to, and my head is playing nice scenes of a life closer to Nora, Peggy and Aunt Sarah, but there's a part too that will permanently feel it needs to be in Kelvedon," she looked up at him, her silky grey eyes wore just the slightest sheen and the end of her nose seemed a tiny bit too rosy.

"I'm being daft, I know. Can we wait to make the moving decision until Nancy returns? She's lived here all her life it would be harsh to up sticks before she's back."

He smiled at her, glad that he could at least get his teeth into selling the garage. It would do no harm to call George later and tell him to keep an eye out for properties. Alma had always wanted to move to Kent, still close to London but leafier, perhaps they could all find homes there, he'd start putting feelers out. Kissing her lightly on the forehead he said, "One thing at a time, then," before dashing out to put 'for sale' adverts in the press.

* * *

A tanned, poised young lady danced down the gangplank at Southampton, untroubled by the height of her heels and resplendent in a scarlet dress with closely fitted top, held in tightly at the waist by a wide black belt and from which the skirt sprouted full of petticoat-stiffened movement to graze her shapely mid-calves. Nancy returned to Britain having left every residual trace of the gauche country girl buried in the soil of India. The question of relinquishing her childhood home was already without teeth as she had spent the voyage back discussing West End auditions with her fellow entertainers, eagerly assuring them she had two aunts in London with whom she could stay whilst she searched for a lucrative part. In her handbag she was armed with the address of the best media photographer in the capital and she intended to pause in Soho for a full set of modelled pictures before continuing her journey up to Essex.

Photos in hand she stepped off the train, her smile slicing across the platform as she saw her huge little brothers standing behind her parents. Her Dad was staring at her but she realised he hadn't recognised her at all and her theatrically made-up eyes were laughing at him when he registered that he was looking at his own daughter. Holding her away from him to study the transformation, he enfolded her into his arms whispering into her hair, "You look amazing my girl!" as she breathed him in and remembered how warm it felt to be completely safe.

The twins ceased clowning and set about unloading her luggage, shouldering her burdens with obvious pride and processing behind while her parents took one arm each walking her slowly home and never allowing her to stop talking. By the time they had tumbled through the front door at Brookside, Nancy had already confessed her need to be closer to London, leading her father to admit that although he had half promised her mother he would abstain from all house-hunting until she returned, George had mentioned a pleasant property in Sidcup that he felt they should look at, especially considering it was just two minutes away from George and Alma's new home in Orpington.

"And when were you going to tell me?" her mother queried in mock indignation.

"I did ask if you were free on Thursday," he replied.

"But you didn't say why!"

"I mentioned visiting George ..."

* * *

The boxes were all packed and the twins were directing operations as the entire contents of Brookside was loaded into the removals van. The family's Singer Saloon would be driven by Nancy with the van following all the way to Sidcup. They would soon need to get on the road if there was to be any chance of beds being made that night, but Dorothy had vanished.

Instructing Nancy to make a final cup of tea for everyone using the china they had left out for breakfast, Harold headed for St. Mary's. Although she rarely went to church he knew she would be there, he had felt her anguish building over the weeks of preparation, in fact it had been one of the reasons he had insisted on moving so swiftly, amputating her from Kelvedon with a sharpened axe rather than a butter knife.

Opening the wooden gate he walked along the path until he could see the pale oblong of stone. It was no longer bright white marble, more than a decade had passed since the stone mason put it in place so weather cracks and moss were cautiously taking up residence. He saw that fresh flowers had been placed in the holder but Dorothy herself was no longer there. He moved towards the porch, trying to stifle the crunch of his shoes on the gravel, not wishing to disturb her within the church, hoping there was still time for her to leave of her own volition rather than be forced by the click of the latch and his appearance through the doorway. Sitting alone on the rough wooden bench waiting for Dorothy, his mind began to still. The past weeks had been so feverishly hectic that the sudden quietness made him feel faintly disembodied. Kelvedon had been good to them, it had provided the perfect haven, a vital escape route, but they didn't need to escape any more, all those terrors were dead and buried, they could go back to London now, a respectable married couple, heads held high.

* * *

Inside the church Dorothy was feeling unnaturally calm, so peaceful that she was unsure if she still needed to breathe. For weeks she had felt as if her chest was being ripped in two different directions but as she had placed her flowers on the grave, which was now more than twice as old as her son had been, there came an unexpected certainty that she was not, in fact, leaving him, that he would always be kept protected in her heart, and in her dreams she could continue to cuddle him. Walking slowly backwards from the grave her gaze never leaving its cold solid cross, she only turned away once she was through the porch entrance.

She had not intended to enter the church but she still suffered a residual pain from the bar of iron that seemed to have been stuck between her temples for the past two days, and the idea of sinking into a pew for a moment beckoned her in. A great hall of silence greeted her, a silence so broad that her own thoughts seemed noisy. There was only one: "Thank you" that Pat and Nancy are back safe; "thank you" that the boys never had to fight; "thank you" that finally we can move back to London and I am no longer frightened; "thank you" that my children have a bright future despite what Harold and I did, free from the stigma which could have blighted them if we had been discovered; "thank you" that we survived together, that we were right, that whatever it was that drew us together remained strong enough.

She rose, half bobbing to the altar before she turned to move up the aisle her heels clattering along the floor. Just before she reached the door it opened towards her and Harold held the heavy portal wide with his arms outstretched so she could walk through them, "Time to move on," he said gently.

Nancy had finished packing the final fragile items around the twins in the Singer and began to pull out of the close. Harold and Dorothy, perched proudly upright in the Wink, were dwarfed behind the removals van as they brought up the rear, hands held across the seat, rejoining after every gear change.

* * *

8 St. John's Road, Sidcup. 1947
(Dorothy: 52, Harold: 53, Nancy: 24, Twins: 17)
It was surprising how good these new electric irons were, Dorothy thought as she used it for the first time before her solitary enjoyment of the BBC's music programme was blasted out of existence by a tornado dressed in yellow and black which smashed through the front door, down the hallway, whirling into a tap dance in front of her while singing, *"There's no business like show business, Like no business I know!"*

"Mother! I'm in the chorus *AND* you won't believe it, they're making me Miss Toye's understudy! I'll be playing Winnie at least once a week to two thousand, three hundred and fifty-eight people a time, having knives thrown at me, singing two duets and hopefully not stumbling in the dance routines." She executed a pirouette landing gracefully in a heap in front of the ironing board, looking up at her mother while waving jazz hands.

"What's wrong?" worry replaced elation in her voice as she saw the tears coursing down her mother's cheeks.

"I'm just so proud of you," her mother said pulling Nancy from the floor and into her arms where they swayed together, "so incredibly proud," she murmured as the smell of burning cotton began to fill the kitchen.

* * *

The terracotta façade of The Coliseum towered overhead its great globe turning hundreds of feet above them as Harold and Dorothy stood in line waiting to take their seats in the front row of the dress circle on the opening night of *Annie get your gun*. Entering the auditorium Dorothy held her breath, her eyes darting around the sumptuous red and gold décor, a great field of stalls beneath and two tiers above the one she stood on, plus half a dozen plush half-moon boxes, all filled with elegantly dressed people, every one of them there to watch the musical her daughter was understudying the lead dance roll in. When the curtain rose her pride dissolved into apprehension as the huge revolving stage leapt into life and she was unable to find her child among the greasepaint and the crowd. She watched Wendy Toye's performance as Winnie closely, becoming increasingly amazed that her Nancy had the nerve to undertake such a role. How would it feel to look out from there at the ocean of expectant faces, conscious that if she put a foot wrong or failed to hit a note, more than two thousand paying customers would register her fault?

Midway through the first act Harold seized her arm, "There!" he whispered pointing to the right hand side of the stage. Raising the opera glasses to her eyes she saw Nancy, dancing for all she was worth, the grin on her face telling the world she was exactly where she wanted to be.

* * *

The following year Wendy Toye headed for Paris leaving the roll of Winnie to Nancy and her own understudy for the rest of the one thousand, three hundred and four performances. The men who nightly haunted the stage door left generous tokens of their appreciation but were rarely repaid with even a glimpse of their star as Nancy's attention was absorbed by a doctor she had met in India who had sought her out when he returned. She took to leaving the theatre almost before the patrons had vacated their seats, tossing her costume onto a hanger, hurrying out into the night without removing her stage make-up in her quest to spend an hour with Jimmy before the last train home.

The first time she snatched extra moments by avoiding the cold cream, the sound of her spiked footwear on the paving stones awoke the need to defend territorial rights in some other night-time workers, and her rush was halted by two ladies sporting similar make-up who blocked her way.

"Eh bitch, you're in the wrong place," the taller one spat, tossing a head of bottle-blonde hair as her partner blew a long stream of cigarette smoke into Nancy's face.

"Just turn around and get back to whatever pitch you came from," the second ordered, poking Nancy's chest with a single curved red-lacquered nail.

Confused and beginning to become frightened, Nancy wished she'd asked Jimmy to come to the theatre, "I'm just going to meet my friend," she offered, attempting to keep the waiver from her voice and wondering why there was never a policeman around when you most wanted one.

"Oh, 'igh class trade is it?" bottle-blonde said with a sneer.

"I'm a dancer at The Coliseum, I need to get home."

"Sorry doll! thought you was movin' in on our location, name's Bess," she said sticking out a hand, "an' this is Daff, you won't be sayin' nuffin' to the coppers will yer?" a pleading tone replaced the open aggression of the moment before.

"No, of course not," Nancy said, relieved that they hadn't wanted her handbag, "but I really am in a hurry."

Embarrassed by their mistake Daff and Bess made it their mission to ensure the working girls with bases from the theatre to the station treated Nancy like passing royalty, each calling out to her as she travelled through their zones ensuring she was protected from unwanted male attention and arrived safely at her front door unmolested every night.

Whenever Harold and Jimmy fretted over her nocturnal rambles through London's least salubrious parts, Nancy would toss her shiny dark curls and laugh, giving them a wink and only half comforting them by her assertion that the entire prostitute population of London was looking after her so there was nothing to fear.

* * *

1950
(Dorothy:55, Harold:56, Nancy:27, Twins:20)

Light streamed through the upstairs window illuminating Dorothy's face as she lent in towards the dressing table mirror, she hesitated, setting down the powder puff and placing her index fingers below the sides of her jaw bone. Gently pushing upwards she acknowledged the bounce of the two drooping flanks that had developed either side of the centre strip. When had her face divided so definitely into three sections, she wondered, and how had she failed to notice that it had occurred? Her chin was still flattish underneath and somehow this profile had fooled her into believing that the double mini-landslip hadn't happened, it was like when she had first caught glimpses of patches of horribly crinkled skin on her upper arms and the backs of her thighs as she passed the long mirror, she had erased them with quick muscle tensing, and convinced herself they had been banished for good, yet almost unconsciously she had started to purchase only tops and dresses with sleeves ending below the elbow and skirts that hung lower than the eyebrow of flesh that had affixed itself above each knee. Now the 'eyebrow' and the unwanted upper arm skin revealed themselves every time she undressed as if they had grown to full maturity by germinating beneath the top soil of more restrained clothing, and covering them up had just encouraged them to take on a clandestine life of their own. But the three-part face could not be hidden, it sat in front of her, undisguiseable proof that whatever age she felt in her head, reality was going to stare back at her every morning. She felt it was rather rude of her body to be so blatant, especially as her mind currently enjoyed the sensations of freedom and spontaneity it had lost during the years their children were dependent, and this had allowed her head to believe she had reverted to the age she had been when she first met Harold.

Nancy had married her Jimmy and was set up as a doctor's wife; Peter was working as an accountant's apprentice and John was studying to become a dental surgeon; all changes that had allowed her and Harold to slip backwards in time, luxuriating in an unhurried life, playing tennis doubles with George and Alma, going to the theatre and dining out whenever the whim took them; lying in bed with a tray of tea and the newspapers in the middle of the week, filling the sheets with toast crumbs. Yet among this backsliding towards their youthful selves, somehow their bodies had been left behind.

Trying to smooth out the creases splaying out from the corner of her eyes, she pondered on whether Harold's blindness to the death of beauty's bloom might the same as hers. She knew if she asked him she would be unable to believe his answer, not because he was necessarily lying but rather that the evidence of visual kindness seemed far too convenient. When she looked at Harold his thinning hair and the slightly thickening waist did not register as a change because his eyes and the shape of his mouth were still those of mischief and good humour that she had always known. In fact, when she caught sight of photos of him in his thirties she would feel a frizzon of apprehension that she had ever made decent life decisions alongside someone so obviously young and inexperienced, looking at the old pictures it seemed a miracle that they had guided their lives to this point, and yet they had arrived unscathed despite all the years of worry that their guilty secret, still so deeply unacceptable, would be unearthed. The fears of a leak to Kelvedon's townsfolk had haunted them, if even a whisper had got out it would have been impossible to ignore, like steam emerging from a pressure cooker, first in small unremarkable bubbles, then creshendoing to a shrill whistle, forcing itself through the consciousness of everyone around until the lid was removed and the insipid contents inspected. But it hadn't leaked and they had been safely married for more than a decade, while their circle of society remained pleasantly untroubled by a past of which it knew nothing.

She considered the judgements that would have been levied against them and their children if Jean had discovered their address, or some slip had alerted the neighbours so fingers of suspicion clawed their way into their lives dragging the truth out into the street for every bored individual to pick over. It would not have been solely people like the Docwa sisters who would have slammed the family as dangerously lacking in morals.

At least it was behind them now and if the price of time safely passing was that much of her body appeared to have moved south, then so be it. She lifted up the powder puff, dabbed it in the pot and began to fill in the deeper rivers of age, brushed her permed grey curls into place around her collar line, grabbed her sports bag and went to join her friends at the tennis club.

* * *

1957
(Dorothy: 62, Harold: 63, Nancy: 34, Twins: 27)
At eleven shillings a week, Harold expected the television screen to be almost free of snow. He had already sent back two sets to the rental shop

and Dorothy was concerned he was on the verge of returning the third just as Nancy's two daughters were hours away from arriving for the weekend.

"It's much better than the last one," she tried encouragingly.

"But every time I sit down it goes off a bit," he grumbled.

"I'm sure it will be fine. The children will be delighted," she said looking round at the newly arranged living room where the fireplace had been sidelined from its previous position of focus by the introduction of the grey and black box.

"You just want to make sure there's a set here on Sunday night so you can see that Bruce Forsyth you like so much!"

"Rubbish! I honestly think the reception is fine and I want it here for the children's programmes. As for *Sunday night at the Palladium* you said yourself how nice it was to have a presenter who didn't speak as if he had three plums in his mouth."

"All right Granny, we'll keep it, at least for the weekend."

"Don't! I'm still not used to it. Maybe we should get them to change to Uncle Harry and Auntie Dot like your Dad did!"

"You'll always be a glam gran to me," he said giving her a hearty whack on the backside which appeared to jiggle the delicate aerial again creating a further on screen avalanche.

Returning to the kitchen to ice the cake she had made for her granddaughters' tea, she thought about the young television presenter with his big oblong head and the crinkly eyes that descended into elongated bracket lines either side of the great mouthful of white pearlies that were forever ad libbing throughout the programme. Could the popularity of normal men like him begin to cause a shift away from the rigid expectations people still clung to in her country? The previous year she had been sad, but not surprised, when pretty Princess Margaret was forbidden to marry her war hero beau because he was divorced. Part of her had believed the country had learned from Edward the eighth's abdication that it was better to accept the power of love than fight against it, but perhaps there were going to be certain things that were immoveable. Was it Oscar Wilde who had said people's attitudes towards war would never change until it was perceived to be vulgar? Perhaps people's attitudes towards love would be set in stone until it was recognised as beautiful instead of reckless or too cringingly personal to be honestly acknowledged.

With a final elaborate swirl of her fork over the chocolate butter icing, she had not had time to wipe the worktop before the doorbell clanged and the shrieking dual reminders that, once again, the generations had moved on, hurtled down the hallway.

* * *

1959
(Dorothy: 64, Harold: 65, Nora: 68, Pat: 37, Aunt Sarah: 94)
"I think you should come up," Nora's voice came down the telephone to Dorothy. "I may be over reacting but Aunt Sarah's cold isn't getting any better and she was odd after Pat left last night, like she believed she wouldn't see him again."

"I'll be on the next train," Dorothy replied. In a few months her aunt would be ninety-five and although she was as mentally agile as ever, she had consented to move into Nora's home when she fell ill with a heavy cold which was unusually compliant of her. The stairs were easier than her own and either Arthur or Nora was always there to give any physical help she might need, whereas it was impossible for Peggy to be constantly around.

By mid morning the three sisters were sitting in Pat's old bedroom with Aunt Sarah propped up on a heap of pillows and cushions, her face flushed and even her gnarled hands, with their bloated arthritic joints, showed a dusky pink through the brown spots, however she was openly pleased to have all of them with her. Reaching out her tender-jointed fingers she clasped the wrists of the two nearest nieces anchoring them to her side while her rheumy eyes fixed them all in place.

"I've been so very lucky," she announced, continuing before they had a chance to interrupt. "When I was young I was very determined not to have a life like my sisters with babies coming every year. All I could see was the poverty it brought them and the constant struggle, I completely overlooked the family, the feeling of belonging. By rights I should be an uncared for lonely old woman battling to get through each day, and yet even though I never had a child of my own I have been blessed with a host of nieces who have shown me more kindness than my girlhood self ever deserved."

"From the moment I arrived in Maddox Street," Dorothy said, laying her free hand on top of her aunt's, "you told me 'people make their own luck'. We don't come to you because we're good people, we're here because we love you. And we love you," she said, a definite quiver invading her voice, "because you've always been loveable. I caused a fair few hiccups for you during my life but even when I disappointed you, you never made me feel you wouldn't want to see me again, that you no longer cared. Every one of us feels like your adopted daughters, because you always made us feel that way." Her voice was so low it was doubtful Aunt Sarah could make out the words, but Nora was rubbing her sister's back as she spoke and Peggy nodded slowly while holding their aunt's other hand.

* * *

Dampness appeared in the outer edges of Sarah's eyes as she gazed down on the silver hair of the child Edward had chosen to live with them more than half a century before. He had been such a wonderful friend, Sarah thought, and it seemed far too long since she had been with him, yet even now she could clearly picture his bearded face, the eyes that looked straight into her core, the way he would consult his pocket watch when he wanted extra time in which to formulate an answer to a question. He may not have been physically with her for thirty-five years, but he seemed as real in her mind as if he had just popped out for a loaf of bread.

* * *

The four women continued to chat quietly, leaving nothing important unsaid, until it was clear their aunt was becoming tired. Dorothy lingered an extra fraction of a second as she bent to kiss her aunt's cheek, breathing in the unique personal scent of comfort as her lips stayed on the warm wrinkles that felt like a baby-soft eiderdown beneath her touch. She drew back, drinking in every contour of the peaceful semi-dozing face that meant so much to her, and her mouth refused to form the word 'goodbye' as she left the room.

* * *

1960
(Dorothy: 65, Harold: 66, Nancy: 37, Twins: 30)
Rationally Dorothy knew she and Harold had become the older generation, but in her head it didn't seem possible. Life must be like a race track, she thought, where the car starts off slowly, straining to power through the gears until it gets faster and faster as it heads for the final chequered flag. The twelve months since Aunt Sarah's death seemed to be the length of a couple of days, while remembered childhood day trips lasted weeks and summers lasted for ever. Now months flashed past and winters dissolved into spring almost before Harold had time to re-string their racquets ready for the first match of the tennis season.

The weather had looked dodgy when Harold drew back the curtains that morning, "I don't know if we'll get a game," he'd said as she lay there opening her eyelids a crack at a time to the new day, but they had got on court and although they hadn't won, the loss wasn't an embarrassing one.

Arriving back home still in their whites she'd gone to boil the kettle while he'd settled into his chair. She thought he'd put the radio on while she was preparing the tea tray but the house remained quiet and as she handed him the cup and saucer he raised his head from his chest, an anxious look in his eyes.

"I feel a bit odd, Bill."

CHAPTER TWENTY-TWO

His face contorted, right hand clutching his chest as the tea cup fell from his left its boiling contents searing their way down Dorothy's shin as she ran for the telephone.

Kneeling beside him she began by assuring him help would arrive in a few minutes, but his total lack of response liquefied her voice from telling into begging before it decomposed completely into a pleading litany to him, to the souls of her family, to any earthly or unearthly power capable of reversing the inertia that had snatched every scrap of vitality from her protector leaving her knees patterned by the carpet pile, clasping an empty husk with which to shelter from a dimly known world. The ambulance men replaced her fruitless entreaties with action, firmly removing her as they ripped open his shirt, one feeling for a pulse while the other pumped his chest, firing questions at her with the rapidity of popping corn, still eliciting information as they deftly rolled him onto a stretcher and began making for the door.

She followed seemingly attached by a tow rope, unable to deviate from his path even to pick up her hand bag, put on her coat or turn to lock the front door. Within minutes they were at Queen Mary's hospital and the smoothly dashing stretcher men must have cut her umbilical cord, leaving her drifting to a stop in the middle of the reception area as they disappeared through wide surgical doors. She sagged above the grey lino floor, her long spine too shocked to hold her shoulders back, her head so confused it looked like a balloon, liable to bob in response to the slightest breeze. She hung there in her tennis whites with her old green cardigan on top until a matron almost barrelled into her, realised there was a problem and gently lead Dorothy to a telephone from where she called Peter's house. His wife answered, running over with concern, Peter would be on his way home from work, she would go and meet him at the station, get him to come as soon as possible and, yes, of course, she would ring Nancy and John immediately.

Once in the waiting room it was impossible to escape the pale blue tiled walls and the cloying smell that left her feeling as if she were drowning in an enclosed swimming pool filled with disinfectant. Every sense was assaulted by reminders of intense sanitation so that it was impossible to retreat from the certainty that she would only be there, stuck to a hard plastic chair, chilled in her unsuitable clothes, and surrounded by the stillness of worry, if something was very, very wrong.

A man with a small child entered the silent sanctuary, taking seats at a respectful distance. She attempted to pull the pleated skirt lower then stretched the cardigan until opposite sides affixed themselves over opposite breasts imprisoned in place by her arms firmly crossed across her stomach. The seat's frigidity seeped through her clothes and was absorbed by her skin from where it travelled into the depths of her muscles invading her pelvis and lower back throughout the eternity in which the man shushed the child, until they were dispatched to a different area of the vast swimming pool of hygiene.

Eventually a man looking no older than her sons, but dressed in the authority of a white coat, stood before her. He seemed to have been trained in unhopeful compassion so his eyes poured our sympathy while his mouth remained a line, mechanically spewing forth words like "extensive damage", "greatly weakened" and "little chance of recovery." He led her to Harold's bedside leaving instructions to call the nurse should anything change.

The arms and torso exposed above the starched white sheet seemed shrunken as if her champion was being surreptitiously removed from beneath, or she herself had turned into a Brobdingnagian woman staring down at her diminishing hero. Perched on a chair she watched his shallow breathing, with each small exhalation a tiny drop of life might be leaving, mingling so completely with the air in the room that she could not catch it and put it back inside him.

Taking his hand in hers and laying it beneath her cheek on the crisp linen she closed her eyes and eased her aching back, lying forward while the rest of her continued to be punished by the plastic chair. She had ceased to consider time and her weariness had left her incapable of stemming the dam burst that washed silently across the three hands and soaked into the pillow. A fourth hand began to stroke the top of her hair and a husky voice whispered, "It will be all right Bill."

* * *

But it hadn't been "all right". She passed the night in Peter's spare room where the different scents and noises mingled with the unfamiliar mattress and bed covers to heighten the surety that in just a few hours she had slipped out of her habitual world into some wretched parallel universe where everything looked the same but had been overlaid with such deep sadness that even the sun's rays which finally filtered through the flowery curtains and released her from the need to remain shackled to the bed, had become cheerless, acting purely as a despondent reminder of what had once been.

She insisted on being dropped at her house, half convinced that if she were left in her usual surroundings the phantom life she was experiencing would dissolve away like a bad dream after a brisk walk. She picked up three buttons and retrieved the cup and saucer from the living room carpet noting the beige tea stain beneath them, evidence of the previous day's events that she was still attempting to confine to the realms of nightmare fantasy. Drifting through the rooms she discovered an intense revulsion towards touching anything. The kitchen was no longer for preparing sustenance when there was only one to sustain; the bed no longer for lying on when there was no one to share it with; her dressing table and wardrobe no longer places for preparing herself when there was no one to please. She wandered into the garage and looked at the cars she would never drive; in the hallway two tennis racquets lent jauntily against the wallpaper, stark reminders of activity so abruptly ended.

Hours later Dorothy stood in front of Harold's writing desk, unmoving, not wishing to pull down the solid wooden flap to reveal the jumble of bills, cheque books and rental contracts she knew to be inside, a den of financial confusion she had never needed to venture into and which she now realised she believed to be terrifying and unmanageable. The electricity bills had been paid, the plumbing mended, the television rented, the coal ordered, the lawn mower serviced, the boiler cleaned and a plethora of household necessities undertaken without her knowing anything about them, she had never even written a cheque. Accounts at the greengrocer, the butcher, the hairdresser and the fishmonger had always been magically settled. There was cash kept in one of the bedroom drawers for smaller expenses but she had never considered how it got there, the nuts and bolts of going to the bank and asking to withdraw funds from an account were as alien to her as what their actual bank balance was.

Pulling out the straight-backed chair in front of the desk she sat and extracted the ridges of wood on which the top would sit when she opened it. A scattered paper mound about the size of a Victoria sponge cake faced her as she peaked over the lip of the lid. The top piece had rows of figures and an underlined total which caused panic to creep up her throat making her almost gag. Perhaps she should shut it and wait for Peter to help, an accountant must know what was meant to be done. She dropped the lid back into place hiding the mound.

The small of her back rounded downwards as she thought of Peggy who had been forced to run her own home singlehanded for years, she seemed all right, she never appeared to have floundered over the task. Even in her bruised state it struck Dorothy as unnecessarily weak to just assume Peter would arrange the payment of her daily bills. With a deep sigh she opened the desk fully and began slowly working her way through the pile, sorting each paper in a manner that seemed vaguely logical. Once the hillock had been restructured into five neatly paper-clipped piles she began to investigate the contents of the drawers beneath. Sitting on the floor with the middle drawer opened in front of her she took out a yellowing foolscap Post Office form: "This is the last Will of me, Harold Willand of "Brookside", Kelvedon in the County of Essex. I give devise and bequeath all my real and personal estate whatsoever and wheresoever in their entirety to my life's partner, Dorothy ..."

She remained cross-legged on the floor, tears that had been wet on her cheeks dried into trails of salt, the paper still clasped between her fingers when Peter let himself in and gently took it from her as she wordlessly handed it to him.

* * *

"Good Morning. Mrs Willand?" Miss Berrill of Hugh-Jones solicitors queried.

"Yes."

"I'm phoning from Hugh-Jones, we were all so very sorry to hear of your husband's death, he was a lovely man," Miss Berrill got through the sentence all the time kicking herself for trotting out such an inadequate platitude. "Your son brought Mr Willand's will into me today and I just need to confirm a few things."

She was managing to keep her tone light but was exceedingly grateful she had the anonymity of a telephone rather than being forced to question the newly widowed woman face to face.

"The wording of the will is a little unconventional so I hope you'll forgive the nature of the enquiry but were you and Mr Willand married?"

"Yes, yes of course we were," a voice tremor was evident down the line but Miss Berrill was unable to glean if it was from grief or indignation.

"That's wonderful, in that case would you be kind enough to ask your son to drop in your marriage and birth certificates so I can proceed with the paperwork. Thank you so much for your help Mrs Willand. Goodbye."

* * *

Dorothy dropped the handset as if it had burnt her and stood staring down at the apparatus, cheeks incinerating, the expression on her face registering the same level of revulsion as if the solid black prism had mutated into a fresh steaming pile of dog excrement. Backing away from it she sank into a squat against the far wall, her mind racing through scenes of cringing embarrassment. Miss Berrill's voice sounded as if she was of mature years, a competent lawyer at an established firm which Harold and Charlie had trusted. Did lawyers have to be discreet in the way doctors did? Could she ensure Peter never saw the marriage certificate with its wholly unacceptable date? Somehow she must remove Peter, in fact all of them, from helping with Harold's estate any further, there must not be the slightest possibility that they could discover anything other than what they had always believed: their parents met, married, moved to Kelvedon and lived happily ever after, full stop, the end, without any rearrangement of the order.

Her body kept flushing with bouts of prickly heat as she pictured the faces of her children if they were ever confronted by her marriage certificate, she even considered burning it but it was too late, far too late, now the eminent Miss Berrill had asked to see it she had no option but to send it in. The image of Nancy loomed in front of her, a questioning look in her eyes but also shades of hurt and with an expression of mistrust. She remembered their talks before Nancy left for India, the advice she had given her on behaviour, saving herself for marriage, about faithfulness and not taking chances, and her daughter had sat before her nodding solemnly in agreement believing absolutely in the sanctity of her parents' marriage, never thinking for one moment she herself might be classed illegitimate. It seemed so unfair that this one piece of paper could make the bond she had with Harold degenerate into something slightly sordid, lowering their relationship from the status of soul mate down to closet lover so that her children's spouses might seize on the facts during future arguments as opportunities to insult, embarrass or manipulate her precious babies – for that's what they were, yet somehow she had failed to protect them and instead of making her offspring strong by the loving upbringing she and Harold had provided, she had handed the weapon of social unacceptability to anyone who might now find out and decide to torment them.

Discovery had been her greatest fear when they were born, but in the last twenty years she had believed herself safe, that the secret could no longer be unearthed. One long green piece of paper was about to wreck not only her own fairy story but that of all her children, and for what? None of the love, the laughter and the happiness had changed, that was all securely anchored in the past, but the four digits '1.9.3.8' on the paper somehow wiped out all the good replacing it with a thin layer of smut. She wouldn't let it happen to her children or to Harold's memory, she just wouldn't.

* * *

Alma was so alarmed by the sound of Dorothy's sobs on the phone that she and George left before even completing the washing up. The first priority appeared to be to remove Dorothy from St John's Road so that Peter, who lived only a few streets away, would not walk in and witness her total disintegration. The couple helped her to pack a bag and gather all the necessary documents before soothing her sufficiently so she could call her children and, in her brightest tone, announce she was going for a long weekend away with the Weiss's and would see them on her return.

Once safely back in Orpington the three of them spent the evening writing and rewriting draughts of two letters to be sent to Miss Berrill, refusing to drop into their beds until Dorothy was finally satisfied that the tone and content was as clear as they could make it whilst retaining at least a semblance of dignified respectability.

* * *

Dear Miss Berrill,
The accompanying letter from my oldest friend Mr. George Weiss will help you to understand why the Will made by my late husband Harold Willand was so badly worded.

I have enclosed my Birth Certificate and my Marriage Certificate, and trust that these documents will help.

My thanks for the kindly attention.
Sincerely
Dorothy Willand

* * *

33, Crofton Lane,
Orpington
Kent
Dear Miss Berrill,
I was asked by Mrs Dorothy Willand to help establish proof in the solution of the ambiguous Will, left by her husband and give all the facts as I know them.

As the oldest friend of the Willands – folks I have known and been very close to for 50 years, meeting almost weekly during most of this time – I am probably the only person (outside the families) who knows the secret that was the cause of that Will being made at Kelvedon and in the form it was written.

    Dorothy Willand was already married to a Mr. Nicolai when she joined Mr. Harold Willand at his house and business at Kelvedon, this was in 1922, her marriage to Mr. Nicolai was in 1915. I well remember meeting her at the Kelvedon Station in 1922.

    She was known to the local customers and traders as Mrs. Willand.

    Her daughter Nancy was born at a Hammersmith Nursing Home. Later her twin sons Peter and John were born at Witham, Essex. All three children were registered in the Father's name - my wife and I acted as Godparents.

    It was not until 1937 that Mr. Nicolai died, and Mr. Harold Willand was able to marry – Dorothy Nicolai. See Marriage Certificate.

    WHY? In spite of my close contact with Mr. Willand he never told me of his neglect to produce a new Will after his legitimising his connection with Dorothy, I cannot say, but, the need now to furnish proof might raise some suspicion in the mind of son Peter – who is doing all the work to clear up the Estate – it is the dread of his Mother, who does not want the children to learn of her lapse which might class them as illegitimate. Your assurance of this please will help to comfort her worrying mind.

    My thanks.
Sincerely
George F. Weiss, M.P.S.

* * *

Dear Mrs Willand,
Thank you for your letter dated 5th September enclosing the certificates and the letter from your friend Mr. Weiss.

    Unfortunately, under British law, a marriage renders any previous will null and void unless it was made with the specific intention of putting matters in place prior to an imminent wedding, which, given the time lapse between the making of the will and the marriage, cannot apply in your case. Upon your marriage the secure position your husband had made for you so many years before was unwittingly wrecked and due to this it is necessary to revert to dividing the estate according to the Administration of Estates Act 1925 which allows you to retain the marital home absolutely but decrees that the rest of the estate must be divided between you and your children.

    I will begin work to this effect and you have my assurance that I will not disclose the reasons behind this alteration to your son Peter or any other party.
Yours sincerely
Ena Berrill

* * *

Maybe it would be all right after all, she could sell the house and live on the proceeds, just tell the children she knew their father would have wanted them to have the money, and leave it at that. She would be fine, all her sisters survived on far less than she would receive. If Miss Berrill kept her word they could all still believe in 'happily ever after'.

* * *

"Mother, I think we have a problem, the solicitor's sending through weird forms about legacies from Dad," Peter's cheerful voice down the line made her stiffen and her breath come in short gasps. "I phoned her and told her she'd made a mistake and Dad's will was quite clear, it was all to go to you, and she told me she was doing the right thing and you knew all about it."

"Your Dad told me before he died he wanted you three to have something," she offered.

"It doesn't sound like that, Mother, these funds are coming straight from Dad's estate. The solicitor can't act against what's in the Will, she'd have to give everything to you and then you would fulfill Dad's wishes. I don't think she's doing that. Perhaps she's incompetent and has mixed it up with someone else."

"No, I'm sure she's not."

"Don't worry Mother, I'll go in this afternoon and sort it out."

"I'd rather you didn't, I'm sure she knows what she's doing," her voice had become trembly and the lower part of her abdomen was performing painful somersaults which left her wanting to sprint to the bathroom.

"It's OK Mother, she probably just needs me to clarify things."

* * *

Peter strode up the path, crashed through the front door dropping his brief case in the hallway as his mother's face appeared around the living room door. She smiled at him nervously, such a handsome man, a typical rugby player frame topped with a head of thick wavy hair but without the crooked nose and cauliflower ears that were the usual hallmark of the sport. The only visible injury was a chipped front tooth which, like Nora's, gave him a rakish grin to compliment his eyes which laughed and winked even when he was tired, as she could see he was now.

"Hi Mother," he said bending down to hug her, "What an afternoon!" he exclaimed, prompting her to hasten towards the kitchen and spring into action with the kettle. He followed her in, leaning on the door frame as she prepared the tray.

"That woman's going to be the death of me! She wouldn't take my calls all day and when I got there she refused to talk to me! I demanded to speak to one of the partners and they had the cheek to tell me that the only person their office would speak to was you! You'll have to write to them Mother or we'll never get this mess sorted out."

Her hand remained on the milk bottle but none of its contents were being tipped into the jug. Standing up from his lean-to position he walked up to her putting his sturdy hands onto her thin upper arms, feeling her tremble.

"Mother? What is it?"

Her frail body seemed to be tearing itself apart from within as great shuddering waves swept through, forcibly bending her chest as she drew away from him unable to seek comfort from anyone.

"I'm sorry Mother, I'm so stupid, I know what a time you've had since Dad died and then I go heaping my troubles on you, I'm so sorry, please don't worry, I'll sort them out, I'll go to the Law Society if I have to. Please Mother, come and sit down, honestly it's nothing to worry about, you need to take it easy, it's all been too much." But as he reached to guide her into a chair she pulled away again curling into herself, it was as if between warming the tea pot and pouring the milk she had fallen over an edge and there was no way back.

"Tell me what I can do," he begged. "Would you like to come and live with us? We'd take care of you. Whatever's troubling you, we can sort it out."

A peculiar rasping voice came out of almost closed lips, "No, it can't be sorted out."

"Of course it can, Mother, there's always solutions, sometimes they're difficult to see when you're tired and upset."

"No," she said, adding "Please would you phone Miss Berrill and tell her we're coming in."

* * *

He looked at the droplets falling regularly off her chin, her whole form seemed smaller, for the first time ever she was unable to look at him and he began searching back in his mind for any hurt he might have inadvertently caused which could have produced such a violent reaction.

"It's in North London Mother, they'll be closing by the time we get there, please, just tell me what's upsetting you."

"I'll wait in the car," she said taking her coat from its hook and picking up her handbag leaving him no option but to comply.

Throughout the entire journey she sat, head bowed, occasionally sneaking her drenched hanky up to her eyes and nose. The afternoon school exit melted into early rush hour traffic as Peter oscillated between concern over his Mother's emotional rupture and mild irritation with her for failing to spit it out in the familiarity of the kitchen saving him hours of driving and enabling him to get home for dinner at a reasonable time.

The signs for Finchley gave way to the broad street of Ballards Lane itself. Finding a space close to the law firm he opened her door, helping her from the car but she shook her arm free from his, walking slowly and alone towards the solicitors as the proprietors of the line of small shops that flanked it began to pull down their shutters and remove their aprons at the end of the day's trading. Passing beneath the sign of Hugh-Jones & Co, she did not even acknowledge the young typist at the reception desk who half rose to stop her before being soothed back into her chair by Peter's hurried explanation. Like a condemned prisoner running towards the execution block, she gave only a cursory knock on Miss Berrill's door, beginning to turn the handle before the person within had called out to come in.

"Please don't wait, I'll lock up," Miss Berrill said to the receptionist as she closed her office door. "Won't you sit down?" she asked gently, but as Peter sank into the furthest seat in front of the broad oak desk his mother remained upright, her face seeming even more ashen against the red rims around her eyes. She began to speak immediately and although her voice quivered she was clear and audible throughout the catalogue of facts she recited. She made no attempt to save herself with sentiment, there was no initial reference to her age at the time of her first marriage, or to the war or Jean's friendship with her uncle, she painted no pictures to soften the edges of the disgrace and betrayal she claimed she was now handing him, leaving neither of them a cubby hole in which to hide away from the shocking truth.

When she finished the silence threatened to grow around the room and digest them until Miss Berrill abruptly truncated it.

"So your father's will is invalid because your parents' marriage took place after it had been made. Consequently, we've had to revert to the law governing intestacy which is why you and your siblings will inherit a significant proportion of your father's estate."

Peter raised his head to look at the lawyer, it felt strangely heavy as if he'd just made a wild rugby tackle and missed, crashing to the ground before he could get his hands out in front of him to break his fall. "But Dad wanted Mother to have it all. I know Nancy and John will want that to happen, what do we do to ensure his wishes are carried out?"

"No, please Peter," she began, control deserting her again, "whatever you think of me now, please don't tell John and Nancy, I'm begging you."

Rambling almost incoherently about losing everything, Peter moved towards her, pressured her to fold into a chair and, hardly even grazing her, laid his index finger against her lips. Although the touch lasted only the tiniest fraction of a second its intimacy shocked her into silence.

"He's my twin, Mother," he said kneeling before her, "You can't ask that, it's not possible."

"I'm so ashamed," she mumbled, head hung low. Taking one of her cold wrinkled hands in his, trying to force her to look at him as he peered up at her from beneath.

"You would have had far more to be ashamed of if you'd wasted your life with someone you didn't care for just because you were too frightened to do something about it," he said.

"If your brother and sister agree, we just need you to sign your parts over to your Mother," Miss Berrill interjected in an attempt to steer the meeting back to the business at hand.

"That won't be a problem," he replied, trying out his most winsome smile with full eye twinkle, and only just managing to restrain himself from a wink before he added, "I'm very sorry if I was impolite, or even downright rude, earlier on today."

She rewarded him with a half grin, "Don't mention it."

Stepping onto the chilly pavement where the street lamps were already obscuring the stars that filled the clear evening sky, Miss Berrill locked the door and shook hands before she turned away down the road.

Placing a heavy arm round his mother's fragile frame Peter walked her towards the car kicking his way through the deep covering of autumn leaves.

"Well Mother," he said giving her a bone-crunching squeeze, "I never thought you had it in you! Fancy a drink?"

Dorothy outlived Harold by 17 years, she never had another partner nor stopped mentioning any daily incidents that would have amused him. After Harold's death, John drove The Wink back to his home in Saffron Walden, he used it for several years before eventually selling it to a couple of students at Cambridge University. By 1961 Dorothy had sold her house in Sidcup and bought a ground floor flat next door to Nancy's home at 25 Shorncliffe Road, Folkstone. This move allowed her to enjoy a very active role in the lives of two of her five grandchildren right up until her death from a stroke in 1977. *Dancing round raindrops* is dedicated to her ten great grandchildren and the front cover shows one of her great grand daughters who seems to have inherited her blithe spirit; 101 years separate the young women on the front and back covers of this book, yet both have an intolerance for prejudice and an irrepressible desire to "live happy", just the way they are ...

"... *Don't forget, you are the only one* ..."

A word of thanks ...

To my father, John Willand, and his brother, Peter, many thanks for their painstaking answers to my interminable questions. To my cousin, Caroline Richards, a whopping thank you for clearing out her junk cupboard and being the best surrogate sister I could have.

Without the support and forbearance in my wackier moments of my husband, Pete, and our children Chris, Alice and Nick, I wouldn't have managed to write anything at all, thank you guys, you're the best.

To Rebecca Winfield of Luxton Harris Ltd, thank you so much for pointing me in the right direction and dragging me off my historical hobby-horse.

A big thank you to Pam Gravett for her excellent research and for being a great email buddy.

I also owe a debt of gratitude to Ruth Kent, Jenny Elliot, Dorothy Pickford, Pacho Loruvacia, Axel Verdier Varamo for his help with cover design and Nigel King of Hugh-Jones & Co for his advice on points of law.

Without all of these people *Dancing round raindrops* would not have evolved into what it has become, however all the errors and shortcomings the book has are mine alone and do not reflect in any way on the superb help and guidance I received from all of those mentioned above.

Published Resources

Collett's Farthing Newspaper by Rex Sawyer. ISBN: 0-946418-22-5
Kelvedon Speaks by Ruth Kent. ISBN: 13: 978-0953551613
Dad's Army: The Home Guard 1940-1944 by David Carroll. ISBN: 07509 26104
Victoria's Final Decade. Looking Back at Britain 1890s by Jeremy Harwood.
    ISBN: 978-0-276-44395-4
Edwardian Summer: Looking Back at Britain 1900s by Tony Allan
    ISBN: 978-0-276-44396-1
The End of a World: Looking Back at Britain 1910s by Jeremy Harwood
    ISBN: 978-0-276-44397-8
Decadence and Change: Looking back at Britain 1920s by Jonathan Bastable
    ISBN: 978-0-276-44398-5
Depression years: Looking back at Britain 1930s by Brian Moynahan
    ISBN: 978-0-276-44399-2
War and Peace: Looking back at Britain 1940s by Jeremy Harwood
    ISBN: 978-0-276-44250-6
Road to Recovery: Looking back at Britain 1950s by Brian Moynaham
    ISBN:)/(-0-276-44249-0

Made in the USA
Charleston, SC
20 April 2012